More Praise for *Measuring and Improving Social Impacts*

"Measuring social impact is a topic at the top of so many agendas yet with so little real insight about how to make it real, actionable, and meaningful. *Measuring and Improving Social Impacts* is a practical guide for maximizing and amplifying impact. A must-read for those grappling with how to define and evaluate success."
—**Paul Bernstein, CEO, The Pershing Square Foundation**

"*Measuring and Improving Social Impacts* offers a useful and timely review of the many measurement approaches available to nonprofits, foundations, and impact investors. Epstein and Yuthas provide practical step-by-step guidance along with real-life stories that show how measurement is applied in action and leads to better results."
—**Fay Twersky, Director, Effective Philanthropy Group, The William and Flora Hewlett Foundation**

"Although this looks like a thorough guidebook for people starting in the field of social change, it is likely to trigger considerable thinking among those who have been involved in philanthropy and the practice of social change for a long time. The desire to bring about social change is quite simple, but doing something about it can be quite complicated—this book helps you to simplify things to achieve your goals."
—**Madhav Chavan, PhD, CEO, Pratham Education Foundation**

"A fascinating read . . . very valuable to corporate foundations like mine that are grappling with effectiveness at the foundation level and also understanding and measuring the added value for the corporation and its employees."
—**Vidya Shah, CEO, EdelGive Foundation, Edelweiss Group, India**

"Epstein and Yuthas provide a lucid and compelling framework—a logic model—for investors, civil society actors, corporate leaders, and policy makers to use resources more effectively and yield better social results."
—**Rohini Nilekani, Chairperson, Arghyam**

"This book is an excellent reference point for social impact investing. Epstein and Yuthas have meticulously researched an impressive cross section of companies, nonprofits, foundations, and individuals to build credible metrics and analytical tools, and they offer useful insights to maximize impact."
—**Zarina Screwvala, Founder-Trustee, Swades Foundation**

"Epstein and Yuthas offer a clear and highly accessible approach to measuring and creating social impact. Drawing on a diverse array of examples from around the world, they demonstrate that there are no quick fixes and that systematic measurement is essential."
—**Alnoor Ebrahim, Associate Professor, Harvard Business School, and author of the award-winning *NGOs and Organizational Change***

Measuring and Improving
Social Impacts

Measuring and Improving
Social Impacts

A Guide for Nonprofits, Companies, and Impact Investors

MARC J. EPSTEIN

and

KRISTI YUTHAS

Berrett–Koehler Publishers, Inc.
San Francisco
a BK Business book

Berrett-Koehler Publishers, Inc.
235 Montgomery Street, Suite 650
San Francisco, CA 94104-2916
Tel: (415) 288-0260   Fax: (415) 362-2512
www.bkconnection.com

Ordering Information

Quantity sales. Special discounts are available on quantity purchases by corporations, associations, and others. For details, contact the "Special Sales Department" at the Berrett-Koehler address above.
Individual sales. Berrett-Koehler publications are available through most bookstores. They can also be ordered directly from Berrett-Koehler: Tel: (800) 929-2929; Fax: (802) 864-7626; www.bkconnection.com.
Orders for college textbook/course adoption use. Please contact Berrett-Koehler: Tel: (800) 929-2929; Fax: (802) 864-7626.
Orders by U.S. trade bookstores and wholesalers. Please contact Ingram Publisher Services, Tel: (800) 509-4887; Fax: (800) 838-1149; E-mail: customer.service@ingrampublisherservices.com; or visit www.ingrampublisherservices.com/Ordering for details about electronic ordering.

Berrett-Koehler and the BK logo are registered trademarks of
Berrett-Koehler Publishers, Inc.

Printed in Canada

Berrett-Koehler books are printed on long-lasting acid-free paper. When it is available, we choose paper that has been manufactured by environmentally responsible processes. These may include using trees grown in sustainable forests, incorporating recycled paper, minimizing chlorine in bleaching, or recycling the energy produced at the paper mill.

Library of Congress Cataloging-in-Publication Data

Epstein, Marc J.
Measuring and improving social impacts : a guide for nonprofits,
companies, and impact investors / Marc J. Epstein and Kristi Yuthas.
    pages cm
ISBN 978-1-60994-977-8 (hardback)
1. Investments--Moral and ethical aspects. 2. Social responsibility of
business--Evaluation. 3. Nonprofit organizations--Evaluation. I.
Yuthas, Kristi. II. Title.
HG4515.13.E67 2014
658.4'08   dc23

                    2013046278

First Edition
18 17 16 15 14   10 9 8 7 6 5 4 3 2 1

Project management, design, and composition by Steven Hiatt / Hiatt & Dragon,
San Francisco   Copyediting: Steven Hiatt   Proofreading: Tom Hassett
Illustrations: Klaus Brinkmann   Cover Design: Wes Youssi, M80

Contents

Preface

All organizations have social impacts: some are positive and some negative. *Measuring and Improving Social Impacts* is about how you can learn to make decisions that will improve the positive social impact of companies, foundations, nonprofits, and impact investors. In our work with organizations that are interested in impact, we've taken on a variety of roles—sometimes we've served as consultants and advisors, and sometimes we've served as researchers attempting to better understand organizational challenges and to develop or evaluate solutions. As professors, we also have our roles in the academy, researching and writing in addition to teaching and working with students, many of whom share their work experiences with us.

We began our careers focusing on two sets of issues: performance management and ethics. We were trained in performance measurement practices and have applied them broadly in both for-profit and nonprofit organizations. Whether the focus of the organization is on improving the financial bottom line or on improving society, similar issues arise. Organizations want clear answers to questions such as: What are we trying to accomplish? What do we need to do to accomplish these goals? How do we define success? How can we measure success? How will we know when we have succeeded? and How can we do better over time?

What we have seen is that too often, in both for-profit and nonprofit organizations alike, the answers were not clearly understood. In many cases, the questions weren't even clearly articulated. We have focused our work on helping organizations explore these questions to better define, measure, and improve performance.

Throughout our careers we have also focused on the ethical dimensions of organizations. We're concerned with questions such as How can various types of organizations use their resources to address social ills? In our work on corporate social responsibility and sustainability, we help organizations develop ways to manage social, environmental, and financial performance simultaneously. We show businesses how they can improve their social impacts while also looking out for shareholder needs.

Marc has authored or coauthored twenty books, and both Marc and Kristi have published extensively in the areas of corporate social responsibility and sustainability, nonprofit governance and performance measurement, and improving organizational social and financial performance. We have worked in Africa, Asia, and South America with organizations specializing in microfinance, microentrepreneurship, global health, and education for the poor. This international work has allowed us to collaborate with the best for-profit and nonprofit organizations in the world in dozens of countries over many years. All of this work has contributed to the ideas integrated into this volume.

Building on our previous work, we embarked on an enormous additional task for this book. We wanted to understand the views and approaches of the world's leading experts in impact measurement and to better understand how they address the difficult problem of measuring and improving their impact. This project took us to places like New York, Seattle, San Francisco, London, and Mumbai. We talked with small and large foundations, nonprofits, and companies as well as impact investors and high-net-worth individuals.

The result—this book—is about all aspects of social impacts. All organizations have impacts, positive and negative, intended and unintended. Companies can produce products that improve or damage society—or both. Nonprofits can create jobs for some and displace jobs for others. Or they can provide services that have only minor impacts relative to the resources used to create them. Organizations can easily make the mistake of operating in the dark—lacking clarity about the impacts they create or lacking the rigor to produce the impacts they desire. These organizations can benefit from developing better measurement systems that can help them succeed in their missions and improve their impacts.

In retrospect, it seems like we have been preparing to write this book our entire careers. We did not know it when we began the project, but this book has turned out to encompass the work we have been doing for decades. In researching and writing it, we learned a great deal about the importance, processes, and mechanics of deciding what impacts really matter, and then measuring and improving those impacts. Whether this is your first time thinking about impacts or you have years of experience working in the field, you'll learn new things as well.

We are grateful to the more than one hundred leaders whom we interviewed for this project. We especially want to thank Praveen Aggarwal, Sabina Alkire, Anish Andheria, Steve Aos, Doug Balfour, Clara Barby, Steve Beck, Dan Berelowitz, Jeff Bernson, Paul Bernstein, David Bonbright, Amit Bouri, Jeff Bradach, Paul Brest, Arjav Chakravarti, Leni Chaudhuri, Cindy Chen, Michael Chertok, Neelam Chhiber, David Colby, Carmen Correa, Claire Coulier, Monisha Diwan, Poornima Dore, Toby Eccles, John Elkington, Jed Emerson, Richard Fahey, Mike Feinberg, CJ Fonzi, Matthew Forti, Cynthia Gair, Russ Hall, Laura Hattendorf, Lucy Heller, Anne Heyman, Jeremy Hockenstein, Kai Hopkins, Bart Houlahan, Alex Jacobs, Hannah Jones, Tie Kim, Sean Knierim, Tris Lumley, Steven Lydenberg, Anna Martin, Steven McCormick, Carol McLaughlin, Sunil Mehta, Zarina Mehta, Hari Memon, Eve Meyer, Sumit

Mitra, Laurie Mook, Will Morgan, Jodi Nelson, Rohini Nilekani, Sara Olsen, Sally Osberg, Paresh Parasnis, Alexander Pope, Kevin Rafter, Mike Rea, Larry Reed, Gabriel Rhoads, Katherina Rosqueta, Deval Sanghavi, Zarina Screwvala, Vidya Shah, Durreen Shahnaz, Devi Shetty, Paul Simon, Rishi Singh, Lynne Smitham, Sean Sokhi, Padmini Somani, Divya Srinath, James Stacey, Nalini Tarakeshwar, Ben Thornley, Pearl Tiwari, Brian Trelstad, Melinda Tuan, Fay Twersky, Steve Viederman, Sunil Wadhwani, Havovi Wadia, Brian Walsh, Michael Weinstein, Peter White, Allen Wilcox, Peter York, and their colleagues for their time in sharing with us their individual and organizational experiences in measuring and improving social impact. We cannot thank them enough for sharing their work with us as well as their important concerns and contributions for improving social impacts. We would also like to thank the Rice University Shell Center for Sustainability. The Center's generous funding supported our field research and many other aspects of this project.

This book has taken more hours than we want to count. But it could not have been completed without the assistance of others. Hannah Sijia Chen is a bright and diligent researcher who was at the center of this project. Not only her great research support but her work in the management of all of the information from both the published research and the field and interview notes was critical. We are extremely appreciative. We are also grateful for the substantial and excellent administrative support provided by Tatianna Aker at Rice University. Samuel Ireland, Tim Hutchinson, and Maria DeWitt also provided assistance and contributed innovative ideas to the project.

In addition to the experts in organizations and our assistants at the universities that were so critical to our work, we want to thank all of the colleagues who have been so helpful in forming ideas and providing important feedback as we were developing this project; these include Klaus Brinkmann, Cindy Cooper, Srikant Datar, Jesse Dillard, Linda Firth, Francisco Montgomery, Scott Sonenshein, and Sally Widener.

Organizations interviewed for this book include:

Absolute Return for Kids (ARK)
Acumen Fund
Ambuja Cement Foundation
Arghyam
B Lab
Bill & Melinda Gates Foundation
BRAC
Bridge International Academies
Bridges Ventures
Bridgespan Group
Center for High Impact Philan-
   thropy
Chevron Corporation
Children's Investment Fund
   Foundation
Dasra
Developing World Markets
Digital Divide Data
Earth Capital Partners
EdelGive Foundation
Edna McConnell Clark Foundation
Escuela Nueva
Geneva Global
Godrej Group
Gordon and Betty Moore
   Foundation
Home Depot
Industree Crafts
International Centre for Social
   Franchising
James Irvine Foundation
John D. and Catherine T.
   MacArthur Foundation
KaBOOM!
Karisimbi Business Partners
Keystone Accountability
Kiawah Trust
KL Felicitas Foundation
Legacy Venture

Liquidnet For Good
Magic Bus
Markets for Good
Mercy Corps
MSCI, Inc.
Mulago Foundation
Narayana Hrudayalaya Hospital
Narotam Sekhsaria Foundation
New Philanthropy Capital
Nike
Nissan
Omidyar Network
Oxford Poverty & Human Develop-
   ment Initiative
Pacific Community Ventures
PATH
Pershing Square Charitable
   Foundation
Plan International
Pratham
Procter & Gamble
Robert Wood Johnson
   Foundation
Roberts Enterprise Development
   Fund/REDF
Robin Hood Foundation
Rockefeller Foundation
Shujog
Sinapi Aba Trust
Sir Dorabji Tata Trust
Skoll Foundation
Social Finance
SpringHill Equity Partners
Swades Foundation
VillageReach
Washington State Institute for
   Public Policy
William and Flora Hewlett
   Foundation

We want to thank Neal Maillet and the terrific team at Berrett-Koehler Publishers, whose efforts greatly improved this book. We also are appreciative of the extremely helpful comments of the external reviewers of the book: Kendra Armer, Kathy Scheiern, and Mal Warwick. They all made important contributions to the project.

This book is dedicated to our families. We thank Marc's family: Joanne Epstein, the Firestone family (Simcha, Debbie, Emily, Noah, and Maya), and the Zivley family (Scott, Judy, Amanda, and Katie). We also thank Kristi's family: Kiley, Jackson, and Michaela. Without their patience, support, and humor this book couldn't have been completed.

Marc J. Epstein
Houston, Texas

Kristi Yuthas
Portland, Oregon

September 2013

Introduction

You are on a hero's journey. You have decided to invest your most valuable possessions—your time, your money, your knowledge—to help others. Not content to sit back and watch, you have joined the effort to tackle some of the world's most difficult challenges: challenges such as poverty, health, climate change, and security. You know that you face enormous odds. Social and environmental problems in both developed and developing countries are immense, and the resources we have available to address them are wholly inadequate to the task. Some of the institutions that help address these problems—governments, NGOs, and corporations—are unable or unwilling to devote anywhere near the resources needed to make meaningful and lasting headway in eradicating serious social problems. Yet you are not giving up. Against all odds, you continue to work diligently or invest generously in the causes you care about, believing that your gifts will make a difference, that you can change the world. And you can.

This book will serve as a guide on that journey. It will help you turn scarce resources into meaningful investments that will, in turn, make significant improvements in society. We have written this book to help you and others like you create the most meaningful impact possible with the resources you control.

There are over one million nonprofit organizations in the United States alone and millions more across the globe. The number, breadth, and depth of these organizations have grown significantly in recent years and will continue to grow. Rapid growth is occuring in social enterprise and impact investing. As social investments flow in, it is essential to figure out ways to make sure that the money will have an impact. The impact investing industry can learn the lessons gained through decades of governmental and nonprofit investments. Both up-front investigation and ongoing assessment are needed to ensure that your investments are on track to create the desired impact.

Traditional profit-oriented corporations, too, have become much more interested in understanding and managing their impacts. Social issues no longer take a back seat to profits, and companies have many boundaries, such as avoiding child labor, that aren't subject to cost-benefit analysis. Almost all of the world's largest companies now routinely monitor social impacts and produce annual sustainability reports. The expectation that companies will contribute to society has never been greater. India has just passed a law that requires large companies to contribute 2 percent of their profits to social causes or publicly explain why there were unable to do so.

But growth in the number of organizations and faith in the good intentions of everyone involved are not enough. Organizations need to develop the ability to know whether they're making a difference and to know how to invest wisely so that they can do better over time.

While working with organizations and industries attempting to create social benefits, we have been surprised over and over again by the difficulties that investors and organizations face in their efforts to make social change. These unpleasant surprises relate to the roadblocks organizations and the social sector encounter in their attempts to produce positive impacts. As Table 1 shows, however, for each surprise there is an emerging opportunity to overcome obstacles and improve performance.

Table 1 Surprises and Opportunities

Unpleasant Surprise	Opportunity
Lack of organizational capacity for performance measurement	Demand for clear social impact strategies and action plans
Lack of incentives and market discipline to develop advanced social impact measurement systems	Pressure to develop measurement systems and increasing resources available for doing so
Lack of serious, significant investment in the social sector	New business and investment models that draw resources into impact markets
Focus on performance measurement is often small subset of organizational impacts	Development of integrated impact models and marketplaces for social impact data

This book is designed for people who are serious about social change and want to put their resources to work in the most effective way. Although the book is packed with a variety of tools and techniques, its core message is simple. To make an impact you'll need to:

- Define what success means to you, and
- Figure out how you'll know when you've achieved it.

Once you've made these key decisions, you'll find it much easier to evaluate your current progress and make changes to improve your performance.

Many investors and service providers are guilty of fooling themselves about the impacts they are making. They do this by assuming that good intentions lead to meaningful actions, by confusing the amount of action with the quality of results, and by basing important decisions on instincts instead of evidence. Perhaps you are guilty of some of these habits; if so, this book will provide you with valuable tools for overcoming them.

One common problem is defining success in terms of what the organization produces rather than the impacts that result. Table 2 shows some examples of goals based on an organization's outputs

Table 2 Goals Based on Outputs versus Goals Based on Impacts

Goals Based on Outputs	Goals Based on Impacts
We want to deliver meals to 10,000 homeless people.	We want to reduce hunger by 5%.
We want to provide 1 million insecticide-soaked bed nets.	We want to reduce malaria by 5,000 cases.
We want to convert 10,000 families from cooking with wood to cooking with gas.	We want to reduce residential CO_2 emissions by 50%.
We want to teach reading to 500 primary school students.	We want to increase literacy in the village by 10%.

compared to goals based on the impacts those outputs create. The distinctions here can be subtle, but it is essential that we focus on impacts for the following reasons: actions don't always have the anticipated results, instincts aren't always correct, and without understanding impacts it is difficult to improve them.

Humans are fallible. Psychological research has shown us over and over again that what we see and hear is strongly influenced by what we believe. Whether we believe the economy is getting better or worse might be influenced by whether we have a job. Whether we believe a school system is good or bad might be influenced by how much our own children seem to be learning. And whether we think our organization's free meals are reducing hunger might be influenced by the heartfelt thank-yous we received when we last served food.

This book will help you gain clarity about the impacts that matter most to you, and it will provide you with methods to measure and improve those impacts. Even for long-term impacts like reducing global warming or poverty that are difficult to measure or to attribute to any one investment or organizational initiative, you'll discover methods for evaluating your potential and actual contributions. Indeed, our purpose is not to try to turn you into a "randomista"—industry slang for those who believe that conducting scientific experiments, or randomized control trials, is the only way to know whether your outcomes are producing impacts.

While such methods can be useful in certain circumstances, there are many ways to use both logic and other forms of intelligence and evidence to evaluate and prove the impacts you are making.

This book's architecture is based on the Social Impact Creation Cycle. We developed the cycle to describe the steps that we believe are most necessary for creating and improving impacts. The cycle is introduced and described in chapter 1 and the steps in the cycle are discussed in depth throughout the book. The cycle is based on the five most fundamental questions faced by companies, and nonprofits, and investors seeking to maximize their social impact:

1. What will you invest?
2. What problem will you address?
3. What steps will you take?
4. How will you measure success?
5. How can you increase impact?

To address these questions, we have developed frameworks, described short case studies of organizational best practices, and provided guides to action. In addition, we have developed an online companion to this book, the Social Impact Self-Assessment tool. The tool will help you answer these five questions and assess your progress on the social impact creation journey. Further information on this self-assessment tool can be found on page 213. The book is divided into five sections:

Part 1: What Will You Invest?

Chapter 1, *The Social Impact Creation Cycle*, describes the Social Impact Creation Cycle and explains how it is used in subsequent chapters to help you define, measure, and improve social impacts.

Chapter 2, *Understanding the Investor*, explores the complex set of motivations that affect investor and donor decisions and the resources that investors can contribute to create impact.

Part 2: What Problem Will You Address?

Chapter 3, *Understanding the Problem*, considers ways investors can choose social causes to support, the approaches for addressing these causes, and the populations or regions to target.

Chapter 4, *Understanding the Investment Options*, surveys options for structuring and targeting investments and describes alternative roles, both active and passive, investors can take in those organizations.

Part 3: What Steps Will You Take?

Chapter 5, *How Social Impacts Are Created*, summarizes the basic avenues through which organizations create positive and negative social impacts—through products and services, through operations, and through investments.

Chapter 6, *Linking Actions to Impacts*, describes the essential ingredients for planning and guiding impact creation: missions, strategies, theories of change, and logic models.

Part 4: How Will You Measure Success?

Chapter 7, *Measurement Basics*, explores basic technical and behavioral concepts associated with measuring performance in general and social impacts in particular.

Chapter 8, *Measurement Approaches*, inventories and describes basic approaches to impact measurement and provides examples of tools used by leading organizations.

Chapter 9, *Measuring Your Impact*, builds on the impact planning discussed in chapter 6 and the measurement foundations in chapters 7 and 8 to provide guidance on how organizations can measure and report social impact.

Part 5: How Can You Increase Impact?

Chapter 10, *Social Impact Measurement Maturity*, describes a five-level maturity model that can be used to assess the qualities of existing impact measurement systems and to guide development of more effective systems.

Chapter 11, *Amplifying Your Impact*, explores ways to increase impact by innovating, scaling your organization, and contributing knowledge and resources to industry and sectorwide efforts to promote impact.

Chapter 12, *Call to Action*, summarizes the significant opportunities that exist to dramatically increase social impact through a careful implementation of the Social Impact Creation Cycle.

The Social Impact Creation Cycle and the book's chapters integrate the experiences from our substantial work in this field, an extensive examination of literature in numerous related fields, and the findings from a large field research project on the measurement of social impacts that included visits and interviews with dozens of leaders in the United States, the UK, and India. The project included both investors and investees. It covered government agencies, nongovernmental organizations, social enterprises, corporate sustainability leaders, and company managers interested in the impact of their ordinary products, services, and supply chains. It also involved leaders in public foundations, corporate foundations, and private family foundations—both large and small. It included some organizations that had well-developed monitoring and evaluation departments, and others that were struggling to create them. All of these organizations—even those known for being measurement experts—discussed a significant need for a book that could provide better guidance on identifying, defining, measuring, and improving social impacts.

You will find many new topics and discussions here that are based on our work with these organizations and are unique to this book. Our affiliations with universities have provided us a vantage point that has yielded powerful insights. Rather than focusing on any particular grantor or grantee, we were able to travel extensively to work with organizations on the ground in many countries. In addition, our university experience has helped us thoroughly ground our work in previous academic and managerial research.

American Express
American Institute of Philanthropy
Annie E. Casey Foundation
Ashoka
AT&T
Bank of America
Beijing LangLang Learning Potential
  Development Centre
Best Buy
Better Business Bureau
Betty Ford Center
Big Society Capital
Calvert Investments
Campbell Soup Foundation
CARE International
Charity Navigator
Children's Aid Society
Chrysalis
Coca-Cola Company
Code for America
Connected by 25
Coordinated Action Against Domestic
  Abuse
Creative Commons
Dana-Farber Cancer Institute
D.A.R.E. (Drug Abuse Resistance
  Education)
Domini Social Investments
Endeavorl
Exxon Mobil
Foodcycle
Foundation Center
Gill Foundation
Girl Scouts
GiveWell
Global Impact Investing Network
Goldman Sachs
Grassroots Business Fund
GreenXchange
Guidestar
Habitat for Humanity
HLL Lifecare
Hope Consulting
Houston Food Bank
Intellecap
International Labour Organization
Jewish Vocational Service
John S. & James L. Knight Foundation

JPMorgan Chase & Co.
Kickstarter
Kids Wish Network
Korean War Veterans National
  Museum and Library
Kresge Foundation
Laura and John Arnold Foundation
Law Enforcement Education
  Program
LifeSpring Hospitals
Locks of Love
Meyer Memorial Trust
Mothers Against Drunk Driving
Naya Jeevan
Newmont Ghana Gold Limited
Oddo Securities
Patagonia
PUMA
Raising Malawi
Root Capital
Royal Bank of Scotland
Social Impact Exchange
Society of St. Andrew
Sunlight Foundation
Taj Hotels Resorts & Palaces
The Gym
Tipping Point Community
Toms Shoes
Triangle Consulting Social Enterprise
Triodos Bank
UK Ministry of Justice
Unilever Indonesia
United Nations Children's Fund
  (UNICEF)
US Agency for International Develop-
  ment (USAID)
US Department of Health and Human
  Services
US General Accounting Office
US National Taxonomy of Exempt
  Entities
Venture Philanthropy Partners
Vestergaard Frandsen
VisionSpring
Wal-Mart Stores
Wellcome Trust
Wells Fargo
World Wide Fund for Nature (WWF)

The book is relevant to organizations, large and small alike, that are ready to step up to the challenges of improving their social impact. This includes those with a poor history of measuring social impact along with those with strong leadership that understands the importance of measurement in increasing their social impact. An extensive list of organizations interviewed is included in the preface. In addition, selected examples from a number of organizations (listed on the facing page) are also included in this book

Individuals working in foundations, NGOs, companies, governmental agencies, and social investment firms need better guidance for practice. Program managers in both developed and developing countries and other staff need more guidance on improving operations to increase impact. Even beneficiaries and hands-off donors can benefit from thinking more rigorously about social impacts. By following the steps in the Social Impact Creation Cycle, both investors and organizations can become more rigorous in defining success, understanding the causal relationships between actions and the desired impacts, measuring these impacts, and amplifying the impacts they and other social-purpose organizations can create for the environment and for society.

Over the past decade, stories of wasted money and "dead aid" have been told repeatedly—often with the conclusion that it may be better not to participate in social change at all and to let market forces prevail. But environmental and social problems aren't going away, and the world needs the resources of nonprofits, corporations, and social investors along with the operating expertise of socially concerned organizations now more than ever. These resources must be employed in the smartest, most impactful ways possible—and this needs to happen now. Let's begin that journey.

Part 1
What Will You Invest?

1

The Social Impact Creation Cycle

Every nonprofit, every company, and every investor creates social impacts. If you're reading this book, you are likely among those looking for ways to increase their impacts in order to contribute to social change. When you decide to invest in social impact, you are embarking on a journey that is uniquely your own—no two individuals or organizations begin or end up at the same point, for reasons you'll soon see. This book will serve as your companion and guide, leading you through the complex maze from the initial investment to the changes you seek.

The book is organized around the concept of a cycle, which helps you maximize your social impact by making deliberate and well-informed choices at every step in the journey from investment to impact. We will guide you through these steps and the factors you'll need to think about as you move through each one. Whether you are new to investing in impact or have been doing it for decades, it's important to make sure that the decisions you make are consistent with both your rational beliefs about how impact is most effectively created and your emotional feelings about which impacts have the greatest value. The method we present here provides you with a way to integrate the important components of your interests into a logical and cohesive whole.

The Social Impact Creation Cycle is designed to help you plan for and create the impacts you care about and to avoid creating negative impacts along the way. If you're an investor, donor, or volunteer, understanding this cycle can help you make sure that the organizations you invest in understand and can deliver on their intended impacts. If you're a company or nonprofit, working through the cycle will help you attract the resources most valuable to you and use them most effectively. No matter who you are, the Social Impact Creation Cycle can help you develop the big-picture understanding of how social investments lead to social change.

All kinds of organizations struggle with targeting and achieving their social impact goals. Philanthropic organizations make difficult resource allocation decisions trying to determine which social impact investments and/or donations will maximize benefits for their targeted communities. A foundation may need to decide whether to invest in a for-profit dairy, a nonprofit primary school, or a social enterprise–based health program. A sovereign wealth fund or government agency may reflect on optimizing the social bottom line of its activities for the neediest citizens. Even when a decision is made to invest in a sector such as health, should that investment be in combating malaria or attacking HIV/AIDS? Should the foundation promote new research or concentrate on making proven treatments available? Should it invest in Africa or in the US? Individuals face the same dilemmas when they assess their own social investments. The choices are many, and they are often difficult.

Corporations must often make trade-offs between sustainability and financial performance as they face decisions related to labor practices, environmental responsibility, community activities, and the like. The identification and measurement of the social impacts of these corporate activities often have significant implications for management decisions. Making this work more difficult, inconsistencies in measurement often arise, depending on the corporate function doing the measuring. For example, the sustainability function's metrics may differ from the corporate foundation's metrics, while both may contradict the viewpoint of those running the business's daily operations.

Individuals in the growing field of impact investing face their own challenges as they try to identify social enterprises and other organizations that can produce social impacts while meeting financial return targets. In fact, among the most critical challenges all these actors face is measurement. Social impact is a primary focus of their activities, yet these organizations and individuals are often unclear about how to measure and then improve their impacts. While projecting and measuring financial results is commonplace, most organizations find social impact measurement significantly more difficult. But demands for more careful and complete analysis of impacts are increasing rapidly. One survey shows that more than 80 percent of fund managers agree that impact measurement is important in raising capital,[1] while over 70 percent of grant makers think that foundations do not receive enough performance assessment information.[2] Social impacts are now discussed in corporate annual and sustainability reports as well as in NGO progress reports, foundation annual reports, and external reports to donors, investors, and other parties.

But even when organizations formally evaluate impacts, they do not always do it well. Inter-American Development Bank, one of the world's most highly respected development banks, once reported that fewer than one-sixth of its active projects had collected data on beneficiaries, and that only 3 percent had data on impacts on nonparticipants.[3] That information is essential for assessing the social impacts of these projects.

To meet both internal and external demands for performance information, organizations need more guidance. They need a better understanding of both how to make investment decisions that maximize social impacts and how to use monitoring and assessment to determine how much social impact has been created.

Systematic processes for gathering and analyzing information about impacts are often absent. Nonprofit organizations often use financial metrics of efficiency to evaluate performance when what they really need are measures of program and organizational impacts that they do not know how to obtain. Companies and foundations face similar dilemmas. They do not have all the information they need to make decisions related to the social impact of alternative projects.

Resolving these measurement inconsistencies requires a broader evaluation of a project's social impact. What we need is an industrial-strength tool to capture the entire picture. The Social Impact Creation Cycle provides a comprehensive method that can help you work through these issues to gain a better understanding of the social impact of a project, program, initiative, or organization.

Before we take a closer look at the Social Impact Creation Cycle, it is useful to establish a working definition for some of the terms we use. There aren't yet common definitions for these terms, but understanding how they're used here will help you as you work through the book.

Social impacts are the societal and environmental changes created by activities and investments. Societal impacts include such issues as equality, livelihoods, health, nutrition, poverty, security, and justice. Environmental impacts include such issues as conservation, energy use, waste, environmental health, resource depletion, and climate change. The term "social impacts" is used throughout this book to refer to both societal and environmental changes—positive and negative, intended and unintended—that result from investments.

Investments that create social impacts can take a variety of forms, including time, expertise, material assets, network connections, reputation, and other valuable resources. These investments can be donated, loaned, or invested with the expectation of social returns. For our purposes, if you donate or invest money or other resources, you are an investor. You are also an investor if you work or volunteer for an organization that creates social impacts or advocates for a social cause.

Social purpose organizations are entities that exist solely or partially to create positive social impacts. These organizations include non-profits, foundations, social enterprises, impact and social investing funds, social responsibility units within companies, and governmental agencies.

Social impact measurement is designed to identify changes in social impacts that result from your activities. Most organizations measure the outputs they produce (for example, meals served or jobs created). Social impact measurement assesses the ultimate impacts of those outputs on individuals and the environment (for example, on the quality of life, or survival of species).

A *logic model* is the logical sequence of activities and events through which the resources invested are transformed into desired social and environmental impacts. Organizations use logic models to work through this sequence to ensure that it is well supported before they invest resources.

This book is written with the recognition that your resources are valuable and limited, and that you would like to maximize the social impacts you create with those resources. The ideas and approaches described here will help you gain a better understanding of what impacts you hope to create and how you can best contribute to creating those impacts.

Creating and Measuring Social Impact

This book is organized around the Social Impact Creation Cycle shown in Figure 1. The cycle is built around five questions:

1. What will you invest?
2. What problem will you address?
3. What steps will you take?
4. How will you measure success?
5. How can you increase impact?

Figure 1 The Social Impact Creation Cycle

These questions are at the heart of promoting, funding, and managing organizations for maximizing social impact. The cycle applies to funders, whether they are individuals, governments, foundations, corporations, or investors. It similarly applies to operating organizations that provide services or support to or advocate for beneficiaries. Donors and investors focus on how their resources—human, material, and financial—can be best used to produce social impact and which problems should be priorities, while NGO managers and other service providers focus on how to address the social problems they face and how to maximize social impacts. For-profit companies need to focus on identifying and managing the impacts they create for their customers and other stakeholders affected by their actions. But all of these concerns are important enough to be explored by anyone interested in social impacts and the processes through which they are created.

Each group can also benefit from better understanding the interests and challenges of the others. Investors can do a better job when they understand the interests and operations of the organizations in which they invest, and operators can do a better job when they understand the needs and interests of those who fund them.

Some of these topics are rarely discussed, such as the resources and interests of the investor, or why impact measures can't be separated from the values of the individuals and organizations that use them. Also widely recognized but rarely measured are impacts created through sharing best practices and innovations or collaborating on goals. We devote extensive discussion here to those topics that are essential for effective decisions and have typically not been carefully articulated.

Step 1: What will you invest? In this step, you'll first think about your investment goals. Why are you investing? What do you hope to accomplish through your investment? Do you expect social returns alone, or do you want financial returns as well? Do you have other goals, such as strengthening relationships, building your brand, or reciprocating for benefits you have received? You'll also consider what resources you are willing to invest in social change—your time, your money, your expertise, your network.

Step 2: What problem will you address? Next, you'll decide what kinds of problems you are interested in addressing, and whether you will focus on one issue or a portfolio of issues. You will consider which social and environmental causes are most important to you and how you can best serve beneficiaries using the resources you plan to invest. And you'll consider the intervention approaches you wish to support, such as research, services, advocacy, or ecosystem support. You'll decide what types of organizations you're interested in—social enterprises, nonprofits, corporations—as well as how you'll structure your investment in that organization, whether as venture capital, equity, a loan, or a gift. You'll also decide what role you want to play in the organizations in which you invest. Do you prefer to be an outside observer, or do you want to be engaged directly in operations or governance?

Step 3: What steps will you take? Once you have identified your causes, you'll plan for achieving the desired change. Social impacts flow from an organization's mission and culture and can be created by the goods and services offered, by operations, and from passive investments. You'll consider the various ways you'll make an impact through your investments. For desired social impacts you'll develop a theory about which actions can create those impacts, and then generate a logic model or results chain that can show exactly how the organization's actions and outputs are expected to result in positive impacts for stakeholders and the environment. Finally, you'll map out your stakeholders and the effects your organization will have on them, taking particular care to ensure that the interventions you plan are both beneficial to and desired by beneficiaries.

Step 4: How will you measure success? Performance measurement and management systems help you monitor how investments are creating social change. In this stage, you'll consider the purpose of your measurement. Is it to learn how effective your work has been, to communicate expectations, or to satisfy investors' accountability demands? You'll also determine the kinds of measurement approaches that can provide the evidence you seek, whether investigation, analytics, and/or experiments. And you'll make plans for developing a performance measurement system for gathering, analyzing, and using your performance data.

Step 5: How can you increase impact? In this step, you'll evaluate the dimensions of your performance measurement system—the metrics collected, the purpose served, and their relationships with your strategy—with the goal of improving your system to increase your impacts. Finally, you'll consider strategies for growing your organization and its impact. These can include sources of innovation, ingredients needed for successful scaling, and opportunities for collaborating and sharing your capabilities in order to leverage your impact beyond your own organization.

Each element in the Social Impact Creation Cycle in Figure 1 is connected by an arrow, and an arrow connects its last and first elements. The arrows suggest that working through the steps in the cycle is not a one-time process and that you'll return to each question as you repeat the cycle to modify your actions and improve your performance.

The Need for Accountability

Governments are finding it difficult to provide the necessary resources to address social and environmental issues, and the burden is increasingly borne by nongovernmental service organizations, foundations, impact investors, and companies. Those donating to or investing in these organizations are reasonably asking for more accountability for the invested resources—as are beneficiaries and communities that have significant unmet needs. Further, when governments provide tax benefits for these investments, it is reasonable to demand that the money be wisely invested to create as much social impact as possible.

One of the most important activities in which any foundation, NGO, or impact investor can engage is to think through and articulate what achievements are desired and how they can realistically be achieved. A common explanation for lack of effectiveness is that the organization has not been clear enough about its definition of success and lacks a well-defined logic model that would likely lead to that success. Too often we find serious gaps in the logic model and little evidence that activities are likely to lead to the proposed impacts. These logic models need to be supported by empirical evidence, a clear logic, or both. But often they are supported by neither. As you'll see, the Social Impact Creation Cycle helps bring clarity to logic models and thus enhances organizational accountability.

The Impact Measurement Roadmap

Although measuring and increasing social impact are commonly understood to be important, many become mystified by the process of implementing an impact measurement system. Even if you are effectively measuring and managing your impacts now, there are methods to increase your impacts that you might have overlooked. Working through the stages of the impact measurement road map can help you identify these methods and maximize your impacts.

Measuring impacts can be a difficult process and requires careful planning. The Impact Measurement Roadmap, summarized in Figure 2 and discussed in depth in chapter 9, has four steps. In the first step, you'll prepare the measurement foundation by defining the impacts expected to result from the organization's actions as well as other positive and negative impacts. In the second, you'll determine the purpose of your measures and how they'll be used. Based on that information, you'll determine which measures are most critical to your mission and stakeholders, and choose the appropriate metrics. In the last step, you'll develop a performance measurement system for gathering, analyzing, and communicating results and taking actions to improve those impacts.

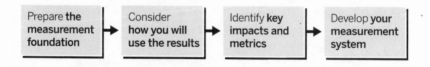

Figure 2 The Impact Measurement Roadmap

Billions of dollars are spent each year by NGOs, governments, and foundations with the explicit intent to make positive social impacts. Many more billions are spent by other organizations such as for-profit corporations that also have significant social impact interests. Too much of this money is squandered. Yes, some is through waste and inefficiency, and that should be eliminated. However, much is squandered by well-intended yet failed attempts to deliver important social changes. That failure can be remedied by careful attention to the five questions we ask in this book.

Although budgets, fundraising, and efficiency are important, social impact is the new bottom line for the social sector. We believe that you can achieve dramatic social and environmental changes through more careful efforts at defining, measuring, and improving your social impacts. Our Social Impact Creation Cycle can provide you with the guidance to do just that.

Action Agenda

1. Determine which of the five questions in the Social Impact Creation Cycle are most important to you right now.
2. Consider how you could improve your current performance measurement system by working through the stages in the Impact Measurement Road Map.

2

Understanding the Investor

What will you invest and what social impacts and other returns do you expect from those investments? Investors face these two key initial decisions when planning their social investments. By thinking carefully about these issues at the beginning of the impact creation cycle, you can maximize the range and depth of your investments and the returns those investments can generate.

A number of organizations recognize the importance of returns to investors and have developed ways to deliver them. For example, some organizations working on behalf of the poor in remote regions show investors firsthand how the resources they provide can change lives. Investors are invited to visit project areas and talk with the people who have directly benefited from their investments. When Sinapi Aba Trust of Ghana began making loans to increase capacity in schools for the poor, the organization invited donors, consultants, volunteers, and office staff to visit the field and see how the investments were working. For many of these visitors, the experience changed their lives. Seeing bright, engaged children in their safe new classrooms gave visible evidence that their investments were indeed making a real difference in the lives of these children. The trip thus gave them an unforgettable personal and emotional experience that forever changed their perceptions of the good that can be done with very small investments.

An often overlooked but critical factor in navigating your social impact investment journey is an understanding of your motivations for investing. This is the first step in making sure that the outcomes you achieve match your intentions. Who are you? What do you care about? What would it take to consider your investment a success? And what will you invest?

This chapter lays the groundwork for answering those questions. Before deciding on a specific cause, project, or partner in which to invest or reinvest, it is essential to recognize your motivational drivers so that your investment outcomes will truly reflect your investment goals. Taking stock of your goals prepares you to make smart, impactful investments that are consistent with your own particular values and interests. Understanding your investment profile also provides stability and continuity to your activities because they are anchored in the essence of your identity as an individual and an investor.

If you're investing on behalf of an institution, reviewing motives will help you ensure that your organization's social impact investments will be consistent with your organization's charter and culture. You'll also run into fewer surprises in outcomes and be less likely to have to backtrack on your investment choices.

You can start the investment process with your own investor preference profile to clarify your vision. Rather than investing out of habit or under the influence of others, begin by identifying what social impact investing means to you. If you are working with an organization, a mission statement will help define the direction of your impact investing and the expected bottom line of your investments.

A clear definition of purpose helps to prioritize potential outcomes that a particular investment might achieve for you or your organization and helps to identify opportunities where you can use your particular skills and interests to make the most impact. Understanding why you invest will help you determine the types of resources you are willing to offer, which can include much more than just money. Experience, advice, or hands-on project-level involvement can all create impacts.

What Motivates Social Investment?

In 2011, Wal-Mart made cash donations to social causes totaling $342 million—more than 4 percent of pretax profits. The company gave more than twice that amount, $617 million, as in-kind donations,[1] and Wal-Mart and the Wal-Mart Foundation gave more than $1 billion in 2012.[2] Other companies also made huge contributions to social causes in 2011: Goldman Sachs gave $337 million, and Exxon, Wells Fargo, Chevron, Bank of America, and JPMorgan Chase all gave more than $200 million. Whether they invest directly in impact or not, companies are increasingly attuned to the social and environmental impacts they create through their normal operating activities. Ninety-five percent of the world's largest 250 corporations now track and report publicly on the social impacts they create—a reflection of the growth in impact-related investment and a willingness to make impacts more transparent.

Individual gifts in recent years have been equally spectacular. The Giving Pledge has enlisted more than one hundred of the world's most wealthy and influential individuals. On the list, you'll find multibillionaire and Microsoft cofounder Bill Gates, Facebook founder Mark Zuckerberg, hedge fund chairman and American business magnate T. Boone Pickens, and founder, chairman, and chief director of Lucasfilm George Lucas.[3] What is The Giving Pledge? It's a commitment made by the world's wealthiest and most influential to donate a majority of their wealth to philanthropic causes. These individuals' donations are huge, as are the donations of their foundations. Since 1994, the Bill & Melinda Gates Foundation has awarded over $26 billion in grant money toward causes including fighting infectious diseases such as malaria and tuberculosis and funding education programs across the United States.[4]

Smaller investors are also generous in their giving. In the United States, more than two-thirds of the money contributed to charitable causes comes from individuals or households.[5] In total, donations added up to nearly $300 billion in 2011 nationally,[6] of which 82 percent were from individuals.[7] In addition, an estimated 10.7 million people are employed in the social sector,[8] and about 64 million Americans volunteered their time to social causes in 2012.[9] Governmental agencies (13.2 percent of the total US economy according to the US Bureau of Economic Analysis) invest vast resources in pursuit of social causes.

Are your investments creating valuable social impacts? It's impossible to tell without a clear understanding of what you're trying to accomplish. Considering your reasons for investing is a good place to start.

Values Drive Investment

What motivates organizations and individuals to be so generous? Why do people crack open their wallets to give their hard-earned money to someone else? When an individual contributes money to a social cause, he or she is making a statement—either public or private—about what is important and valued. In this sense, all social investment is value-driven: giving is a manifestation of one's beliefs.[10] Investors' values drive their social investments regardless of the form or scale of those investments, and whether they are acting alone or as agents of an organization. For investors who have shifted their focus from the act of giving or investing to the outcomes and impacts of those investments, values are perhaps even more important.[11]

What do individuals and organizations hope to achieve through their investments of money, time, and other resources? And what do they expect in return? The answers to these questions are as varied as the people who invest. In most cases, the investor has multiple goals in mind: social impact is the goal that unifies them. Interest and investment in social impact have gained momentum, and contributing to positive social change is at the top of the agenda for an increasing number of individuals and organizations.

Throughout this book, we broaden the use of the term "investment" beyond traditional monetary investments by expanding the range of returns that investors seek and the resources they invest. The social impact investors for whom this book is written seek social returns on their investments, which may complement or totally supplant monetary returns. They expect some kind of social or environmental change to result from their investments. Additional returns that flow from engaging in social investment include personal returns, such as pride in giving or enjoyment of the process of investing.

Goals of Social Investments

Social impact is rarely the only motivation driving investor involvement, and it is useful to both investors and recipients to explore these goals and make them explicit so that investments can best deliver on these goals. A foundation pursuing a social change mission in public health, for example, might make investments in research on aging, caretaker training, and services for the elderly. But that same organization might also invest in local arts organizations in the city where it is headquartered. Thinking about a full range of returns helps make sense of this commonplace practice.

We can think of investment returns as falling into four loose categories: identity returns, process returns, financial returns, and social impact. Figure 3 lists examples of the kinds of returns that characterize each category. There are natural overlaps and interactions among the items we list here, but investors will find that some of these outcomes are more important than others for a particular investment decision.

Each investor is unique, and more than likely, you'll discover that several motivation factors are at work, but the priorities you give them form the driving characteristic. For example, you have agreed to join a university advisory board because you want to help the university improve its impact. But upon reflection, you

Identity Returns	Process Returns
• Reciprocity • Satisfaction • Reputation	• Knowledge • Experience • Relationships

Financial Returns	Social Impact
• Profits • Increase in value	• Societal • Environmental

Figure 3 What Motivates Social Investments?

might recognize that the more important reason is that you wish to give your time to the university because you received so much during your student years. Alternatively, your primary interest in serving might be the opportunity to work alongside other high-profile members of the community with whom you would like to develop relationships. Thinking through these goals before deciding where and how to invest and reinvest can help ensure that your investments deliver the results they are intended to deliver.

In addition to financial returns, which are well understood and carefully managed by individuals and organizations of all types, and social impact, which is the focus of this book, we as investors have personal and emotional reasons to invest that are not effectively captured in terms of financial or social returns. *Identity returns* are a direct and often personal reflection on the identity of the individual or organization making the investment. These returns surround our raw desire to give and the emotional benefits that motivate and result from the pursuit of social change. Institutionally, they can include financial return substitutes such as marketing benefits like "branding" (Nike's "Just Do It" campaign, for example) or aligning products with a cause, such is the case with Coca-Cola's alliance with World Wildlife Fund, which is designed to preserve freshwater resources and increase Coca-Cola's water usage efficiency.

Process returns reflect the relationships the investor has with the investee and the transactional and relational gains that accrue to each as a consequence of their relationship. They reflect collaboration and benefits to the organizations involved rather than direct impacts on the final beneficiaries of these investments. *Financial returns* represent increases in cash flows and asset values over time, and *social impacts* represent the social and environmental changes the investor wishes to pursue.[12]

Identity Returns

Identity returns include the personal or emotional returns that accrue as a result of the investment. Many investments are made as a result of an urge to give or may flow from a desire or felt obligation to "give back" in gratitude for the benefits or advantages that have been received. The investment or gift may be motivated by altruistic impulses that are integral to the investor's identity or personal happiness. Reputation among peers and community members can also be a personal return that results from the investor's generosity. For an organization, attaching its name to a social investment can improve the reputation or brand value of the organization. Identity returns fall mainly into three categories:

- *Reciprocity.* The sense of an obligation to repay the community for one's good fortune, or a specific organization for benefits received.
- *Satisfaction.* The emotional benefits associated with the act of making the investment.
- *Reputation.* Community recognition and branding resulting from alignment with certain social investments.

Reciprocity. For many, giving to social causes is akin to settling an obligation or following through on a responsibility to repay for one's good fortune or benefits received from society. Family members and friends of loved ones who have been stricken by disease may support further efforts toward helping others suffering from that disease in gratitude for the support they received. Graduates may express thanks to a university for the education they received. Some expatriates give most to affiliated communities—their home country or the country from which they emigrated, or to institutions in immigrant communities.[13] In some cultures, it is customary to donate a portion of income earned. In several, there is an expectation that a portion of one's time will be spent in service to others. In others, the act of giving contains a spiritual element and is a means through which to express and strengthen spiritual connections and obligations. For example, some Indians give significantly to temples,[14] and nearly half of large individual donations in Asia go to religious institutions. Thus in addition to the direct social benefits to beneficiaries, the investor receives the benefit of feeling that a debt has been repaid or paid forward for the benefit of an organization and the community affected by it.

Satisfaction. From the satisfaction of writing a check to the joy of opening an email and learning about a social impact partner's success to the awe experienced when seeing firsthand the impact of the investment, emotional benefits provide a payoff for the hard work and generosity underlying an investment. Sometimes referred to as a "warm glow," emotional satisfaction can be a result of either the investment itself or the payoff from that investment. While social impact is the goal, satisfaction can be a direct benefit from the act of giving, or it can be a second-order effect that results from the perceived social impact.

Reputation. The people responsible for making investment decisions are social, emotional beings. Thus, the personal outcomes associated with a social investment may also have value for the investor. Participation in fundraising, for example, is an activity that investors may feel portrays them as people worthy of respect within the community. Businesses believe in the substantial benefits of "branded" social involvement. A business may gain brand recognition or be perceived more favorably when it is associated with a social cause. High-profile individuals or organizations may invest strategically to enhance their own reputations by associating themselves with a well-regarded organization. Naming a building or receiving public recognition for a donation, for example, can result in reputational outcomes that can benefit both investor and investee through many avenues.

Thinking ahead about the emotions attached to various aspects of the impact journey can help both in designing interactions and in assigning value to the range of outcomes that may result from the investment.

Process Returns

Process returns are those benefits that flow from the process of engagement in a project. Some investors value the learning opportunities offered through involvement in an investment, such as the acquisition of new knowledge about how a particular operation works on the ground. Others gain from the investing experience itself, as they engage in activities that contribute to the creation of impact or as they interact with beneficiaries. Social investing may also translate into new relationships and networking opportunities. there are three broad categories of process returns:

- *Knowledge.* The information and learning acquired by investing in or working with an organization.
- *Experience.* The skills and understanding gained as a result of the investment.
- *Relationships.* The personal or business relationships formed or strengthened by the collaboration with the target investment.

Knowledge. To the extent that investors are actively engaged in participating in or following the activities of investees, they can enhance their learning and knowledge in a variety of cause- and sector-related areas. Lessons from one set of circumstances can often be applied in another, and innovations can result when learning crosses conceptual or contextual boundaries. The culture of engagement and passion found among many organizations involved in the pursuit of social causes can also be an important source of insights for investees. Because social purpose organizations frequently work in extremely resource-constrained or high-risk, dynamic environments, they often develop the capacity for rapid learning, innovation, and transformation that can be enlightening and useful to investors operating in other environments.

Experience. This can be a strong draw for many investors, since the lessons learned are often transferable to other life situations. They enjoy learning new things or experiencing the differences between theoretical solutions and real results on the ground. Some may be in it for the challenge of evaluating a problem and implementing the solution while learning from experts who instruct them along the way. For both individual and organizations, gaining experience in a particular field can be a major purpose of an investment. It may, for example, be a pilot process where the investor is interested in acquiring the specific workable skills in order to better understand the social impact of the experience, which could be helpful in future projects.

Relationships. Many investments have strengthening relationships as an objective. Religious giving or giving to causes supported by friends or colleagues can build relationships, as can serving on the board or staff of a social purpose organization. The relationships can result in a broad range of benefits for both the investor and the investee. For the investee, these relationships can enhance performance of the board or staff or can provide access to a broader network of investors and resources. Thinking through how investments are likely to affect relationships for both investor and investee can support more effective allocations of resources and effort. From a "deal-making" point of view, an

investor may receive tremendous benefits from board appointments, high-powered relationships and networking opportunities,
and the like. For example, a senior executive may make a substantial investment in a project and in return be named to the
target organization's board of directors, where he or she can form
collegial relationships with other corporate leaders and improve
his or her social and commercial standing. Supporting a cause
promoted by an associate can strengthen relationships with that
associate that can result in benefits for the investor and for the
investees they support.

Financial Returns

Corporations, impact investing funds, and even foundations and
nonprofits seek two bottom lines at once: financial performance
and social performance. Financial performance can come from
cost management alone, or can be generated through revenues or
increases in the values of assets in which investments have been
made. The line in Figure 4 shows the range of financial returns
typical for various types of investments.

The line shows a continuum from donations that have no
expected returns of capital all the way to "financial first" investments, which yield commercial rates of return on the investment.
Many donations and grants are simply gifts and yield no financial returns to the investor. Charitable organizations have become
increasingly entrepreneurial, however, and their own operations
often have revenue-generating components. Although revenue
may not cover all of the organization's expenses, this model places
them on the part of the continuum in which a portion of the capital invested is returned in the form of financial gains, reducing the
demand for ongoing grants or donations.

"Social first" investments hold the middle ground. Investors
expect all or most of their capital to be returned, but are willing to accept a rate of return lower than the commercial rate
that would be expected based on the riskiness of the investment
and general economic conditions. Investors at this level are often

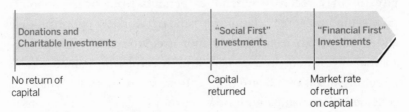

Donations and Charitable Investments	"Social First" Investments	"Financial First" Investments
No return of capital	Capital returned	Market rate of return on capital

Figure 4 Various Types of Investments

referred to as impact investors, and the capital they invest is sometimes referred to as "patient capital" when it is recognized that
the investment may yield a return, but only in the distant future.
Many impact investors are willing to sacrifice financial returns
because they value the social impact the investment creates. Social
enterprises similarly fall into this space. They intentionally seek
a combined bottom line in which financial concerns are not the
only priority. Social and environmental returns are considered to
be among the organization's key priorities, and may be built into
the organization's charter or mission. Impact investors and social
entrepreneurs may pursue this middle-ground strategy primarily
because they wish to maintain capital for future investment, but
most social-first investors believe that a quasi-market model is the
optimal way to take the first step toward providing long-run solutions to some social problems.

Investments with returns that are equal to or higher than the
market rate of return on investment can be thought of as traditional commercial investments. However, use of the term
"financial first" investments suggests that financial considerations
do not stand alone, and that social concerns also represent significant investment objectives. For example, microfinance has promised investors favorable rates of return, but most investors are also
concerned with the impacts of microfinance services on impoverished communities.[15] While financial-first investments may have
access to traditional capital markets, they have prioritized social
impact as a positive goal to be sought rather than a potential risk
area to be managed.

For example, SpringHill Equity Partners is a US financial-first investment manager that is committed to maximizing financial returns while achieving measurable and lasting social impact for its partners. SpringHill searches for small businesses in Africa that serve the poor. For each of its investments, SpringHill targets an annualized return of 10 to 20 percent and generation of a social benefit worth six to twelve times the money it invested.

Traditional corporations and their investors have various motives for valuing social impact. They may be financial-first investors, seeking social returns as a valuable goal independent of financial returns. Or they may be "financial-only" investors who prioritize social impacts because they recognize its increasing importance to stakeholder groups that have the power to influence them financially.

Financial returns may come from a variety of sources that are related to social impacts—reduced energy, materials, or logistics costs, increased brand reputation and customer loyalty, or even reduced cost of capital as investment funds screen out corporations that are seen to be particularly damaging to society or the environment. In contrast, Mulago Foundation funds high-performance social enterprises. The foundation's investment strategy focuses solely on maximizing social impact, so 95 percent of its social impact portfolio is philanthropic, with the remainder being loans.

Social Returns

Throughout this book, we describe methods for defining, measuring, and increasing social returns. We assume that since you've selected this book, you already consider social impact to be a primary investment consideration. Since the remainder of this book is about social returns, we won't go into depth here. But we will discuss trade-offs between social and financial returns. To do that, we'll need some kind of social metric. Here, we'll use a simple rating system to demonstrate how a rating of this type can be useful for evaluating investment opportunities.

Impact First/Financial First Portfolio: KL Felicitas

KL Felicitas Foundation employs a disciplined impact investing strategy to support global social entrepreneurs and social enterprises in addressing poverty.

Its impact investments break down to two general categories:

- *Impact First Investments:* aim to optimize social or environmental returns. Some of them focus on new and high-risk areas in the hope of sizable social or environmental returns. KL Felicitas' Impact First Investments include **Program Related Investments (PRIs)**, which provide low-interest financing, equity investments, etc., and **Corpus Impact First Investments (CIFs)**, which are PRIs made directly from KL Felicitas' corpus.
- *Financial First Investments:* aim for optimized financial returns that generate some social or environmental returns at the same time. KL Felicitas' Financial First Investments include **Mission Related Investments (MRIs)**, which financially support programs aligned to KL Felicitas' mission; **Sustainability Investments (SUIs)**, which offer equity investments to companies or funds focused on sustainability; and **Social Component Investments (SCIs)**, which are equity investments in funds that cycle their profits into social programming.

Source: KL Felicitas Foundation (2013) "Impact Investing Overview," http://klfelicitasfoundation.org/impact-investing-overview/.

Imagine a rating system in which each project is evaluated according to the degree to which it satisfies the investors' social objectives. Our imaginary investor has these potential projects to evaluate:

- Project 1: Fund loans to build for-profit healthcare clinics in Zambia.
- Project 2: Make a grant to support a Nepalese girls' school.
- Project 3: Fund water distribution projects in Tunisia.

To help compare the alternatives, the investor rates them on their social objectives and then plots the resulting social returns score against the expected financial return of each investment. Table 3

Table 3 Comparison of Expected Social Impacts and Financial Returns

Expected Social Impact	Project 1	Project 2	Project 3
Criteria for this investment:	*Clinics*	*School*	*Water*
Addresses difficult-to-serve clients in impoverished regions	6	6	5
Link between actions and outcomes has been evidenced	7	4	7
Capacity to continue program after our investment ends	7	2	5
Total Social Impact Score	20	12	17

Expected Financial Returns	Project 1	Project 2	Project 3
	Clinics	*School*	*Water*
Return on investment	20%	2%	30%

shows how this investor has rated each of the three projects on its social and financial returns. On the criterion of whether the three options would benefit difficult-to-serve clients, the investor gives the first two projects scores of 6, and the third a score of 5. All three projects are capable of reaching difficult-to-serve clients. On the second, which asks whether the intervention had been proven, the investor rated the school project quite a bit lower than the others. That suggests that there was more evidence that the intervention would lead to success for the clinics and the water projects. Finally, on the third, about whether the project could be sustained beyond the investment period, the clinics scored high, the school scored very low, and the water project was in the middle. Overall, the clinics project achieved the highest social impact score, and the water project was second.

Next, estimated financial returns were calculated, and the water project scored higher than the clinics project. Because no single project was highest on both financial and social performance estimates, the investor must now decide which project is superior— the clinics project with a social impact score of 20 and an estimated return of 20 percent, or the water project, with an impact score of 17 and an estimated return of 30 percent. As with all decisions involving social impacts, there is no objective way to determine which project is best—that will depend on the investor's values and interests, and on the specific goals for this project.

Once the expected social performance of each investment has been evaluated, the investments can be plotted on a graph to help the investor see which investment provides the better combination of social and financial returns. Figure 5 shows how the plot might look for this investor.

It is useful to note here that the expected financial returns are an objective estimate that could be made by a financial analyst. This estimate would remain the same regardless of which investor funds the project. Social returns, however, are value based and will vary from investor to investor. Each investor determines his or her own unique set of impact factors that will be used to rate the investments.

Another investor might have completely different criteria for rating the social impacts of these investments, such as which investment empowers girls and women the most or which project best promotes health. This investor might rate the water project highest on social impact, on the basis that access to clean water will reduce disease and free girls from the lengthy daily walk to carry water for the family. No two investors will have identical values, so each must think through his or her own values and preferences in determining social impact priorities. This is an important point, and one we'll revisit.

What Will You Invest?

At first glance, this is an easy question to answer. When we think about investing in social impact, we think primarily about investing time and money. The size and influence of the social sector is often characterized by the number of people working in social organizations and the amount of money given to or spent by these organizations.

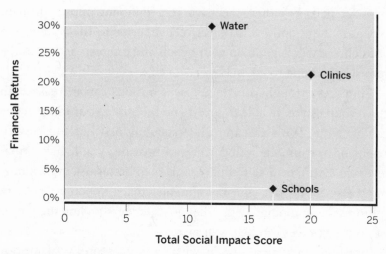

Figure 5 Projects with Different Levels of Return

But thinking about investment only in terms of time and money can paint a picture that is far too narrow, leaving out resources that can be uniquely valuable in creating impact and restricting the amount of impact you are able to create. For example, you may have medical knowledge that can be used in a crisis, you may have access to a building that can be used as a meeting place, you may have a group of colleagues whom you can invite to support a cause, or you may have the business expertise necessary to advise the investee.

Here we'll ask you to take stock of your resources. You'll identify everything that you or your organization has available that might be useful in creating impact. We'll also ask you to think about resources you have that are uniquely valuable, either because they are rare and hard to find, or because they match the needs of a particular recipient.

For example, imagine that you're a dentist with time that you're willing to devote to create impact. You could package food at a local food bank, donate your services to be auctioned off for a church fundraiser, or train dental assistants to provide basic, low-cost care to impoverished people with no access to dental care. These three options might require the same investment of time on your part, but they can have very different impact profiles. None of these options is objectively superior to the others, and your choice will depend on your beliefs and interests as well as the returns you hope to create.

Thinking through your investment options can increase both the resources you're able to invest and the value your investments can generate. With a clearer understanding of what you have to offer and the unique value you can provide, you'll have more leverage. You'll be able to put resources to better use in maximizing the social impact your investments create. When your desire for impact is combined with other goals, understanding the power of your resources can help you increase those returns as well.

Investors must first decide what resources are available for investing. For some, this is simply a matter of deciding how much cash they have available. But you may have a variety of other resources that can be useful in creating social impact. Figure 6 describes some of these resources.

Reputation

Reputation is a powerful resource that is often underappreciated. It's difficult to put a monetary value on reputation, but that doesn't mean that this resource isn't valuable. In fact, sometimes an investor's reputation is the only thing a recipient needs to create impact. An endorsement by a well-respected individual or organization can change everything for a particular organization or even for an entire cause. Betty Ford, wife of US president Gerald Ford, received a great deal of publicity when her struggle with chemical dependency became known in the 1970s. By using her reputation, she was able to gain support for building a clinic and helped reduce the stigma of seeking treatment for dependency problems.

You don't have to be internationally known to have an impact. Your willingness to support a cause can be influential to people who know you—business associates, community members, family, and friends. When kindergarten teacher Joni Huntley donated her hair to Locks of Love, a charity that provides hairpieces for children undergoing medical treatment, many children and parents decided to donate their own hair. In turn, some of their friends and acquaintances donated as well. Many social-purpose organizations don't do extensive advertising, so gifts that lead to increased publicity or a more valuable brand name can be very valuable.

Organizations often have well-known brands that are linked with their reputations for good work. Attaching their name to a project or cause often adds a level of acceptance and legitimacy. Some foundations have been asked to invest a single dollar in an organization, just so that organization could include the foundation on its list of supporters and thereby enhance its credibility.

An investor's network of relationships carries great value. Helping an investee make connections with individuals or organizations in the investor's network can open up a pool of contacts who can provide needed information, assistance, or support. The relationships and networks an investor has formed are sometimes referred to as "social capital," which is arguably more important than financial capital in many situations.

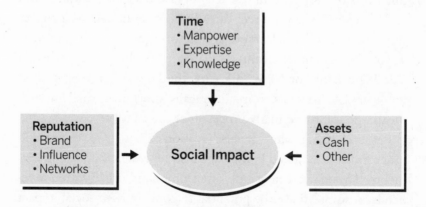

Figure 6 Resources That Can Create an Impact

Time

Working in the social sector is perhaps the most significant investment an advocate of social change can make. Employees making careers in social sector organizations invest their most valuable assets into driving social change—their time, energy, intellect, and emotions. Volunteers also invest time to drive change. They are called to fill a number of positions and responsibilities that either can't be afforded or can't be completed without their help.

Along with time generally comes expertise. While little previous experience is needed for some activities, such as piling up sandbags to protect a village from flooding, most investments of time are made much more valuable because of the knowledge that is invested along with the time. Employees, of course, build expertise and institutional knowledge, which makes their investment of time especially valuable. Volunteers often fill in gaps by providing knowledge, perspectives, and work products that can greatly complement, expand, and diversify the body of resources available for creating impact.

Knowledge developed through investments of time can be stored, shared, and used over again. This knowledge can take the form of policies, procedures, techniques, decision-making tools, and the like. These resources can also be exceptionally valuable to organizations that lack direct access to organizational expertise. Toyota, for example, recently donated its production expertise to The Food Bank for New York City, the largest antihunger charity in the US. Toyota's efforts drastically shortened wait times for meals and improved many processes at the charity.[16]

Research briefs, white papers, position papers, case studies, and other kinds of codified knowledge also represent valuable investments. These investments are often time- and organization-independent, so they have the potential to contribute to social impact in a broad range of circumstances.

Formal intellectual property (IP) can also be invested. An example of the vast impact of IP investments is the GreenXchange program, initially devised by Creative Commons in conjunction with Nike and Best Buy. The program provides a way for companies that have developed sustainability-related patents to share their intellectual property freely without extensive negotiations and legal contracts. Participants in the program can make their patents available for use by organizations, especially in relationship to their research and development functions, in order to enable widespread creation and use of green technologies and models.

Assets

Money, of course, is needed by all individuals and organizations seeking to make a social change. Even if money isn't required to directly produce impacts, it is needed to publicize the program to potential beneficiaries. Obviously, money can provide impacts in many different ways. Later, we'll explore the implications of how monetary investments can be structured—through loans that must be repaid, for example, or donations that do not.

Some investors are able to provide large lump sums of money that can be used for one-time capital projects or large investments that would otherwise be out of reach. Large investments can also be more efficient than many smaller ones, because organizations typically incur fewer costs in securing and managing the investment.

But the timing of monetary investments can also affect their value. Money that is provided in a stream over time can enable the investee to make long-term commitments that wouldn't be possible under more volatile budgetary conditions. Sometimes an infusion of cash that comes right at the beginning of a project can be valuable in getting the project off the ground and making it acceptable to more risk-averse donors. The first investment in a project on the website Kickstarter, for example, can open the gates to further exploration and support by other investors. The final investment needed to launch a project can also be valuable. Money provided at that point can help avoid delays and stress, and can change the emotional climate surrounding a project.

Other assets can be converted to cash as needed by the investee or as specified by the investor. They can also enable the recipient to avoid cash outflows. Gifts of stock, equipment, vehicles, artwork, and the like are common. But assets can also be invested in the form of long-term loans. Rights to use property such as land can be granted in circumstances where the investor wants to retain rights but also wants to use the asset to generate impact.

Communications and technology companies have offered their assets to create impact in times of need. In the event of natural disasters, many technology companies help by enabling people to better manage aid logistics and support communication. For example, AT&T and other wireless services providers agreed to use their phone lines and processing equipment to enable their customers to make donations to Japanese tsunami and Hurricane Sandy victims.

Even assets that might otherwise be discarded can create an impact in the hands of the right recipient. The Society of St. Andrew is a US nonprofit that gleaned (gathered and gave away) over 30 million pounds of food in 2012. In the United States, one-half of all food purchased is wasted.[17] The organization trains restaurant employees on food storage so that their food waste can be stored properly and then picked up by the Society of St. Andrew and given to poor people. Taking a full inventory of investable resources and identifying where those resources are likely to be useful can help investors maximize the impact they are able to create.

Investors who wish to maximize their returns need to spend time thinking about what returns they'd like to see and what they can invest to achieve those returns. By building an investment strategy firmly grounded in both a clear understanding of the range of returns desired and a complete inventory of resources available to invest, you'll be well positioned to achieve your personal goals and maximize the social benefits of your investments.

Action Agenda

1. Decide what kind of returns you want from your investments: identity, process, financial, and/or social.
2. If you're seeking financial returns, decide if you're willing to put social impact first by accepting lower-than-
   market returns on investment.
3. Take an inventory of valuable resources you can invest to
   create impact: your reputation, time, and assets.

Part 2
What Problem Will You Address?

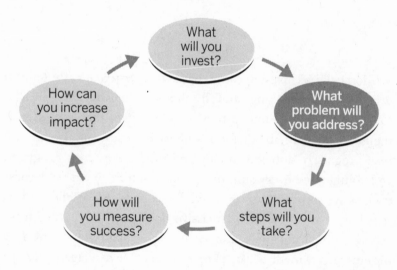

3

Understanding the Problem

We don't always invest in causes based on a systematic, thoughtful process. But by thinking carefully about which issues matter most to us, we can direct our resources to initiatives that best address the issues we care about. John, a physician who was also an avid hiker, regularly donated money and time to outdoor programs and volunteered every summer to build and maintain wilderness trails. One summer, however, his focus changed. While he was traveling in rural Mexico, a massive flood cut villagers off from access to medical care. He immediately went to work providing the emergency medical care people needed. He bandaged wounds, splinted broken bones, and even delivered a baby. This experience changed his thinking about the kinds of impact he would work toward in the future. Today, he spends time every summer traveling to villages that lack medical care to deliver medications and medical services to people who need them.

This physician faced the same range of issues we all face. Investment is needed in every social sector. Education, environmental causes, foreign affairs, religion, the arts, and many more causes can benefit greatly from increased investment. So which issue is most important? Organizations and advisors provide their own rankings, but ultimately the choice is determined by our values.

As a result of our culture, belief systems, interests, and experiences, we may hold very different views about which issues are important and about how to best address those issues. While there have been countless efforts to develop a universal set of social impact indicators, the fact is that our views of social impact and how to achieve it may not be consistent. Even if two people have community safety as their most important goal, one may seek to enhance safety through gun ownership rights while another may seek safety through gun control—and they would be unlikely to invest in the same organizations or programs.

What is really problematic, however, is that many people invest without even thinking about whether and how that investment will result in positive social impact. This may be fine for a purchase of Girl Scout Cookies or donations to a school auction. But when you're making more significant investments, you need to carefully consider whether the investment is consistent with your values, beliefs, and goals. This is as true for organizations as it is for individuals. An organization's charter, mission, and culture can provide both direction for and constraints on investment choices.

One of the biggest decisions you'll make is which problem to address. This decision will determine the contours of your subsequent choices on how best to approach the problem and how to measure progress toward the solution. Clarity here will help ensure that the resources you invest in a cause will result in changes that are most meaningful to you. We'll consider this decision from the perspective of both the beneficiaries and other stakeholders.

What Motivates the Choice of a Cause?

For-profit organizations may focus on the financial impacts of their social investments—making sure that these investments are consistent with the organization's brand and stakeholder interests. American Express, for example, gets most of its revenues from travel expenses, so its corporate social responsibility efforts focus

in part on improving tourism.[1] American Express has funded
Travel and Tourism Academies in secondary schools since 1986
to train students for tourism industries: travel agencies, airlines,
hotels, and restaurants. The program boosts profits by improving
educational opportunities for local employees.

Foundations and nonprofits may have charters that determine
general investment targets. For example, Robert Wood Johnson
started the Johnson New Brunswick Foundation, which gradually
developed into the Robert Wood Johnson Foundation, the largest
public health philanthropy in the US. Although its programs vary
over time, the general purpose of the foundation is to contribute to social change in the health and health care fields. Swades
Foundation, an Indian foundation founded by prominent media
leaders Ronnie Screwvala and Zarina Mehta Screwvala, focuses on
empowering rural India.

Some organizations use filters to narrow their investment activities. The Gordon and Betty Moore Foundation has four filters for
screening philanthropic endeavors:

1. It is important.
2. It makes a difference and has enduring impact.
3. It has measurable outcomes.
4. It contributes to a portfolio effect.[2]

Individual donors are driven by many of the same considerations as organizations. The importance of the problem and the
value the investor can contribute to solving the problem are key
considerations. As we discussed in chapter 2, individuals invest for
a variety of different reasons. Interests, preferences, and passions
play a role, as do background experiences that have influenced
the investor. Investing in social impact can sometimes be a hap-
hazard process, driven by the timing of a request or the charisma
of the person making the request. Nonetheless, the perceived
importance of the problem and needs of the beneficiaries form an
important undercurrent. What ultimately draws all social inves-

tors together is the desire to make an impact by supporting efforts toward positive social or environmental change.

The Potential for Impact

Deciding on an appropriate cause takes into account the values and capabilities of the investor. But investors don't always explore where their resources can have the greatest potential to effect change even though the promise of social impact is the primary reason for the existence of many social purpose organizations and the primary reason many investors decide to engage in the sector.

Some investors have unique capabilities or resources that can be more useful in solving some problems than others. For example, the Rockefeller Foundation, one of the biggest private foundations in United States, has the capacity to bring people together to work jointly on large social issues. The foundation holds learning forums and constructs communities of practice for its grantees and partners to share experiences, highlight lessons, and improve mutual learning.[3]

There are so many social and environmental needs that it can be difficult for investors to sort through them and decide which problems to target. As a result, investors are commonly moved to invest in a particular cause or organization as a result of personal relationships they have formed with leaders and other investors, their appreciation of the competence and expertise of potential investees, or the urgent demands of a global crisis. All of these are valid reasons to invest, as long as they are consistent with the investor's values and, most important, the social returns sought from the investments.

Giving thought to which problems you want to help solve will ensure that the investments you make are targeted toward valuable social and environmental changes. You can—and should—revisit the question of which problems to solve before every major investment decision and periodically over time. Reflecting on priorities in this manner will help you to balance your investment portfolio and to ensure that it continues to match your priorities.

Table 4 Social Responsibility Framework

Millennium Development Goals	Scientific Consensus on Life Support Systems	UN Global Compact
Poverty and hunger	Climate disruption	Human rights
Universal primary education	Extinctions	Labour
Gender equality and empowerment	Loss of ecosystem diversity	Environment
Child mortality	Pollution	Anti-corruption
Maternal health	Human population growth and resource consumption	Business for Peace
HIV/AIDS, malaria, and other diseases		Financial markets
Environmental sustainability		Business support for development
Global partnership for development		UN–Business Partnerships
		Supply chain sustainability

A number of frameworks can help you think through the various global problems in need of social investment solutions. Some try to cover all possible categories of causes, such as governmental taxonomies like the US National Taxonomy of Exempt Entities. Others focus more narrowly on an important goal. Three examples of focused frameworks are summarized in Table 4.

The United Nations Millennium Development Goals focus on the elements necessary for global economic development. The United Nations Millennium Declaration, signed in September 2000, commits world leaders to take actions to reach development goals. Each goal has specific targets and indicators. More than 190 UN member states have agreed to try to achieve these goals by the year 2015. The Scientific Consensus on Maintaining Humanity's Life Support Systems in the 21st Century (known as The Consensus) identifies factors that pose the highest immediate risks to the prosperity and survival of humans. The Consensus also outlines solutions for each of these problems. More than 2500 scientists from around the world have endorsed The Consensus so far.[4] The United Nations Global Compact is a corporate citizenship initiative from the United Nations. It encourages corporations around the world to embrace sustainable and socially responsible policies. The Global Compact is supported by six UN agencies, trade unions, and civil society groups.

In addition to these global problems, there are many local problems in need of investment. In addition to worrying about general problems, social investors also focus a great deal of attention on problems affecting those in their own communities. Local political, social, and environmental causes are continuously seeking resources, and investors may be able to have a greater impact when they invest locally. Investors may also be more familiar with the activities, capabilities, legitimacy, and effectiveness of those organizations operating in their local regions.

No one can tell you as an investor which problem is most important. But it is possible to gain additional information to help you narrow down the issues. Some philanthropy centers provide lists of critical causes each year. Some organizations provide guidance on the most promising solutions in a particular issue area, such as childhood obesity. And some attempt to provide lists of the world's most pressing problems. Once you begin narrowing down the choices, this research will help to provide answers to your unique questions.

Consider Methods for Solving the Problem

Once you have identified the problem you want to address, you need to consider various approaches for solving it. Some problems can be addressed directly by giving or selling goods and services to beneficiaries. But there are many additional methods of addressing social problems and of helping to build market or governmental solutions to those problems.

Here we explore six common methods for creating social change. The top three boxes in Table 5 show solutions that focus primarily on single organizations or initiatives: innovation, service delivery, and capacity building. The bottom three boxes list solutions that extend to multiple organizations working on the same problems and include industry-level investments designed to facilitate broad development and implementation of solutions that benefit multiple organizations within or beyond a sector: research, advocacy, and infrastructure.

Innovation is distinguished from other methods for addressing a social problem because it refers to new, untested solutions. Innovations can be associated with any aspect of running an organization that creates impact, including product and service innovations, operational innovations, and innovations in business models, such as is common in social entrepreneurship. For example, the Oshman Engineering Design Kitchen at Rice University provides space for undergraduate students to design innovative solutions to real-world engineering challenges. It collaborates with large engineering firms and other disciplines at Rice University such as the Jones Graduate School of Business to develop solutions—for example, low-cost healthcare technologies that can be commercialized in developing countries. The John S. and James L. Knight Foundation, a nonprofit private foundation with an endowment of more than $2 billion, provides significant support for media innovation. Its five-year, $24 million initiative, the Knight Community Information Challenge, aims at increasing local community news and information. More than seventy-six projects have been funded to use media and technology to help communities get informed in a creative way.[5]

Service delivery is the provision of goods or services directly to customers or beneficiaries. These services can be delivered on a for-profit or not-for-profit basis to fill unmet needs and provide benefits that result in positive social impact. Universities and hospitals are common examples of service delivery organizations, but the range of services is broad. For example, a nonprofit based in

Table 5 Six Solutions to Social Problems

Innovation	Service Delivery	Capacity Building
Developing and testing new business models, products, or processes	Providing goods and services to directly address social problems	Helping organizations improve their ability to make an impact

Research	Advocacy	Infrastructure
Developing knowledge about problems and solutions	Promoting understanding or legislation with beneficial social impact	Providing networking and technical support that enable greater impact

Mumbai, India, called Magic Bus uses sports and games as a way to provide training in gender, leadership, health, and livelihoods. Magic Bus works in marginalized communities and has reached over 150,000 children since its inception. The Beijing LangLang Learning Potential Development Centre is a social enterprise that addresses learning disabilities among primary school students in Beijing. The center has educated over 20,000 parents about dyslexia and helps them create a better learning environment for their kids.[6] Schoolhouse Supplies in Portland, Oregon, uses a hybrid model. The organization assembles boxes of supplies needed in various classrooms, and parents purchase these boxes online rather than shopping for individual items. The profits from this activity are used along with donations to provide a warehouse where teachers can shop for free supplies for their classrooms.

Capacity building refers to efforts to improve the knowledge, skills, and abilities of an individual or organization. Improved capacity enables organizations to deliver services and other outputs more efficiently and effectively. Capacity building generally seeks to increase managerial and administrative skills, enabling an organization to improve its performance and thereby create greater impact. Dasra, a leading Indian strategic philanthropy, empowers philanthropists and social entrepreneurs with training, consulting, funding, and networks to create large-scale social impacts. Incubators like the Portland State Business Accelerator help social entrepreneurs develop start-up organizations by providing technical and administrative expertise and connections to funders, talent, and other resources.

Research is designed to generate new knowledge geared toward creating greater impact in the future. Research includes traditional research and development work that results in new products, technologies, business models, etc. We differentiate research from innovation here, because it typically involves testing, such as testing the validity of an intervention or viability of a delivery method. Once an intervention has been tested, it can more reliably be duplicated or shared as a way to increase social impact. For example, the Dana-Farber Cancer Institute is a Boston-based nonprofit that conducts research on cancer diagnosis, treatment, cure, and prevention. The results of this research are disseminated widely and used in the institute's education and patient care programs.

Advocacy work is also critically important for creating impact. In many cases, social purpose organizations exist because of a policy-related failure. Many nonprofits in India—for example, Industree Foundation in the natural fiber sector—help impoverished citizens to demand the resources owed to them by the government. Organizations throughout the world work to enact laws that protect or support people or the environment. The William and Flora Hewlett Foundation, one of the biggest US private foundations, has an Environment Program that funds organizations that work on climate change and air quality policies. Although the outcomes may not be readily visible to investors, policy-focused organizations push constituents to engage in thoughtful conversation and negotiation about important social topics.[7]

Infrastructure or ecosystem interventions are investments that strengthen a network, industry, or sector. Support for and connections among social purpose organizations can be essential for sharing and leveraging best practices and other resources, as well as for benchmarking and improving performance. Markets for Good, a collaboration of the Bill & Melinda Gates Foundation, the William and Flora Hewlett Foundation, and the financial firm Liquidnet, bridges the information gap in the social sector by providing a technological backbone for storing and exchanging information on social impacts.[8] Markets for Good believes that if the structure of the social sector is strengthened, then there could be a better information flow among the organizations that could potentially generate much greater impact.

The Target Market

In focusing investments, a number of additional factors may be important to the investor, such as the social and demographic characteristics of the beneficiaries (see Figure 7). One of the most important factors is the geographic location or region you want to focus on. For example, you may want to support social change in a small community or region where you live or have affiliations, or you may be interested in investing in a broad region or country in which social change is needed.

When the target for change involves people, the selection of socioeconomic status can also be important, and investors may decide to focus on the destitute, the poor, the middle class, or other groups. Investors may also have a preference for targeting individuals, families, villages, or larger communities. Investments may target a particular life stage as well—prenatal care, infants, preschoolers, etc. And they may target girls or boys, women or men. Various racial and religious groups can be a focus, as can various occupations and social interests.

Investors may also choose to target a particular stage in the lifecycle of a problem, whether on preventing a problem, detecting the problem, solving it, or regaining ground after the problem

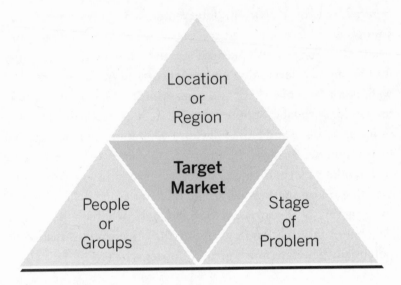

Figure 7 Target Market Characteristics

has been addressed. For example, someone interested in reducing breast cancer could invest in research, cancer screening, delivery of treatments, or support for affected patients and families.[9]

As with causes and interventions, you may have preferences relating to these categories, and if so you should make them explicit because it will help guide your investment choices.

Breadth of Investments
Depending on their investment goals and values as well as on the resources they plan to invest, investors may pursue various investment strategies. They may focus on a single solution to a social problem, on multiple solutions to a particular problem, or a broad portfolio of causes (see Figure 8).

Solutions
Some investors are very specific in the interests they target and seek to make a meaningful social impact through a trusted solution. Organizations with this approach include Mothers Against Drunk Driving, a nonprofit that seeks to reduce drunk driving among

US high school students; Foodcycle in the UK, which invites local student groups to develop ideas to feed hungry people; Bridge International Academies, which creates schools in Africa to provide affordable, high-quality primary education; and Habitat for Humanity, which builds affordable housing. KaBOOM! builds playgrounds to help American children have a healthy, happy, and successful future. Even when your focus is very specific, there will usually be a number of different organizations, programs, or initiatives with a similar focus. You can decide on which of these investments to pursue based on a number of factors, including the ability of the intervention to generate impact. As with other investment decisions, reviewing what returns are expected from these investments and what resources are available to invest should help guide your choices. In some areas, it is possible to find or commission studies of various service providers to enable more accurate comparisons and thus more effective investments.

Causes

Cause-related investors seek broader solutions by focusing on multiple approaches to solving the same problem or include a broad range of related problems. There are many methods available to address a specific cause—including providing direct services to individuals in need and supporting development of tools and resources that strengthen that sector. Cause-related approaches generally include investing in multiple complementary methods. For example, BRAC, which is the largest nongovernmental development organization in the world and is based in Bangladesh, provides education, health, financial services, and other services to help alleviate poverty.

The Children's Investment Fund Foundation in the UK focuses on seven impact areas for children, including childhood survival, educational achievement, and nutrition and hunger. Robin Hood Foundation applies multiple strategies to alleviate poverty in New York. Pratham, the largest NGO in India, does research on illiteracy around the country, develops and delivers literacy solu-

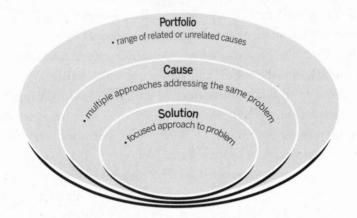

Figure 8 Breadth of Investments

tions in a variety of languages, and promotes development by working with governmental agencies, schools, and local volunteers to develop the infrastructure for delivery.

When the resources available for investment are substantial, the investor may seek to have a direct and measurable impact on the desired social change. One such approach is known as "catalytic philanthropy," which seeks to create large-scale, meaningful, and enduring change. Catalytic philanthropists think beyond choosing which organization to fund. They choose a social issue they truly care about and then leverage their skills, connections, and resources to develop a solution.[10] For example, when Thomas Siebel, the founder of Siebel Systems Inc., decided to deal with methamphetamine abuse in Montana, he did not simply give funds to one nonprofit in the field. Instead, he researched the problem and found that teenagers were not aware of the harm the drug can do. As a result, he started a TV campaign that demonstrated how the use of methamphetamines can destroy families and loved ones. The TV ads were brutal and the impact was significant. In two years, Montana dropped from fifth to thirty-ninth in US rankings for methamphetamine abuse.[11]

Portfolio

Perhaps the most common approach by individual investors is to invest in causes that both create social change and are meaningful to them personally. In some cases, they have a clear understanding of how these gifts are associated with objectives such as reciprocity, satisfying obligations, or building a network. Gifts to local churches and schools, an alma mater, and research on a salient disease may all be included in a portfolio of unrelated investments. Some organizations have a very broad strategy. For example, the William and Flora Hewlett Foundation sets as its mission working to solve social and environmental problems in the US and abroad, which includes everything from global poverty to climate change, and from education to health and human rights.

Investment in a portfolio of causes can be a meaningful strategy when there are many issues the investor seeks to affect and ample resources available to invest. The Godrej Group, one of the best-known companies in India, consists of seven major companies operating in a diverse range of industries that includes real estate, consumer goods, and industrial engineering. The group's holding company invests heavily in the environment, healthcare, and education—areas in which the organization can have a significant impact on customers and other stakeholders. Initiatives within each area are also diverse. For example, environmental initiatives include platinum-level LEED building certification, wildlife conservation, and a grove of mangroves that functions as a "lung" for the city of Mumbai.

Values

The social changes investors seek are strongly linked to their own values and those of their families, organizational founders, colleagues, and communities. These values, in turn, are driven by a variety of cultural, social, experiential, and historical factors. Values differ from individual to individual and organization to organization, and they also change over time.

For this reason, coming up with a universal definition of what is socially beneficial is impossible. Same-sex marriage, for example, might be seen as a social benefit by some and a cost by others. And even those who agree on the benefits of a particular outcome, such as low carbon emissions, may differ about the importance of achieving low emissions relative to other outcomes such as reducing the incidence of poverty or empowering women.

As an investor, you'll need to consider which values and impacts are most central to your own goals and those of your organizations and where your investments can produce the greatest social impacts. You'll need to revisit these goals over time as interests, contexts, and options change.

Action Agenda
1. Clarify your investment mission by determining which social and environmental changes you would most like to see.
2. Consider constraints, such as charters, that guide your choice of problems.
3. Determine where your unique set of capabilities and resources can provide the greatest impact.
4. Choose the methods you will use to strengthen individual organizations or contribute to collective goals.
5. Determine the specific population or region you will target.
6. Decide whether to invest in a specific problem, a broader cause, or a portfolio of causes.

4

Understanding the Investment Options

Social investors have many factors to consider when deciding where and how to invest. Here we'll focus on *how*. The basic choices facing the investor are:

1. How should I structure the investment—as a gift, a loan, or as capital?
2. What kind of organization should I invest in—nonprofit, social enterprise, fund?
3. What role should I take as an investor—hands-off investor, advisor, board member?

Aligning Investments with Objectives

A critical challenge in determining where to invest is identifying specific organizations, projects, and initiatives that align with your investment objectives. While there are numerous rating systems that can provide generic evaluations of organizations, none of these ratings can ensure that an investment opportunity aligns with the unique goals of a particular investor. Thus, to make sure that each investment is capable of producing the desired social impact and associated goals, you must determine for yourself or your organization whether there is a good fit between investment objectives and opportunities.

You should keep alignment in mind when deciding on investment structures or organizational forms. Ensuring alignment is
also important before moving on to the next stage of the cycle,
in which you define and measure specific social impact objectives
and strategies to achieve them. Investment objectives and opportunities should align on at least four important dimensions:

- The social impact mission
- The roles available and resources needed
- The financial risk profile
- Accountability requirements

Social Impact Mission

Alignment on the social impact mission is the starting point for
ensuring that your objectives are in alignment with the expected
outcomes of the investment. The impact provider's mission and
its strategy for accomplishing that mission must be compatible
with your focal causes and your desired approach to pursuing
them. Alignment on these elements helps ensure that your social
objectives are consistent with those of the organization that will
be tasked with accomplishing them. In some cases, the two parties
will be in full alignment on the objectives and how they can be
accomplished. More commonly, your objectives will intersect and
overlap in the area of concern so that alignment exists for one set
of pursuits but not all.

For those investors with a small stake, alignment will be determined by verbal or narrative documentation of the mission sup-
plemented by information about actual accomplishments and
metrics. For significant investments, you can investigate alignment
in greater depth through direct discussions and negotiations and
possibly detailed written documentation. This can be done infor-
mally or through grant applications or due diligence processes.
Sometimes the investee operates as a subcontractor for the investor. In this case, the investor's mission is paramount, and resources
are invested in organizations capable of carrying out the mission.

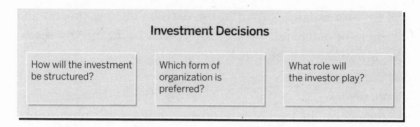

Figure 9 Investment Options

Alignment on mission is in many ways a meeting of values. There is no objective manner for determining alignment, but when both parties are explicit in defining and presenting their social impact objectives, the possibility that both can form effective partnerships is enhanced. More important, the more clarity and transparency an organization can provide with regard to mission, the more able the organization will be to develop systems and practices to effectively pursue that mission, and the more capable the investment community can be in its support. With careful attention to clarity of mission and a serious alignment of values, the parties will be better positioned to avoid the common problem of mission drift, which can occur when an organization shifts away from its purpose—for example, to take advantage of a funding opportunity or satisfy a powerful stakeholder.

Roles and Resources
In addition to alignment on desired social impact, you should investigate the degree to which the investee can meet your other objectives regarding the role you expect to play and the resources you plan to invest. Investors can benefit from making their objectives transparent to everyone on both the investor and investee sides of the relationship. Failure to explore and communicate objectives can lead to disappointment on the part of the investee or even early termination of the relationship. For example, an investor who expects to be involved in strategic decisions may anticipate that the investee desires and values that level of participation. If

the investor is not involved in the decision-making process and decisions or outcomes that are unacceptable to the investor result, the relationship will be at risk.

Financial Risk

Alignment on the level of investment risk is another precursor to a successful relationship. It is important that you are aware if an investee is new and other funding or revenue sources are fragile, so that you can adjust your expectations and actions accordingly. Some investors are concerned with governance and will investigate the financial expertise of the investee's board, along with its IRS Form 990 reports,[1] annual reports, and any audit or accreditation reports that are available.

For individual investors lacking the ability to evaluate fiscal strength, Charity Navigator provides general information about the basic financial status of nonprofit organizations as well as the percentage of expenses they allocate to fundraising and administrative overhead. For a small but growing number of organizations, GiveWell, an American charity evaluator, has performed a detailed examination of key financial aspects of the business, and detailed evaluations are available to potential investors.

Organizational capacity is also an important factor in managing investment risk. The organization must have the capacity to deliver on the promise of creating the targeted social impact. There are many sources for information about organizational capacity, including associates familiar with the organization, results for prior similar initiatives, past performance, clear targets and operational policies, and the like. In some industries, standardized managerial rating systems are available. But in every case, the organization that will be charged with delivering the impact must have a clear strategy for delivering, assessing, and managing that impact, as we discuss in detail in subsequent chapters.

Accountability

Performance reporting—alignment on the manner in which social impact objectives and other desired outcomes will be monitored and reported—is also an important foundation for a successful investment. Before you initiate any agreement, you should make sure that you and the investee agree on a basic philosophy of measurement and reporting. Some social organizations may decide that measuring impact is irrelevant due to the difficulty of linking actions to impacts or because the action–impact link has been well demonstrated in the past. Others will see impact measurement as critical. They will build performance measurement routines into project processes from the beginning and carefully monitor and manage them as the project progresses.

To deliver on the promise of turning dollars and other investments into social impact, alignment between the investor and investment opportunity is important. Individual investors must prioritize alignment if they want to be confident that their efforts and money will generate the returns they seek. Organizational executives and boards have an even greater obligation to answer this question because the resources they control are not their own. The organizational charter, mission, values, and culture provide general guidelines of what matters to the organization. But managers and board members should be in alignment not just on strategy and operational activities, but also on what kinds of social change they want to pursue, which roles and resources must be employed to meet those objectives, and the levels of financial risk and accountability that are feasible and desired.

Ways to Structure Investments

There are many ways to structure social investments, and new investment vehicles are being invented every day. Here we focus on the monetary portion of the investment, although we recognize that money is frequently accompanied by endorsements, advising, and other forms of support. Basic types of monetary investments include:[2]

Grants/donations. Grants and donations are commonly used structures for investments that take the form of monetary gifts to nonprofit organizations. Their use may be restricted to a specific purpose or may be at the discretion of the recipient. They may be given at a particular point, over time, or as certain project milestones or measurable results are achieved. Investors who give grants or donations don't expect monetary returns, but they do expect that the recipient will use their investment to create social returns.

Loans. Loans can be made at commercial rates, but they can also be structured as below-market-rate loans—loans that wouldn't meet the risk profiles of commercial investors. Loans can be structured in various ways, such as allowing a long grace period before repayment is scheduled to begin, or allowing the borrower to make interest-only payments until full repayment is possible. For example, US Federal Direct Loans can be considered to be social investments. By accepting lower-than-market returns on student loans, the government seeks to promote an educated citizenry. Some investments are quite risky, such as investment in the development of a new technology for use in a developing country. In this case, the investor may expect the loan to become a grant if the project or organization is not successful or is unable to repay. Many foundations combine targeted loans with grants for philanthropic goals—for example, the Gates Foundation has a pool of $1 billion for charity investments and loans in addition to its traditional giving.[3]

Angel/venture capital. Venture capital investments can take the form of seed or venture financing with the objective of supporting an organization through its early growth stages until it can become sufficiently stable and successful. In the case of a social enterprise, venture capital may support the organization until it becomes financially sustainable and sufficiently successful to seek commercial investments.

Philanthropic capital typically refers to investments that enable the organization to mature to the point where it is eligible for traditional equity funding. Numerous organizations, including Endeavor, Acumen Fund, Skoll Foundation, Intellecap, Legacy Venture, and Omidyar Network, channel capital to support social enterprises and social entrepreneurs. Patagonia, a California-based clothing company, launched a new in-house venture fund called $20 Million & Change that will invest in start-ups making positive impacts in clothing, food, water, energy, and waste.

Social bonds. In issuing a social bond,[4] a government agency typically supports a nonprofit or private organization's investment in a social program of the kind that requires heavy up-front investment but for which social impacts are highly speculative. Private investors buy the bonds, bearing the risk that the project will not produce the expected social benefits. If the goals are not reached, the investors lose their money. However, if the project's goals *are* reached, the government repays the investors with interest as stipulated in the bond. Pioneers in the field include Social Finance in UK, which issued the first social impact bond in September 2010 for a prison recidivism program. Goldman Sachs invested almost $10 million in a jail program in New York City in 2012 through social impact bonds. In 2013, Goldman Sachs, together with Chicago investor J. B. Pritzker, invested about $7 million in Salt Lake City's childhood education program.[5] Government agencies elsewhere have also started exploring the possibilities. The UK, US, Australia, Canada, and Israel all have begun social impact bond programs at various levels.[6] Pay for Success Bonds issued by the US government were budgeted at $100 million for 2012 to support successful initiatives in education, juvenile justice, workforce development, and other fields.[7]

Credit enhancement. Credit enhancement supports nonprofit or social enterprises with a funder's strong credit profile to help create a way to guarantee repayment. This support can take several different forms. One of the most common is loan guarantees. Kresge Foundation has budgeted $13.5 million to guarantee its grantees' loans with its strong credit, thus lowering their borrowing costs.[8] Root Capital, a nonprofit social investment fund that finances rural businesses producing natural products in Africa and Latin America, uses future sales contracts as collateral for its loans. If the small business fails to repay the loan, the contract is forfeited to Root Capital. The buyer in the contract pays Root Capital instead of the small businesses. In this way, Root Capital solves the financing problem for small rural businesses—and its program has experienced a repayment rate of over 99 percent.[9]

Impact investments. Impact investments can refer to any of the investment types described above and often have risk/return profiles that make them unattractive to commercial investors. Although many investments promise positive financial returns, the returns may be lower or the investments more risky than similar market investments. These investments can be structured in common ways, including grants, loans, or equity investments. They increasingly also include a variety of alternative investment vehicles, such as loan/equity hybrids that convert loans to equity when impact milestones are met or link interest to revenue generation. Layered investment stacks may combine grants, equity, and debt in the same investment package.

The Acumen Fund, a US-based nonprofit global venture philanthropy fund, provides different types of financial support to its investees. More than half of its investments are in the form of equity, and about one-third of them are debt/loan guarantees. Only a few investments are made as grants. At the same time, Acumen Fund leverages its resources and attracts money of about four times the size of its own investments from non-Acumen sources to fund its investees.

Impact investments can be relatively hands-off or, as with venture investments, the investor may play an active role in managing or providing consultation to the organization. In all cases, impact investments are expected to produce significant social returns. Impact investing funds provide opportunities for pooling investment capital. Impact investment funds tend to emphasize social impact more heavily, often expecting investees to have clearly articulated social missions. Some focus on a particular impact area, while others seek more diversified portfolios.[10] Triodos Bank in Europe has, for example, launched a number of financial products for companies, projects, and foundations that focus on sustainability.[11]

In recent years, impact investing funds have grown dramatically. In 2012, fifty-one fund managers in a survey reported raising $3.5 billion, and they target $5.7 billion in 2013. The impact investment industry aims at $9 billion in 2013, and predicts a $200 billion to $650 billion market opportunity in the next decade.[12]

Types of Organizations

Every organization creates social impacts, whether or not it does so intentionally. Social investors in the past typically provided gifts to nonprofits or invested for dual social and financial returns using a social screening process.

Calvert Investments, for example, has used social screens for many years to screen out investments in organizations with potential negative social impacts—investors may, for example, wish to screen out extractive industry organizations, organizations operating in countries known for human rights abuses, or companies that manufacture guns.

Today, investment managers offer a wide range of positively screened funds—funds that intentionally invest in market leaders that offer significant social as well as financial returns. For example, Calvert manages one fund that invests in organizations providing alternative energy and another that invests in organizations working to increase access to clean water. There are also impact investors who gear all of their investments toward a particular impact. SpringHill Equity Partners, for example, invests

Omidyar Network: The Venture Capital Model

Omidyar Network (ON) is a philanthropic investment firm with a mission of unlocking individual potential through the power of markets. It applies the best practices of the venture capital industry to philanthropy and achieves its goal by investing in sustainable charities that have solid business plans.

ON provides grants to nonprofits to spark innovation and invests debt and equity to scale up their ideas. Grants nuture nonprofits' potentially impactful ideas by subsidizing goods and services and spurring investments in risky ventures. For example, ON-supported Creative Commons grants copyright permissions, enabling more public sharing of creative works. For-profit ventures such as ON do good by leveraging the power of the market. Using grants as well as investments, they deliver desired social impact in difficult socioeconomic environments. The aggressive growth of microfinance illustrates the complementary role of grants and business. Most microfinance institutions were grant-funded when the industry first started in the 1980s. As their commercial viability became clearer, business investors stepped in and helped fuel their further development.[13]

in large alternative energy projects that have a long payback period and are therefore unattractive to most standard private equity investors.

Social impact investments can be made through a broad range of organizational forms. Some of the forms most commonly associated with making and managing social impacts are:

Nonprofits. Nonprofit organizations are controlled by boards of directors and do not have stockholders. Nonprofits exist to address social issues rather than to provide financial returns. Any profits generated by these organizations are not distributed to employees or founders; instead, they are retained within the organization and used for funding social projects.

Foundations. Foundations are nonprofit organizations that typically support other nonprofits to achieve their mission. Foundations usually give grants, but they may also become involved in social investments. Some foundations work alongside their grantees to support capacity building. Foundations can also leverage the resources of their grantees in the same field by holding meetings to share experiences. In the United States, the Internal Revenue Code distinguishes between private foundations and public foundations. Private foundations are usually funded by an individual or a family, and donors have more control over their giving. However, private foundations also face more restrictions and enjoy fewer tax benefits than public foundations, which raise money from the general public. There are also corporate foundations, which are established by a corporation to create social good. They often receive a portion of revenue or consistent funding from the corporation.

Social enterprises. Social enterprises are revenue-producing organizations with social missions. These organizations apply business strategies to optimize their social impacts while seeking financial returns in order to make their impact sustainable. LifeSpring in India, a for-profit maternity hospital chain in India set up by HLL Lifecare Ltd. (an Indian government enterprise), and the Acumen Fund (a US-based nonprofit global venture philanthropy fund) are examples of successful social enterprises.[14] If its business model proves to be effective, a social enterprise can be replicated and spread widely.[15] The Gym Group, a low-cost gym chain in the UK that started in 2008 and now operates in over forty sites, is a profitable example of a social enterprise. It yields a 50 percent internal rate of return and a 3.7 multiple for Bridges funds, while delivering social impact. Since more than half of the gyms are located in underserved areas, The Gym creates jobs for low-income people and improves both health and well-being in local communities, with about one-third of its members being first-timers.[16] There are over 60,000 social enterprises in the UK, employing almost 1,000,000 people and contributing more than £24 billion to the economy.[17]

Corporations. Corporations may become involved in the social sector through their corporate social responsibility (CSR) programs or their daily operations. Corporations enhance their social responsibility by supporting local communities and programs related to their fields as well as by regulating their manufacturing processes. More than two-thirds of large companies in Europe and the US report on their social performance. India recently passed a Companies Act that requires companies of a certain size to contribute at least 2 percent of their profits every year to CSR activities.[18] Some corporations establish units create social good and devote revenues, skills, and time to doing so. Liquidnet For Good is one example. Founded by Liquidnet Holdings, a financial technology firm, Liquidnet For Good supports initiatives like the Agahozo-Shalom Youth Village, which protects and nurtures orphans in Rwanda, and Markets for Good, which is using Liquidnet's expertise to create an information exchange for social purpose organizations.

Investment funds. Some investment funds operate with a social purpose. Fund managers invest in social enterprises or other social purpose organizations using the collective capital from investors. There are numerous examples of impact investment funds, and many have shown evidence of effectiveness in terms of management and impact. ImpactAssets publishes the IA50, an annual index of fifty top-tier impact investing funds.

Government agencies. Government has a special role to play in the social sector because it has the power, reach, and influence that no other organization has. The Community Development Financial Institutions (CDFI) Fund is a program of the US Treasury Department that promotes community development. The CDFI Fund provided hundreds of financial assistance grants since its inception, and generates about twenty times the amount it has funded in nonfederal government investment to targetted areas.[19] Government in the US also uses other subsidy programs, including Low Income Housing Tax Credit and HOME Investment Partnership.

Public–private partnerships. Public–private partnerships are arrangements between private and governmental entities. Typically, a project is funded wholly or partly by the private entity, which bears much of the economic risk of the project. Returns on the investment come directly from governmental agencies or others who pay for using the assets or services. These vehicles are able to fund projects that would be difficult for governments to take on due to the debt and risk characteristics of the investments. Swades Foundation, a foundation that empowers people in rural India, promotes Private Public Community Partnership, which combines resources from communities, government, corporations, and NGOs to create self-sustaining villages.

Choosing the Right Organization
After clarifying the mission, investors need to choose specific organizations in which to invest. Charity research organizations are designed to help investors make these choices. These organizations study, rate, and recommend organizations with good and sustained social performance, enabling more effective spending and greater social impact. Leading organizations in the field include B Lab, Charity Navigator, and GiveWell. Numerous rankings of corporations and nonprofits on a range of social, environmental, and governance factors are available as well. Table 6 lists organizations that provide ranking information and Table 7 lists rating systems and indexes.

In selecting an appropriate organization in which to invest, two aspects are particularly important: the potential for creating impacts and management capacity. As we emphasize throughout this book, organizations vary dramatically in their ability to make an impact. At the highest level, we can make comparisons of the type and relative global importance of impacts. Numerous recent discussions in the press argue that social impact investments should be directed toward pressing large-scale problems like poverty and climate change rather than less life-threatening causes like historical preservation or school enrichment programs. But

GiveWell

GiveWell, a US-based nonprofit charity evaluator, started out in 2007 to evaluate, rank, and recommend charities. It focuses on the charities' evidence of effectiveness, cost-effectiveness, transparency, self-monitoring, and need for funding. Results of evaluations are reported publicly on GiveWell's website to support investor decision making. For example, in its most recent update for VillageReach, a US nonprofit focused on distributing medical supplies in remote areas, GiveWell published a detailed description of VillageReach's progress. GiveWell stated clearly the challenges that VillageReach is facing, how much funding it needs, and what it has achieved. GiveWell especially praised VillageReach's effort on transparency and impact measurement.

even among organizations addressing a specific issue, such as child immunization, there are enormous differences in performance and impact. One organization might provide immunizations for a single school using the same amount of resources that another uses to immunize an entire village. Or one organization might offer a prison training program that reduces recidivism by 3 percent while another program with the same number of training courses and students reduces recidivism by 30 percent. Lofty aspirations and delivery of services are not enough. Organizations should be able to demonstrate the impacts they have made or are capable of making.

In addition to evaluating current performance, you'll want to make sure that the organization has the capacity to continue its successes into the future. Internal and external problems and opportunities will cause organizations to change course frequently and to revise higher-level strategies on a regular basis. You'll want to confirm that the organization's management has the capacity to deal with these demands. Management should also have the capacity to maintain an effective performance management system and to use the knowledge provided by the system to continually improve impacts.

Table 6 Examples of Information Intermediaries

Organization	Type of Organization	Geographic Focus	Information Provided
GiveWell	Nonprofit	Most developing countries, some US	• Rankings of organizations based on effectiveness, cost-effectiveness, need for funding, transparency, and self-monitoring; based on its own research • Recommendations of 2% of the organizations reviewed
Charity Navigator	Nonprofit	US	• Evaluations of over 6,000 charities based on their financial health, accountability, and results reporting
B Lab	Nonprofit	US-based; worldwide	• Standards for corporate social responsibility, company rankings, and B corporation certifications
New Philanthropy Capital	For-profit	UK, expanding in Germany, India, and the US	• Free reports on different sectors • Customized reports on specific organizations, stresses on program effectiveness
Dasra	Foundation	India	• Research reports on different organizations, interventions, and people • Executive trainings for nonprofit and social business leaders • Events that bring philanthropists, foundations, and nonprofits together
Better Business Bureau	Nonprofit	US and Canada	• Charity ratings and reports • Charity complaints and reviews
Foundation Center	Nonprofit	US-based; worldwide	• Database of grant makers and their grants • More than 11,000 reports, case studies, and other documents on nonprofits on its online resource

Roles Investors Can Play

Investors have a broad range of options in determining the role they would like to play in the organizations in which they invest. So-called "checkbook philanthropists" donate resources at arm's length, or anonymously, and then step back and let the organization determine how best to allocate those resources. Social investors may contribute to funds, which may in turn make financial investments that are managed only from a risk control perspective, as might be the case when investing in large for-profit organizations.

Other investors play a variety of roles in addition to or in lieu of investment of financial resources. Those who invest their time, for example, may take part in some aspect of operating or managing the organizations in which they invest. More and more, people today expect wealthy families to involve themselves actively in the organizations they fund.[20]

One important element in defining the role to be played is the amount of control the investor seeks in relationship to the resources invested and how those resources are managed and used. The role will depend, in part, on the resources to be invested and their significance and value to the investor. Typically, the individual or organization engaged in producing the social change is not the only investor. Other investors can take a variety of roles, from serving on the board or steering committee responsible for directing and overseeing managerial activities to simply providing resources at arm's length.[21]

Contributor. Contributors are donors and grant makers who provide resources and then allow the investee to manage those resources without a high level of ongoing interaction or negotiation between the parties. The contributor trusts the investee to effectively manage the resources and deliver the promised or implied results. This arrangement is typical for investors and investees for whom the resources exchanged have a low level of significance for either or both parties. But the arrangement is also

Table 7 Examples of Rating Systems

Ratings/ Index	Provider	Type of Organization	Geographic Focus	Information Provided
S&I 100	Social Impact Exchange	Membership association	US	Reports on 100 evidence-based non-profits and nearly 16,000 local affiliates
RBS SE100	Royal Bank of Scotland	For-profit	UK	Facts about the financial performance and positive impact of UK social entrepreneurs
Global Impact Investing Rating System	B Lab	Nonprofit	US-based; worldwide	Comparable comprehensive assessments and ratings of companies and funds
KLD Social Ratings	MSCI (formerly KLD Research Analytics, Inc.)	For-profit	US	Environmental, social, and governance research on companies for institutional investors

common where trust in the capacity of the recipient to maximize the value of the contribution is high and the donor places no restrictions on the use of the gift. With grants, it is common for the investor to hold the grantee accountable for operations and outcomes. Interaction between grantor and grantee can take a variety of forms, and ongoing support can depend on achieving of milestones and agreement on future programs.

Contractor. With a contractor, a very different relationship exists. Contractors come into the picture when the recipient operates as a subcontractor to the investor, implementing projects or programs that support the investor's objectives. Granting organizations often have specific social objectives and pursue those objectives through investment in organizations with compatible objectives and appropriate operational expertise.

Champion. For some investors, a significant role is that of champion for the organization or cause. A champion may serve as a public spokesperson, governmental or corporate liaison, donor coordinator, or in a variety of other roles. Champions help investees promote the good work they are doing and help ensure that they receive the recognition and resources commensurate with their capabilities.

Advisor. Investors may also advise the investee in a variety of capacities, including business strategy, risk management, and technical aspects of program delivery. The advisor can play an extensive partnership role, much like that of an angel investor or venture capitalist, or can act as a consultant on specific issues. The advisor can be a funder or an organization with compatible social objectives that shares knowledge and experience with another organization. The Edna McConnell Clark Foundation, a US-based foundation focusing on empowering low-income youth, assists its grantees with business planning, development of performance tracking systems, external evaluation, talent development, and growth capital while providing unrestricted multiyear investment. When US philanthropic investment organization Venture Philanthropy Partners invests in an organization, it begins a long-term, trusted partnership with the organization, providing management advice and expertise together with large-scale, multiyear funding to build the organization's capacity.

Implementor. When the investor is directly engaged in operating the social change initiative, the investor is also the implementor. NGOs or social enterprises that exist to create social change are implementers.

Complementor. One often overlooked role is that of complementor. One organization can help another by investing in complementary goods or services that help an organization accomplish its social mission. An example is a restaurant that stays open extra hours when a fund-raising drive is underway. In the annual Houston Restaurant Week, for example, many participating restaurants donate a specific amount of money to Houston Food Bank for each meal sold, and the Restaurant Week promotes the Houston Food Bank and directs donations to the nonprofit.

Collaborator. Collaboration among investors can also be an important aspect in the pursuit of social impact. While some investors act independently, others participate in a consortium—pooling resources to meet capital needs or to spread costs or risks. Micro-investors who pool resources to make a Kiva microfinance loan or provide capital for a Kickstarter project provide a simple example of how investors can work together to reach a goal. Larger investors, such as those participating in impact investment funds, may pool money to share risks among large portfolios of projects. Foundations may collaborate in performing due diligence on prospective investees or on monitoring and evaluating activities for projects in which they jointly participate.

Action Agenda

1. Evaluate each investment opportunity to determine whether it is aligned with your social impact mission and other investment objectives.
2. Decide how to structure your monetary investments.
3. Decide what kind of organization can best deliver the desired returns.
4. Consider what role you wish to play and how active you want to be in managing the investment.

Part 3
What Steps Will You Take?

5

How Social Impacts Are Created

There are many approaches organizations can take to generate social impact, and different types of organizations create impacts in different ways. These variations are particularly noticeable in the way nonprofits and for-profits produce impacts. Nonprofits and social enterprises focus on the impacts they make through their products and services, while for-profit companies mostly focus on impacts they make through their operations. Some nonprofits thus consider their primary social impacts to result from consumers or beneficiaries using their products, while companies tend to see their primary social impacts coming from the way they source and produce products.

In general, social purpose organizations take a narrow view of their impacts by focusing on their primary areas of influence—the impacts they manage directly and carefully. But all organizations produce secondary impacts as well. The resources they consume, the people they employ, the procedures they carry out, and the products and byproducts they produce can all yield both positive and negative social impacts.

To truly understand your organization's full range of social impacts, you'll need to look more broadly at the ways your operations and products affect society and the environment. You could accomplish this using a simple brainstorming process, but your understanding will be much more complete if you use a more comprehensive approach that can point you to all of the major areas where you are likely to make impacts.

Developing a system to plan and track your primary impacts, as we'll discuss in chapters 9 and 10, will take you a long way toward creating the changes you seek. But you'll also need to be aware of secondary effects if you hope to protect and nurture your positive impacts while managing potential negative impacts. Whether you're investing your time and expertise in the organization as an employee or board member or you're funding the operations of the organization as a donor or investor, you'll need to understand a broader range of impacts than is normally tracked and reported by organizations working in this space.

Understanding an organization's social impact objectives does not mean you'll agree with those objectives. For example, you might find that a low-cost school model that increases attendance relies on rote learning to manage large class sizes and help students pass state tests, or that educating girls results in more young women moving from their village homes into the city.

Depending on their values, stakeholders may view these outcomes as positive or negative. It's therefore difficult to objectively compare the social benefits of these organizations on a single scale, or to give an organization an objective rating or ranking. Organizations need to accurately define and carefully track their impacts and then attempt to make these impacts as transparent as possible. This will enable a broad range of stakeholders to ensure that their values and impact objectives are aligned with the outcomes resulting from the organization's activities.

Mission First

The first step in creating social impact is to be as clear as possible about the organization's social mission—its products, clients, and social change goals. (See chapter 6 for an in-depth discussion of missions.) Nonprofits and social enterprises have social missions, as do foundations and impact investment funds. Corporate units engaged in promoting social change should have social missions as well. The pathways through which these organizations create their most significant impacts vary, but all organizations create impacts in many different ways. Organizations can use three primary pathways to create social change:

- Products and services
- Operations
- Investments

Most organizations direct their primary change efforts toward one of these three paths, choosing the path that best fits the social mission. In addition to their primary goals for social impact, organizations have secondary impacts in each of the three categories. Understanding and managing these pathways will help your organization achieve its primary goals and maintain a positive social profile through all of the areas it touches.

Your organization's social mission is central in driving how the organization will use these pathways to make an impact. At its most basic level, the mission describes the products or services the organization will deliver and the primary beneficiaries to which those products and services will be targeted. The creation of a compelling social impact mission and the act of designing the organization to promote that mission are foundational to all other organizational activities. With a clear mission, your organization will be able to make ongoing changes in myriad ways while staying true to its social change objectives. You can change operational details over time, pursue new strategies, enter new markets, and develop new products and services. If you have a clear mission, these changes will strengthen rather than dilute your organization's focus on its cause and help it resist forces that might cause it to drift from that mission.

A mission is ongoing. It can remain with your organization through changes in the organization's board members, programs, and investors. The mission itself can drive numerous decisions, determining which avenues you will pursue, which values will be primary, which beneficiaries you will target, and which employees you will hire. It also determines what your organization will communicate to its stakeholder groups and to its industry.

An organization with a strong mission conveys a great deal through its very existence. One example of an organization with a strong mission is the for-profit company PUMA. PUMA believes that by being a leader in promoting a sports-oriented lifestyle, it can contribute to a safer, more peaceful, and more creative world. When a mission is sufficiently strong and clear and when the organization builds its identity and culture around that mission, many benefits result. Changes in the environment, technology, competition, consumer needs, and many other factors occur on a moment-to-moment basis. Formal control systems can never fully keep up, but a clear mission, with a culture that flows from it, can provide guidance on how to respond. As a result, hundreds or thousands of small decisions made by staff, investors, and other key stakeholders will propel the organization in a direction that is consistent with achieving the mission.

Mission-based guidance is especially important in difficult-to-serve markets, such as areas that are torn by war, suffering natural disasters, or lack basic infrastructure and institutions, as well as in organizations that change too rapidly to develop a full range of formalized policies and procedures.

Using your mission as a guide, your organization will be more likely to find and assemble the right resources and expertise to accomplish the organization's goals. With these goals in mind you are also more likely to improve productivity: each resource will be allocated and used in a way that furthers achievement of the outcomes you want. At the same time, constituents will be regularly watching for signs that the desired outcomes are being achieved, and they will be alert when there are deviations that could impede success. As they grow, organizations become increasingly dispersed and complex and it becomes more difficult to coordinate activities across a variety of business units, programs, and activities. When members of an organization are passionate about the organization's mission, however, this coordination occurs far more naturally and cooperation in pursuit of the mission is more common.

Impact from Products and Services

Social purpose organizations commonly produce products and services that are intended to make a positive social impact. But products create impacts in a variety of ways, and the impacts are not always positive. The ways products can make impacts include:

- Benefits to customers
- Impacts beyond customers
- Use and safety
- Disposal of products

Products and services may produce impacts through direct interaction with a beneficiary, or can provide indirect impacts, such as through research or advocacy. For example, a woman who receives HIV/AIDS training may adjust her behavior or she may encourage others in her village to adjust theirs. The ways products are used and disposed of are also important. Pesticides sprayed outdoors on crops may have different effects than when applied directly to crops in storage. Leftover pesticide dumped into a river used for drinking water can affect people downstream.

The positive impact of products is generally well understood by the providers. They have seen a significant market gap in which they have identified potential social and environmental problems, and they have provided resources to fill them. When the market fails to provide products and services needed by members of a society, they must go without them or they must substitute inferior alternatives for them. For example, a sick person unable to access healthcare services might substitute home remedies and home care, or might go without healthcare services.

Figure 10 Primary Pathways to Create Social Impacts

Many challenges stand in the way of filling market gaps. Sometimes needed products and services are available in the marketplace but clients can't afford them. In this case, the social purpose organization might provide these outputs at a subsidized price or create a more affordable substitute product or service that the clients can afford. Distribution is another common challenge, especially in developing countries. Many countries lack the infrastructure and economic institutions that could deliver the products to clients who need them. Sometimes a lack of physical infrastructure such as roads and communications networks prevents access. At other times, distribution systems and staff to manage those systems have not yet been developed. Social purpose organizations can sometimes provide the material resources or expertise to help deliver products to the people who need them.

Naya Jeevan is a nonprofit social enterprise that sells affordable health insurance in South Asia. Because of low government spending on public health programs in South Asia, low-income people in this region don't have access to high-quality healthcare and are left vulnerable to medical crisis. Naya Jeevan offers a core health insurance plan that costs only US$2.50 per month per adult and makes proper healthcare available to millions of low-income workers in Pakistan and India.[1]

The product or service needed to address a social problem has, at its core, the potential to enrich lives or the environment. But products and services produced to generate corporate profits also create social impacts. In general, however, companies spend insufficient effort trying to gauge the social impacts of their products. The fact that consumers find the products sufficiently beneficial to purchase and use them is an indicator of their value. But the fact that they are purchased does not ensure that all their impacts are positive. For example, recent debates about health problems associated with cigarettes and fast foods tend to focus on the negative impacts of these products. The positive social value of a large variety of commercial offerings have similarly been called into question—including sport utility vehicles, cosmetic surgery, credit cards, and even college education.

Even when a product has potential benefits, it is possible that consumers aren't using it in a beneficial way. Criticisms of aid programs for developing countries often include stories of providing people with products they don't need or that are useful initially but can't be effectively maintained. Some products can be used in a dangerous manner. For example, some mothers save money by diluting baby formulas with water, which can lead to undernourishment or, if the water is unclean, serious illness.

When a product is used effectively by customers and does increase their quality of life, organizations providing those outputs naturally assume that they are creating positive social impact. Often assessments of the full impact of these products are limited to their expected impact on the intended group of beneficiaries. But other groups are also affected, either intentionally or unintentionally, by the products and services, and their experiences should also be considered.

Introducing new or subsidized products, for example, can affect established industries and markets. As the case of Toms Shoes demonstrates, good intentions don't always lead to positive outcomes. Toms Shoes has a program that donates a second pair of shoes in a developing country for every pair of shoes purchased in developed world markets. While this campaign provides much-needed shoes in many areas, it also has the potential for negative impact. The influx of free shoes can disrupt markets and take business away from local shoe sellers.[2] Such consequences should be weighed when you determine the full social impacts of your products and services.

The impact of some products is a function of the way they are used by consumers. Procter & Gamble has developed cold water detergents that can greatly reduce the environmental impact associated with laundering clothes. Many consumers, however, have difficulty letting go of the belief that cleanliness requires hot water, so the impact of the product is limited by the effectiveness of the marketing and consumer education that goes along with it. A similar problem exists with antibiotics. Consumers often stop taking the antibiotics when symptoms subside rather than taking the full course of medication. This practice can reduce the patient's immunity or strengthen the bacterial strain causing the disease.

For other products, impact is a result of how the consumer disposes of the product after using it. Batteries and electronic equipment can have dangerous environmental consequences when disposed of improperly. And plastic bags, which are used for packaging in many parts of the world, often end up in places where plastics are particularly problematic, like the Great Pacific garbage patch.

Some believe that the overall plusses and minuses of a product can be rated, so that, for example, fresh produce would likely rank higher than cigarettes. Environmental lifecycle analysis provides one way to evaluate the social and environmental costs and benefits of a product. Lifecycle analysis follows a product through the entire production and usage cycle. It examines the manner in which a product is created, used, and disposed of or repurposed at the end of its useful life. Wal-Mart and other large corporations are developing social impact assessments for their products and plan to ultimately provide labeling and other forms of transparency that will allow consumers to use this information in their purchasing decisions.

Impacts from Operations

With every operating decision made, organizations create positive or negative impacts. Many nonprofits fail to consider these
impacts and how they support or conflict with their primary social
impact goals. By ignoring operations, even organizations with the
most sophisticated methods for assessing the impacts of their
primary products can seriously misunderstand the full range of
impacts their organizations generate.

Large corporations throughout the world have begun to report
on the social costs and benefits of their operations. These impacts
may be included in stand-alone social responsibility or sustainability reports, or they may be merged with annual financial reports
distributed to stockholders. Aside from social enterprises, companies typically provide little information for customers about the
social impacts of their products. However, they may well conduct
thorough investigations of the social impacts generated by their
operations. Figure 11 shows some sources of operational impact.

- Product design
- Human resource practices
- The supply chain
- Infrastructure
- Production processes

Product Design

The design of a product or service can affect its ultimate utility and
safety for consumers and others. Product design can help ensure
proper use and disposal, such as single-dose medicine packs or recy-
clable containers. All of the product and service impacts described
in the previous section result, in part, from choices made during
the design stage of product and service development.

Materials used to make products can have significant impacts
and should be chosen wisely. The choice of specific materials may
be locked in during the design of a product. For example, companies building electronic devices such as cell phones often use

| Product Design | Human Resource Practices | The Supply Chain | Infrastructure | Product Process |

Figure 11 Sources of Operational Impact

tantalum, tin, or tungsten in production. These are among the set of materials that have come to be known as "conflict minerals" because they are sourced in northeastern Congo and other areas of conflict that are controlled by warlords. Purchasing materials from these regions is thought to help fuel these conflicts. Purchasing materials from countries with human rights violations or from factories with workplace safety inadequacies can be similarly problematic. For example, floor mats sold to villagers at afford-able prices have counterbalancing impacts if those floor mats are produced using child labor.

Product designers concerned about environmental impact may use dematerialization strategies to reduce the amount of mate-rials used during production. The ability to recycle or reuse a product is also a designed-in characteristic. Some products are designed for easy disassembly so that individual parts can be reused or disposed of separately. Many car makers today design for easy disassembly, resulting in reuse of the majority of parts in some cars. Nike's Considered Design program improves prod-uct sustainability by using better design and production processes. Although the use of environmentally preferred materials some-times increases total materials costs, it can ultimately reduce prod-uct costs by reducing footwear and packaging waste or the use of potentially harmful chemicals that are costly to keep in inventory.[3]

Service designs can also lock in impacts. Location, for example, can affect the base of customers or beneficiaries. Siting offices in rural locations, for example, might make services more accessi-ble to underserved customers. Service processes can also embed impact. Processes that require service workers to speak local dia-lects help ensure that staff will be hired from targeted regions.

Services can also serve as substitutes for products. Cell phone rental programs provide communications access to many who could not otherwise afford cell phones, giving them easier access to family and friends as well as to valuable services like healthcare advice and current crop prices. These programs also reduce the number of cell phones produced, shipped, and later disposed of.

Organizations and even industries can be rated based on the products and services they provide. Environmental and social ratings evaluate some industries as having a more positive social impact than others. For example, extractive industries that use nonrenewable resources rank lower than the education sector, because the overall negative impact on the environment potentially outweighs the positive social impacts of the products these industries produce.

Human Resource Practices

Fair labor practices have long been promoted and are well understood. Organizations such as the International Labour Organization have developed lists of basic labor practices that every company should follow, whether or not the laws of the countries in which they operate require them.

Some organizations create their primary social impacts through their human resource practices rather than through their products and services. Dave's Killer Bread in Portland, Oregon, for example, hires convicted felons coming out of jail who would otherwise have a difficult time finding a job and reintegrating into society. The products, while secondary in this situation, are also designed with positive impact in mind. The breads have low fat and high fiber and protein content, and they use locally sourced organic ingredients. Dave Dahl, the former CEO, was once a convicted felon himself and carefully tracks the success of his employees. He spends a great deal of time speaking with groups interested in learning about his methods and their impacts on the employees and on society. He has won numerous ethics and citizenship awards for his efforts.

In some cases, organizations would like to create social impact through employment but encounter difficulties finding staff with the appropriate skill set. Managerial talent and basic employability skills are lacking in some regions. To deal with this problem, some employers provide livelihood training to help employees become job-ready. Taj Hotels Resorts & Palaces in India, for example, in association with Pratham, provides opportunities for people from impoverished villages to get the training they need to work in a Taj hotel. Training begins with the basics, such as how to tie shoes and use silverware and then builds to higher-level housekeeping and restaurant work skills. The Taj then hires these workers and provides them with basic accommodations until they take their now impressive resumes and find other jobs, perhaps closer to home.

The Supply Chain

Supply chain impacts have received increased attention as corporations continue to contract out both production and service work to subcontractors. Nike, for example, employs more than 40,000 people on six continents, but this is only a fraction of the number of workers employed by Nike's 700-plus manufacturing contractors.

Sourcing locally to reduce transportation-related impacts and support local suppliers is one strategy for creating social impact. Sourcing products from a region in need of economic development is another. In some cases, the use of contractors rather than the company's own employees can be a means of producing social impact. Industree Crafts, a hybrid social enterprise in India that connects rural natural fiber producers to markets, forms rural artisans into producer companies and connects the companies, in turn, to finance capital. Through this process, the rural artisans are no longer workers who are paid by the piece; the artisans instead become the owners of self-sustained community enterprises. Products are sourced from independent microentrepreneurs, who are responsible for managing their own finances, production volume, and quality. Through this process, businesses are strengthened and many ultimately expand their customer base. Industree's social audit shows that the incomes of their artisans have tripled.[4]

Infrastructure

Choosing where to locate facilities like factories can have important social impacts. Some governments actively recruit businesses through free trade zones or by giving them tax and other incentives. Some governments would like to keep large or dirty industries outside their borders. Any infrastructure built to support a factory or other businesses will have a range of impacts.

The layout of buildings can also affect impact, through the materials used in construction, lighting and environmental atmosphere, ergonomic considerations, and many other infrastructure characteristics. All these factors will affect the quality of life for both employees and members of the surrounding community.

When buildings cause environmental damage or disturb community life, companies may compensate with other social projects, such as improving roads, water resources, or schools. Ambuja Cements Ltd., India's largest exporter of cement, has compensated villages for disruptions associated with its plants by providing benefits like job creation for locals, improvements to water resources, and establishment of clinics. Ambuja has also made a number of other infrastructure investments that improve its social impacts. For example, the company pioneered new energy-efficient power technologies that use biomass fuels; it has used rainwater harvesting, wastewater management, and other water management technologies to become water positive; and it has built a port that reduces shipping distances and related emissions.

Other infrastructure developments can have direct positive impacts. Rural borrower networks set up to support microfinance operations can be used for delivery of education, healthcare, or other services. Roads and communications infrastructure built for businesses can provide locals with important access to distant markets or services.

Production Processes

Choices about how goods are produced and services are delivered can also be important sources of social impact. For companies that manufacture products, production choices can have serious consequences, particularly for the environment. In general, organizations concerned with impact focus on both the inputs coming into the manufacturing facility and those leaving. Energy, water, and other resources used during production can be managed and reduced. Emissions and waste leaving the production facility can also generate negative impacts and should be carefully managed. Companies across a range of industries have adopted environmentally beneficial processes. Chevron, for example, reduces greenhouse gas emissions through a process that combines natural gas and carbon and injects them into geological foundations for long-term storage. It also contributes to biodiversity by avoiding accidental introduction of invasive mammal species or weeds in oil field communities.[5]

Impacts from Passive Investments

When an organization has money not needed for current operations, that money is invested in what we'll refer to here as passive investments. Foundations, for example, often have large endowments from which only a small payout is used each year. In some cases, these foundations are intended to exist in perpetuity, paying out in grants only the minimum required by law each year. Other types of organizations also have sums of money that are invested until needed for operating activities. We discuss three types of passive investments here—mission-related investments (MRIs), program-related investments (PRIs), and socially responsible investments (SRIs).

Passive investments are important potential sources for social impact. For example, money can be invested in publicly traded stocks of companies that have primarily financial bottom lines, or it can be invested in companies that carefully manage their social bottom line as well. As we have described, both the products and operations of these companies can have significant social costs or benefits. Ideally, passive investments should be placed in assets that are compatible with the mission of the organization. These investments are known as mission-related investments, and are a form of impact investing. They seek both financial returns and social impact.

Foundations often invest part of their money in program-related investments. These investments are expressly designed to promote the foundation's primary impact objectives, whether or not they also produce financial returns. For foundations required to spend a set proportion of their endowed funds each year, any expense related to PRIs that is less than the return from a market-rate investment can be considered part of the required payout. One common form of PRI is a loan to a grantee at a lower-than-market interest rate. Another is the provision of venture capital or private equity to a social purpose organization.[6]

Meyer Memorial Trust, an Oregon-based private philanthropic institution, has over 10 percent of its assets (more than $70 million) in mission-related investments. It applies a "bulls-eye" target strategy for its MRIs, prioritizing the beneficial investments from the center of the bulls-eye that have direct environmental, social, and economic impact in Oregon. The outermost portion of the target includes investments that contradict the trust's mission. These investment opportunities, if sufficiently large, could shift the balance such that the trust does more harm than good, so to avoid such problems the trust systematically evaluates each opportunity.

For many foundations and other organizations with cash to invest, traditional vehicles such as publicly traded stocks and bonds are used. While these investments may be unrelated to the organization's mission, they may still be socially responsible investments. SRIs are screened investment funds that avoid investments likely to produce negative social impacts. In some cases, investments that promote positive social impacts make up the targeted investments. A clean energy organization, for example, might invest in municipal bonds that fund public transportation rather than in traditional corporate bonds. A maternal healthcare organization might invest in pharmaceutical company stocks or companies with large cancer research budgets. As an owner of stock, the healthcare organization would have access to the same rights as other shareholders, and could engage in advocacy activities, such as proposing shareholder resolutions to influence the activities of the company.

Many organizations continue to invest their endowments and other available funds into standard market investments because they lack the expertise on staff to develop a passive investment strategy related to their mission. In some fields, such as economic development, housing, and the environment, intermediary organizations can be used to manage the funds and ensure that they are directed toward companies that will promote the social impact goals of the investor.[7]

Action Agenda

1. To create lasting social impacts, begin with the mission.
2. Identify areas in which you make the greatest impact—usually products and services for nonprofits and social enterprises, and operations for for-profit companies.
3. Learn how your products affect your users and their communities, both during use and after disposal.
4. Understand the ways in which operations contribute to your impact through your supply chain, the materials you use, your employment practices, and more.
5. Make all investments impactful by putting large endowments as well as other funds into investments with social benefits.

6

Linking Actions to Impacts

Why are you here? What is your organization's reason for existing? What does success mean to you? What would it take for you to be able to say, "Because of our investments, the world is a better place"? It is surprising how difficult these questions are to answer for many social purpose organizations. But if creating social change is important for you, it is essential to envision and describe exactly what changes you seek.

Even if you operate in dynamic environments and have rapidly changing goals, it is important to think about these questions on a regular basis. Without them, you may end up fighting fires or solving the problems that seem most salient at the moment, or you may be pulled to and fro trying to serve the interests of powerful stakeholders. Only when you are clear about the changes you hope to make can you start planning and executing the actions that will bring about those changes.

A good investment program begins with clear thinking about the desired social change. All of the key investors should understand, and ideally agree on, the organization's ultimate mission. For companies, the mission often specifies the products or services to be delivered, the target market, and/or the specific set of customers they would like to see using these products and services. The strategy defines how the organization will deliver products to customers and, in competitive environments, how they will differentiate themselves from competitors in order to capture market share.

Markets provide the ultimate test of whether strategy and products are effective in the corporate world. Feedback received from customers through repeat purchases, or from shareholders, communicated dynamically through the price of the company's stock, is immediate and clear. Corporations respond to this feedback by modifying their strategies, changing their operations, or both. For organizations with social impact goals, it is far more difficult to determine how well the organization is achieving its mission. There is no built-in market discipline to judge or reward effectiveness.

Most nonprofits don't understand how well they are achieving their impact goals, both because they receive little feedback and because their missions are not tied to evaluation. A survey of nonprofits in 2012 found that these organizations rarely track data related to their missions,[1] so they don't know what they've done right and what has been achieved—and consequently they can't learn and develop plans based on experience. In the UK, only about 20 percent of charities use planning models and only 10 percent of small charities are even familiar with them. For their part, donors rarely investigate how effectively their money is spent. They typically do little research before giving, and the research done is often about efficiency rather than impacts.[2] Therefore, nonprofits that are able to prove their effectiveness may not attract more capital than those that cannot. The surprising results of a survey of UK donors showed that only 18 percent of the donors preferred charities that had evidence of effective performance.[3]

For organizations driven to serve both beneficiaries and funders. A clearly defined mission that serves the interests of both groups is essential. The social change mission and strategy define the changes the organization will pursue and the mechanisms it will employ to create them.

To clarify your own mission and ensure that your primary stake-holders are on the same page, it is helpful to define in very specific terms what your desired social impacts will look like, and how you will know whether and when these changes have occurred. This process helps ensure that key stakeholders, who may have different goals and worldviews, are in agreement with you about the specific changes you will need to see to make sure you are accomplishing your mission.

Sometimes it's appropriate to identify key performance indicators that will signal when a change has been achieved. Quantifying the change in this manner works only when the change is clearly definable and is more difficult for organizations that pursue advocacy or have rapidly evolving missions. The process of defining key metrics can help any organization communicate and clarify objectives, because this process forces participants to clearly articulate their views of success.

Social issues tend to be complex, and both the problems and the methods of addressing them change over time. In addition, most social purpose organizations find investment funds scarce. In such conditions, an organization may be driven to try a variety of new programs and approaches, or to pursue projects outside its primary mission to satisfy the interests of influential stakeholders. Being clear about its mission can help the organization decide what to do—and what not to do. Turning away beneficiaries or funders is difficult, but by avoiding the constant pressure to diffuse its objectives the organization can streamline its resources and investments in a manner that best promotes the desired social change.

Mission Statement

Your mission and vision statements don't need to describe all of an organization's objectives.[4] In fact, some argue that a mission statement should contain fewer than eight words. All you need to include in the mission are an action, a target population, and a target outcome.[5] Incorporating only a few elements helps keep the mission focused on your ultimate objective and how you will deliver that value.[6] Swades Foundation focuses on empowering rural India. Its mission is "to create a permanent, irreversible change in the lives of 1 million people in rural India in the next 5 years (December 2017)." This mission statement clarifies the foundation's goal: to create permanent, irreversible change; the served population, people in rural India; and a measurable outcome, 1 million people served by December 2017. The Children's Aid Society, a US nonprofit providing children and youth services, states that its mission is "nurturing the child by strengthening the family." Although brief, the mission statement effectively articulates the nonprofit's objective: nurturing the child; and its approach, by strengthening the family.

Your vision statement is consistent with your mission, but it articulates an ideal future to which your organization can aspire. Arghyam, an Indian public foundation that gives grants for groundwater and sanitation projects, states its vision as "safe, sustainable water for all." The foundation works with various entities to improve access to clean water and sanitation through field projects, research, knowledge sharing, and advocacy. The vision statement points out a clear direction for all of these efforts.

A well-defined, distinctive mission statement supports the success of an organization. When your mission is clear, you'll be better positioned to design an effective strategy for achieving your goals as well as to develop performance measures that are consistent with that strategy. An organization's mission determines what really matters, and its goals define the results the organization must achieve to accomplish that mission.

One example of this need for a clear focus on mission is the Robert Wood Johnson Foundation, one of the biggest and most revered US foundations in the public health sector. In reviewing its work, the Robert Wood Johnson Foundation has acknowledged its failure in some cases to have an effective impact and identified the reason as not having a clear mission. The foundation started out to cure chronic disease and disabilities in the 1980s, and later added two other areas of focus—substance abuse and access to health care in the US. No clear priority was set among the three goals, and they competed with each other for resources. Although the foundation spent over \$1 billion and had many great successes in each area, it acknowledges that its uncoordinated grant-making strategy prevented its huge donations from having the transformative impacts they might have made.[7]

Theories of Change

A theory of change is a theory about which actions or interventions will create the desired change.[8] It defines the problem, the target population, the assumptions underlying the solution, and the expected results.[9] A theory of change works mainly at the strategy level, mapping out the interventions required to create outcomes that will lead to the ultimate goal.[10] Figure 12 diagrams the steps in creating a theory of change.

Determine Your Impact Goals. Articulate the change you are seeking to make: this is your organization's reason for being. When managers and investors are asked about their goals, many are unable to articulate them. Instead, they describe the outputs they seek to create—for example, "We deliver bed nets in malaria-ridden locations." But whether or not this goal is stated, there is an underlying impact objective, or perhaps multiple, competing objectives, toward which the organization is striving. Bed nets are presumably intended to reduce the incidence of malaria, improve health, and possibly increase lifespan or reduce poverty.

Develop a Theory. Determine which activities and interventions can best achieve your goals. Organizations often get stuck focusing on what they can do—which services they can provide, which clients they can serve. But these aren't necessarily consistent with the change they seek to create. New technologies and methods are introduced every day, and there may be better and more efficient ways to achieve your goals. Managers should evaluate the

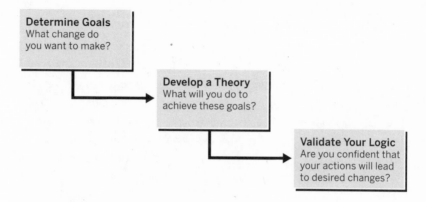

Figure 12 Steps in Creating a Theory of Change

range of options as well as the resources and capabilities they have available or are able to obtain. With a full understanding of what is possible, your organization can develop a theory that links planned actions with desired changes.

Validate Your Logic. After a theory is agreed upon, it should be validated. Your organization can do this in a number of ways. First, individuals with trained judgment and experience in the field should confirm the theorized relationships. Then the organization should look to the work of peers active in the same cause to examine their successes and failures. Trade, academic, and government publications can also be important sources of evidence regarding how well your theory of change holds up. Finally, the theory should be vetted with stakeholders—particularly beneficiaries—to determine whether they, too, buy in to the theory. The process of producing a theory of change is as critical as the end result. It brings every part of the organization together to talk through the tough questions and assess key activities, and it can contribute to building an engaged environment in the organization.[11] Reaching a consensus is time consuming. But it's worth it because it guides team members to think deeply about what they are doing and why it matters.[12]

Case Study: Dasra

Dasra, a leading Indian philanthropy foundation, wants to create large-scale social change. Having this goal in mind, the foundation searched for ways to achieve its desired impact. Dasra believes that if the people working in a social sector have better knowledge, funding opportunities, and advisors with expertise, they will be able to create maximum social impact. With this theory of change identified, Dasra has started several initiatives to equip the philanthropists and social entrepreneurs in India with better understanding and resources, including:

- *Indian Philanthropy Forum.* A platform that involves more than 200 philanthropists who are devoted to creating social good in India.
- *Dasra Social-Impact.* An executive education program for nonprofits and social businesses focusing on sustainability and scalability.
- *Dasra Portfolio Program.* A type of collaborative giving effort of selected organizations that work on one issue together.
- *Dasra Research.* A program that performs in-depth research on different social sectors in India.

Logic Model

The logic model helps flesh out the theory of change. While the theory of change explains *why* we expect our actions to lead to desired outcomes, the logic model focuses on *how* we expect to achieve them. The logic model is also referred to as an impact chain or results chain because each part is linked to the next through if-then logic. The model includes investments or inputs, linked through a sequence of actions and events to the ultimate impact for the beneficiaries. Logic models have also been compared to the strategy maps used by some corporations. A strategy map links learning activities to processes, processes to customer outcomes, and customer outcomes to financial performance— an ultimate goal for companies.[13] A standard diagram for a logic model is shown in Figure 13. The basic logic model contains five components:

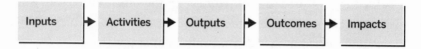

Figure 13 Basic Logic Model

- *Inputs* include both the resourses and constraints that a program faces. Resources are what a program uses to do its work, which may include human, financial, material, cultural, and other resources. Constraints are the internal and external limitations an organization faces—for example, local regulations or lack of capital. The program leverages its resources and works within its constraints to maximize its impacts.
- *Activities* are the steps to be taken in implementing a program or initiative, including the processes, events, and actions. A program uses its resources to execute activities in order to achieve intended outcomes. Activities are the planned work of a program.
- *Outputs* are the direct result of the organization's activities— they are its deliverables. Outputs may include products and services delivered to beneficiaries, including ongoing support for the target population or other completed projects.
- *Outcomes* are the intermediate effects on the target population that are necessary to achieve the desired impact goals. They are the program's direct results on the served population's behavior, attitudes, and skills, or on the condition of specific social or environmental variables. Outcomes are sometimes divided into short-term outcomes, which are outcomes to be achieved in one to three years, and long-term outcomes, which are attainable within four to six years.
- *Impact*, the ultimate goal of a social purpose organization, refers to systematic and fundamental progress on a social issue. Impacts are central to why the organization exists in the first place. Many organizational models leave out impacts,

focusing instead on outcomes as the final objective. But impacts should be included in the model, even if the organization does not have a good way to measure them.

The arrows between each of the five terms form the other important component of the logic model. These arrows represent the linkages between each stage in the chain of results. You can read the logic model as a series of "if ... then" statements. If a program has these resources, then it can carry out the planned activities. If these activities are accomplished, the intended outputs will be delivered. If the program delivers its outputs, then the outcome will be that participants benefit. If the intended outcome is achieved, then impacts—changes in social or environmental conditions—will result. These causal linkages are vital because they demonstrate the underlying logic of the intervention.[14] Every investor or organization seeking to make an impact should be convinced that the proposed resources and actions will ultimately and logically create the desired impacts.

Figure 14 shows a simplified sample logic model for KaBOOM!, which builds playgrounds in "play deserts" where safe facilities for play do not exist. KaBOOM! also provides detailed plans for gaining access to land and volunteers and for building the playgrounds.

In Figure 14, we see how KaBOOM!'s outputs lead to its impacts—healthier children and communities. The playgrounds are KaBOOM!'s final deliverables, both products and services. The outcomes represent changes in actions, beliefs, knowledge, and other factors. In KaBOOM!'s case, children use the playground rather than hanging out on neighborhood streets, and parents form relationships with each other as they watch their kids play. The long-term systemic changes KaBOOM! expects to result from these changes are healthier children and stronger communities.

Each arrow in the figure represents a causal linkage. We expect one variable to influence another, and generally there is logical or empirical evidence available to support these cause/effect relationships. Even when relationships between the variables shown

Figure 14 Sample Logic Model for KaBOOM!

in the boxes in Figure 14 seem confirmed by experience, it is critical to regularly gather data about impacts and outcomes to ensure
that the logic underlying the model remains valid over time.

Logical Frameworks

Logical frameworks or "logframes" include the same basic elements as logic models, but include more specific information
about each link in the chain and provide the basis for determining
work assignments. They are often used as part of an organization's performance measurement and evaluation processes. The
logframe begins with an impact goal and is very specific about the
steps needed to achieve that goal.[15] It includes basic steps from the
logic model, working backward from the impact goal:

- *Goal (Impact).* The goal or desired impact should be clearly
  defined and stated in terms of the specific change desired and
  the specific population who will benefit. Each of the organization's major impact goals should have a separate logframe.
- *Smart Objectives (Outcomes).* Objectives define the key outcomes or changes in the target population that are necessary
  to achieve the impact goals.
- *Key Outputs (Outputs).* Outputs are the organization's deliverables—the products and services provided by the organization to its beneficiaries.
- *Major Activities (Activities).* These are the actions the organization will take to create the outputs.
- *Indicators.* Indicators are the measures or metrics that will
  be used to determine whether each smart objective is being

met. Indicators and the mechanisms through which they'll be gathered are often specified in a logframe, although they aren't typically included in logic models.

Stakeholders

The logic model defines your organization's theory and planned actions. Before implementing your plan, however, it is essential to consider the interests of your stakeholders. Stakeholders are those individuals and groups that can affect or be affected by the activities and outcomes associated with a social investment. The primary stakeholders for most impact investments are the direct beneficiaries of the changes that result from those investments. But social change in an interconnected world is complicated and may involve participation or require buy-in from many different parties.

For any social intervention, numerous stakeholder groups may have information and interests that will directly influence your success or failure in achieving your investment goals. You will need to determine which stakeholder groups are most important to achieving your goals, and you'll need to develop processes through which you can hear and learn from these stakeholders. This information will be key in helping you design interventions that take stakeholder interests into consideration.

Two stakeholders are central to the success of any project: the beneficiaries and the investors. Beneficiaries' perspectives are critical when you're determining whether and how the investment will create impacts. The reasons social purpose organizations and social programs exist is to solve tough problems. Whether the solutions deliver impacts or not is a question perhaps best answered by the direct beneficiaries. In many cases, these are people who, with effort and care, can provide important opinions and insights. In other cases, particularly for broad-scale interventions such as saving rainforests or supporting democracy, the ultimate beneficiaries may be too distant,not yet born, animal or plant species, or other interests not easily represented. In these cases, you'll need to engage experts on the topic when you assess stakeholder perspectives.

Too often, the groups who are intended to benefit from an intervention have no say in whether and how the intervention is implemented. Their interests and concerns are inferred, often by well-meaning individuals who come from very different cultures and circumstances. Many groups are accustomed to putting on a show for any visiting representative of a social organization they encounter, for cultural reasons, out of respect, or in order to secure any type of resource the investor seeks to provide.

As an investor, you should prioritize hearing the real voices of these groups before your social projects move forward. Staff members who work most directly with beneficiaries, communities, and other organizations focused on similar causes can often provide valuable information about how an intervention is or will be received by the beneficiaries. But you should also seek assistance in working directly with your constituents. Keystone Accountability, a charity that helps improve the efficiency of social purpose organizations, provides detailed guidance on "constituent voice"—a process for gathering data from stakeholders and using that data to design and improve interventions.

Chapter 4 discussed the importance of alignment between the interests and values of the investor and investee. It is even more critical for the organization's interests to align with those of its intended beneficiaries. You should be sure that clients and others affected by your actions view the social change as beneficial. In many cases, a mismatch has led to a failed project. For example, one organization in rural Nicaragua was building chicken coops for local farmers. The coops were designed to protect chickens from predators and provide an environment in which they would produce many more eggs. When they returned to assess their intervention, however, the investors found the chicken coops unused. The farmers viewed their chickens as pets and preferred to let them roam free, as they had for generations. For the would-be beneficiaries, having more eggs was not worth caging their pets.

In another situation, huge sums of money were being spent in the US secondary school system without the benefit of reliable input.[16] Many programs have provided funding to schools, but few have been based on a good understanding of how students were receiving the intended benefits. Surveys have been conducted, but the results have rarely been actionable and have often been difficult to understand. The YouthTruth initiative took a different approach that helped engage students in providing feedback by explaining how their feedback would be used to redesign programs. YouthTruth also made it easy for students to share their opinions. The program has proven successful, and 76 percent of students in schools using the program have offered their feedback.

To get effective feedback from beneficiaries, you'll need to consider how to make it easy and worthwhile for individuals to provide feedback, and you must consider how to make sure that the feedback is authentic. Providers and beneficiaries are often from different worlds, and they may have difficulty understanding each other's perspectives. Obtaining feedback as directly as possible using staff who deal most directly with clients using is one helpful approach. Green Empowerment, a US-based nonprofit that works with NGOs around the world to install renewable energy and water technologies, goes a step further. The organization works only in communities in which beneficiaries both request support and demonstrate commitment to a project by contributing a significant portion of the funding. Third parties who are closer to the world of the beneficiaries can also be good sources of information. We have heard stories about organizations that have used "secret shoppers" to ask children of families receiving aid such questions as "Did you eat breakfast today?" and "How many meals did you have yesterday?"

Investors and donors also have an influence on an organization's success. The implementing organization must engage regularly with these groups to ensure that objectives and interests are in alignment. Investors, in turn, may affect or be affected by other stakeholder groups. Thus, whether you are part of an organization working with the beneficiaries or you are an organization's funder, you should make sure that you're informed about other stakeholders and their interests. For example, investors can influence members of their networks, and many investments result from requests or information from friends or colleagues. Likewise, if investors are unhappy with the investment, they can reduce current or future funding and influence others to do the same.

Although investors are a key stakeholder group, it is important for the investee to ensure that interests are aligned. For organizations that rely on ongoing donations or capital investments for survival, it is easy to start treating the funders as if *they* were the clients. Investors' needs come to be seen as primary, and a great deal of energy and attention goes into carefully monitoring and managing this group. Beneficiaries may receive correspondingly less attention as an organization focuses on defining and measuring success in a way that meets donors' interests, and they may blur or shift their focus away from the needs of their beneficiaries.

Stakeholder engagement is a core element in any organization's efforts to pursue its mission. When the investor, investee, and beneficiaries are in alignment regarding the nature of the intervention and the value associated with the ultimate impacts, the investment is more likely to succeed. Returns to all three parties will differ, but their impact goals will be compatible.

Action Agenda

1. Clarify the mission and impact goals to align efforts between investors and implementers.
2. Create a theory of change or results chain to clarify your thinking about how your actions will lead to your outputs, or deliverables, and how your outputs will lead to outcomes and impacts.
3. Validate the logic of your theory by engaging with stakeholders—especially beneficiaries and staff or organizations closest to them.

Part 4
How Will You Measure Success?

7

Measurement Basics

Are we really making a difference? This is the question that all social impact investors ask themselves. Yet in a recent survey of nonprofit executives, only half said that their organizations were collecting data on client outcomes.[1] In another study, more than 70 percent of grant makers agreed that foundations lacked the data they needed to effectively assess their performance.[2] Only about one-fifth of nonprofits report working with professional evaluators, whether internal or external, to evaluate their performance.[3] Many of those that do measure their impact do so only to meet the requirements of funders. And many that don't measure impact mistakenly believe that measurement can only be done quantitatively—an approach that can separate measures from their context and reduce their value. However, those organizations that do measure impact, whether because they choose to do so or because they are required to do so, believe that the services they offer and the impacts they create are improved as a result.

Measurement is the only way to know whether an investment is making a social impact and to determine the significance of that impact. Organizations that have this information are better positioned to adjust their resources and activities to create the impacts they desire.

If you are working for social change, you likely believe in your heart that you're creating positive impacts. You experience firsthand the evidence of your impacts: a child learns to read, a patient is healed by a drug, a river teems again with fish. You see the evidence. You believe that you are doing good. But research has shown that beliefs can distort what we see, and that we are prone to generalize from a very small amount of information. We eagerly grasp evidence that reinforces our beliefs, and we discount or ignore evidence that does not. Anyone who has listened to political debates has seen this in action. So if you're like most people in the social sector, you think that you don't really need evidence because you *know* you're creating value.

But increasingly, board members, investors, donors, and even beneficiaries want proof that investments are truly generating the returns that have been promised. To provide these stakeholders with the proof they desire, and to answer your own nagging questions about whether and where you're making a difference, you need measurement. You need to measure your actions, you need to measure your results, and you need to measure the effects you're having on your constituents.

Why Organizations Don't Measure

Why do so few investors and organizations measure their impacts? Organizations commonly cite a number of reasons:

- Measurement is costly.
- Measures are misleading.
- Measurement is difficult.
- Measures are dysfunctional.

But many organizations don't measure impact because they simply don't know how. They don't know what to measure, they don't know how to measure, and they believe they don't have the skills and expertise to implement a measurement plan and interpret the results.

A number of organizations do measure their activities and out-puts, as well as their income and expenses, and often have highly sophisticated measurement systems in place. Yet at the same time they argue that measuring their impacts isn't possible. There are a variety of reasons underlying these arguments.

For some, the problem isn't measuring the impact per se, but measuring their own contribution to that change. When the rate of smoking among teenagers drops, it is difficult to determine how much of that change is attributable to any particular pro-gram or organization. For some organizations, the impact itself is difficult to measure. How do we know, for example, if we're any closer to Middle East peace as a result of the work of any one organization? In measuring the impact of advocacy and many other challenging areas, however, great strides have been made. Chapter 9 shows examples of metrics that can be used for diffi-cult-to-measure impacts. Although measurements will never be perfect, there are many ways to get closer to understanding the change your efforts have made.

Many organizations believe that measurement is too costly. Allocating resources or hiring staff for impact measurement just doesn't fit into many organizations' budgets. Even when they do have ample resources, many believe that spending them on "over-head" such as impact measurement draws resources away from the very programs that produce the impacts. Or they believe that different projects can't be measured using a single measurement system because successes are defined and measured differently in different areas.[4]

The problem with this logic is that organizations can't really know if they're making an impact from *any* of their investments without some kind of measurement. In the absence of this infor-mation, efforts to increase impacts or improve the efficiency with which they are created will be informed by gut feel or anecdotes rather than evidence. On top of that, it will be difficult to know which investments have been most successful and should be increased, and which are a waste of resources.

The third major argument is that measures can be mislead-ing. By boiling down multidimensional social or environmental phenomena into a few simple metrics, much of the context and complexity can be lost. When that happens the measures can be distorted, resulting in judgments or actions that push the organi-zation in the wrong direction.

While it is true that measures can never fully reflect the underly-ing reality, they can still provide value. If you recognize that metrics are only proxies and use them along with your trained judgment and situational knowledge, they can help bring the underlying real-ity into better focus than if you didn't measure at all.

The final argument, which is often left unstated but is certainly valid, is that measures can lead to dysfunctional behavior. Once a measurement system is established, people might change their focus to managing the measures rather than managing the activi-ties. This is a very real risk and should be considered when you are establishing or changing a measurement system.

The risk of dysfunction, however, is associated not with the act of gathering and reporting measures, but with the way the mea-surement system is used. Metrics used for doling out sanctions and rewards are bound to be managed and even manipulated. But metrics used as a cornerstone of a program for understanding performance drivers can be extremely functional in improving effectiveness.

All these reasons represent barriers standing in the way of measuring impact, and they are formidable enough that many organizations don't even try. But these organizations also need to consider the risks of *not* measuring impacts. The Drug Abuse Resistance Education (D.A.R.E.) program, a US student substance abuse prevention program, provides an example of this risk. The program has been in operation for thirty years and millions of dollars have been spent on it. However, in 2003 a report by the US General Accounting Office, citing several extensive studies of the program, found no evidence of its long-term effectiveness.[5] If people had been aware of D.A.R.E.'s ineffectiveness earlier, the time, money, and other resources devoted to D.A.R.E. could have been employed more effectively.

Without measurement, there is a real risk is that money, time, and other resources are wasted. To keep investing money without finding out if your efforts are doing any good jeopardizes your ability to maximize the effects of the funding you are able to direct toward social problems. Worse still, by failing to measure impact you risk the possibility that your actions are harming the very groups they are intended to help. One published experiment found self-esteem to be lower among students who had been through the D.A.R.E. program, perhaps because they had experimented with alcohol or cigarettes, which had been lumped together with other drugs to be avoided.

One thing is certain—every social program makes some kind of impact on some group of stakeholders. Without measurement, the assumption that all positive impact goals are achieved and all negative ones are avoided goes untested. To maximize the value you can create, you must try to do better.

Measurement Is More Than Metrics

The most important benefit of measurement, and one that is rarely discussed, is that in order to decide which metrics to use, *you first need to understand what it is you're measuring!* Before you start measuring anything, you need to be clear in describing the constructs you want the measures to represent. In this way, the process of measurement forces you to articulate your values and beliefs in a way that other types of communication can never match. Figure 15 represents the relationships between measures and constructs.

Before discussing the practical purposes of social impact measurement, it's useful to recognize one of the most fundamental and valuable aspects of measurement: its role in creating a shared vision that can guide strategies and actions. The process of measurement does this by opening up ideas about impacts to questioning and scrutiny. To agree on which measure will best

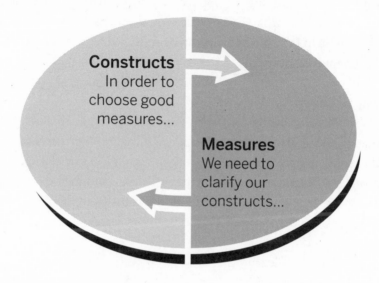

Figure 15 Measures Help Clarify Constructs

represent a construct, we must first agree on how to understand that construct itself. Useful measures rely on a clear understanding of what is being measured. In some cases, it is only after an organization begins to develop measurement systems that it uncovers differences in the way its members think about the real world as represented in the measures.

For example, everyone on the board of an organization that provides education to girls might agree that one of the primary goals of the organization is "empowerment." When asked for ideas about how to measure empowerment, however, it quickly becomes clear that the views of the board members differ greatly regarding what constitutes empowerment. One member believes that the number of girls completing their education is a good metric, another suggests delayed pregnancy and marriage, another favors working outside of the home, and still another insists that participation in family decision-making is the best measure.

The process of creating an impact measurement system can be instrumental in both uncovering these differences in beliefs and values and in creating an opportunity to overcome those differences and develop a shared vision of the organization's impact objectives. In fact, this process can be more valuable than the measurements themselves.

Why Measure?

Investors measure performance for many different reasons. Ultimately, the goal of social performance measurement is to improve the social impacts valued by organizations, beneficiaries, and investors. Measurements are gathered for a number of distinct purposes. Figure 16 shows three of the most prominent of those purposes. An organization can:

- Measure for learning
- Measure for action
- Measure for accountability

Measurement for Learning. Among the most basic reasons to measure impact is to learn. Investors want to understand whether they performed well, and they want to test assumptions about whether actions did, in fact, create the desired results. Without measuring performance and validating assumptions, there is no way to know if the investment is really making a difference.

It is easy to rely on instincts and anecdotes to demonstrate effectiveness. Yet despite the confidence you may feel in your programs and their results, you can still learn a lot from measurement. You can discover when and for whom your programs are most effective. You can explore whether your assumptions hold up for different populations under varying conditions. And you can learn how various aspects of your actions and results interact with one another to produce the impacts.

Measurement for Action. When you develop this understanding about the full nature of your results and how those results relate to other aspects of the chain, you can use this knowledge to take

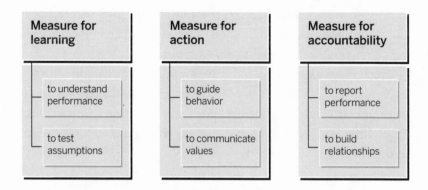

Figure 16 Purposes of Measurement

action. Once you realize, for example, that an intervention works better for one group of subjects than another, you can make adjustments to improve outcomes for the latter or redirect resources to the group for which the intervention has greater impacts. You can also take action that communicates how your organization thinks about performance and how it can be improved. Reporting impacts internally can help communicate what is valued throughout the organization. By sharing and discussing key aspects of performance, an organization can help align priorities and create buy-in so that individual members make decisions and take actions that are most likely to create the impacts that the organization values.

Measurement for Accountability. The third key reason to measure impacts is to enhance accountability. Many stakeholders have an interest in impacts, and they will take action as a result of the impacts they see. Funders, for example, may have an interest in particular impacts, and can increase or withdraw funding on the basis of performance. More than half of fund managers think it's necessary to have impact measurements in order to raise capital.[6] Customers or beneficiaries can exit or can continue their participation and strengthen their relationships with the organization. Regulators and government agencies can provide or withdraw various forms of support. And if an intervention is successful, it can be adopted by another social purpose organization or by a governmental agency or for-profit corporation.

Engaging with stakeholder groups and providing them with the information they deem most useful can improve stakeholder relationships. It can increase trust in the organization's impacts and capabilities and strengthen stakeholder willingness to collaborate in the future.

Measurement Rules of Thumb

Measurement is challenging and costly, and common measurement problems can lead to excess spending or unreliable results. A few basic rules can help investors make the most out of their measurement systems:

1. *Measures should be actionable.* If a measurement won't affect the way you or your stakeholders do things, it's probably not worth gathering. Before deciding to collect a measurement, ask yourself what you'll do once you get that information. If the results don't affect actions, and you don't expect that to change in the future, there's no need to collect them.

2. *Measures should be manageable.* Don't measure too many things. Too many measures can create information overload or increase decision-making costs. A small number of items critical to achieving your goals is usually sufficient. One rule of thumb suggests that managers can manage only ten or fewer variables at a time. When measures are manageable, you can easily formulate a picture of how your investment is doing and make changes as needed to improve that performance.

3. *Measures should be comparable.* If you can use the same measures over time, you'll be able to evaluate your performance against your own targets and you'll be able to see trends in your performance over time. Finding measures that have already been validated elsewhere can also save time and increase the reliability and comparability of your findings. By using measures adopted

by others in your industry, you'll be able to benchmark your performance. Some organizations and industries are already doing this on a regular basis. About a fifth of the organizations targeting homeless issues are using Outcomes Star, an outcome measurement system developed by Triangle Consulting Social Enterprise in the UK. And another UK charity, Coordinated Action Against Domestic Abuse, promotes a shared monitoring tool for domestic abuse professionals and organizations. Resources like these allow organizations in an industry to learn from each other's successes and mistakes. To the extent you can find, use, and contribute to these benchmarking efforts, you'll improve measurement for your own and others' investments.

Monitoring and Evaluation

In the social sector, organizations tend to separate monitoring and evaluation activities from impact assessment activities. Monitoring and evaluation typically refers to measurements of inputs, activities, and outputs, and is used for understanding and managing organizational performance. Impact assessment usually refers to measurement of outcomes or impact, and is often used for reporting or providing proof of effectiveness to external stakeholders. Operational or process evaluation can be treated separately from monitoring and evaluation as well. This kind of evaluation is used to ensure that a program is being implemented as designed.[7]

Monitoring and evaluation covers many different approaches that can be used for many different purposes. Figure 17 shows three evaluation approaches used by Grantmakers for Effective Organizations: developmental evaluation, formative evaluation, and summative evaluation.[8]

Developmental evaluation is the least well-known of the three approaches. While formative evaluation is recommended for *improving* an approach, and summative evaluation for *validating* it, developmental evaluation is used for *creating* innovative approaches to social problems.

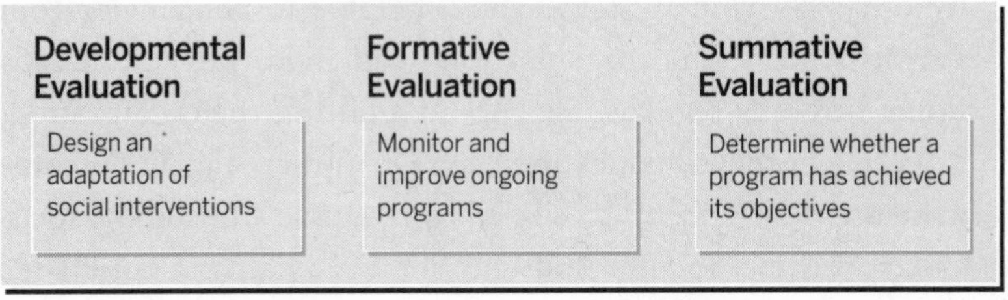

Developmental Evaluation	Formative Evaluation	Summative Evaluation
Design an adaptation of social interventions	Monitor and improve ongoing programs	Determine whether a program has achieved its objectives

Figure 17 Three Approaches to Monitoring and Evaluation

Developmental evaluation is used in situations where an organization is innovating by creating new products and services, programs, or business models. The purpose of the evaluation is to gather data to help design and test the innovations early on. Like a prototyping or agile development approach, in which a model is quickly developed, tested, and refined, developmental evaluation helps organizations make ongoing changes to their approaches as they uncover strengths and weaknesses.

Because results of a new intervention are unpredictable, developmental evaluation examines the relationships between activities and predictable outcomes, but is also alert to unanticipated outcomes. By monitoring outcomes as well as relationships among the various components that make up an intervention, developmental evaluation can help organizations learn and adapt in impactful ways.[9]

Formative evaluation is used when relationships have been more firmly established. When an organization has a clear theory of change or strategy map and wants to monitor and improve execution of that theory, formative evaluation can be used. Formative evaluation often begins early in the implementation of a program and provides feedback to help the organization make modifications to programs. When a program is more mature, formative evaluation can be used to monitor ongoing performance so that continual improvements can be made.

The James Irvine Foundation evaluates program content, outcomes, and refinement, as well as foundation leadership, constitu-

Case Study: The John S. and James L. Knight Foundation

The John S. and James L. Knight Foundation, a US foundation focusing on media and community engagement, has a five-year, $24 million initiative, the Knight Community Information Challenge (KCIC). The initiative aims at increasing local, community news and information using creative approaches. Because the approaches funded are new and the issue addressed is broad and complex, the foundation has decided to use developmental evaluation. Instead of verifying the grantees' performance, the purpose of the evaluation is to provide continuous feedback, check grantees' adoption of results, and get insights on next steps. The evaluators use traditional methods like surveys, interviews, and focus groups, but they note how the program is developing and how its progress advances the entire field.

Source: Preskill and Beer (2012) "Evaluating Social Innovation."

ent feedback, financial health, and organizational effectiveness. The foundation creates feedback loops to use these evaluation results and to enable ongoing improvement. Performance is reported to the board and then shared publicly. This pushes the foundation to test its reporting progress to identify short-term and medium-term objectives and measures that can be tracked and reported accountably.[10]

Summative evaluation is used when an organization needs a judgment about whether or not an approach has worked. This type of evaluation is used when the chain of relationships between actions and impacts is well understood and targets for impacts have been established. Summative evaluation helps to determine whether those targets were met and to establish responsibility for performance. Summative evaluation is often conducted by an external evaluator. Its primary purpose is to prove, rather than improve, the efficacy of an approach, and it may be conducted as a way to make an organization accountable to funders, regulators, and other external stakeholders.

Impact Evaluation

Evaluating a program's or organization's ultimate impact has become increasingly important in recent years. Investors today want evidence that their investments are creating a real difference for the stakeholders affected by them. So-called "evidence-based" investing has been elevated in status, and some investors won't consider investing in any intervention that isn't supported by evidence. Evidence has, in some circles, been equated with scientific testing. In this case, only those projects whose interventions have been linked with statistically significant changes in results in a tightly controlled setting qualify as evidence-based.

Although experimental evidence is valuable, it is only one form of highly reliable evidence that can be used to inform investment decisions. Figure 18 shows three basic sources for gathering reliable evidence for impact evaluation.

Investigation

Investigation is designed to gain an in-depth understanding of people or of a setting. The researcher plays an integral role in investigative research, and he or she must have a strong understanding of the issues being studied and an ability to let go of preconceptions and allow new understanding to emerge through the research process.

Investigative research typically relies on interviews and observations. Interviews range from informal, conversational interviews to highly structured interviews in which the researcher doesn't deviate from a set of scripted questions, except to probe for additional information. Guidelines are developed before the interviews to ensure that respondents are answering the same questions or discussing the same issues. The guidelines are modified over time as new issues come to light that require additional investigation.

Observation involves observing people in natural settings. The researcher provides a rich description of the setting, activities, and people and tries to understand how the people make meaning of their activities and situations. Observation can provide the context

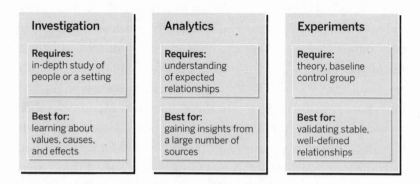

Figure 18 Sources of Evidence for Impact Evaluation

for understanding the information obtained in interviews. It can also provide a reality check on the data obtained under circumstances in which it's difficult to get useful answers from participants. Sometimes, for example, the way participants understand the issue varies too greatly from the way researchers understand it. Participants want to be helpful and provide answers that will please the researchers, but the result can be data that's difficult to interpret. Observation can help the researcher make sense of both the setting and the responses of the participants.

Documents and other artifacts can also be important sources of investigative data. Correspondence or business documents can be useful, as can observing artifacts such as technologies or resources that can confirm or provide greater perspective on data that was gathered through interviews or observations.

Analytics

Analytical methods are used to explore patterns in data. Analytics are used to understand phenomena or to compare expectations with the actual findings. Analytical methods can be used to describe any aspect of an issue, but they typically require numerical data. For example, a farmer might be asked how much fertilizer is spread on crops each season. Analytics often require coding so that nonquantitative data can be quantified. For example, patients might be asked how much pain they feel, on a scale of one to ten, or how strongly they agree with a statement such as "I feel safe in my home." Descriptive information can be compared to benchmarks. For example, a benchmark might be that farmers typically use five bags of fertilizer per hectare, while a survey might find that farmers in this village use three. The information can then be used to look at trends: last year farmers used three and a half bags of fertilizer, while this year they used three. Or it can be used to compare populations: farmers in one village used three bags, while farmers in an adjacent village used four.

The validity of analytics depends on the quality of the data being analyzed. In collecting data, there are two major considerations. First, the data you collect should be representative. Second, your measurements should have validity.

Data should be representative. If you survey only the most experienced farmers for a study of fertilizer use, you might get different results than if you surveyed the entire village. You'll normally survey a sample, so it's important to sample randomly and obtain a large enough sample so that results aren't affected by an unknown variable. For example, imagine that fertilizer use varies with the age of the farmer. By using random sampling, you'll help ensure that you didn't survey only older farmers last year and young ones this year, or experienced farmers in one village and novice farmers in another. If it's not possible to get a random sample, you can use matching: for example, you can survey an equal number of farmers in each experience level.

Data should also be valid. If farmers can't remember how much fertilizer they used and are just guessing, your data won't be valid. To increase validity, you might ask the question shortly after the farmers used the fertilizer, or you might ask the shopkeeper to record how much fertilizer each farmer purchased.

The way questions are asked is also important. A question about the level of pain experienced may be difficult for a patient to answer effectively. To increase the validity of the question, you could add descriptions to the levels of pain: 1=no pain, 10=disabling pain; or you could include pictures: 1=happy face, 10=pained, crying face. It is important to test out questions formulated in this way to make sure they are understandable and answerable.

Analytical methods are used for three basic purposes: to describe various aspects of an issue, to compare these characteristics, or to predict what is likely to happen in the future. Description can include simple counts or means, or it can include ratios or percentages. You can describe a single characteristic, or multiple characteristics. And you can look at how the variables are related or correlated with one another, or you can describe the range and variability of the data. Understanding the data you're working with can help with any further analytics you use.

You can also use analytics to make comparisons of characteristics over time or across groups. You can look for significant differences between and among group members, you can examine changes in characteristics, and you can look at interrelationships between variables.

Finally, you can use your understanding of the data and relationships to predict future conditions. If a variable has changed at the same rate for many time periods, you might expect it to keep changing at that rate in the future. If the relationship among variables has been constant, you might expect it to remain that way. The ability to predict enables you to stay the course if you're happy with the results, or to shift resource allocations and activities if you'd like to change them.

Analysis can be performed by looking at numerical data and trying to find the relationships between your variables. But you can often get a much better and more accurate understanding of the phenomena and relationships by using statistical analysis or data visualization.

Statistics. When analyzing data, you can use statistical techniques that enable you to determine the strength of the relationships

among your data points. For example, you might have data show-
ing that the average number of years that boys attend school is
lower than the average number for girls. A simple means test can
tell you whether this is a real difference, or whether the difference
among the boys is so great that the differences you found in aver-
ages is just a fluke. There are many techniques available for such
purposes, even in desktop computer spreadsheets. Depending on
the nature of the data and problem you're dealing with, you'll
decide how important it is to use correct statistical procedures
and assumptions. When calibrating dosages of a drug, for example, research protocols must be carefully followed. When you're
trying to understand a problem using the best evidence that is
available, you can use basic data gathering and rough analytical
procedures.

Visualization. Data visualization is becoming an increasingly pop-
ular way to analyze and convey information. Data visualization
uses various types of charts, graphics, and maps to represent the
data. Visualization can help the reader see patterns and how those
patterns vary over time or under different assumptions. Visualization can also be used to collapse large amounts of data into
a form that is more accessible. Bubble charts, for example, can
depict four dimensions at once. They typically use the x and y
axes to represent two dimensions, and bubble size and color to
represent the other two. Even for people well-versed in statistical
analysis, data visualization can be an effective way to develop a
deep understanding of an issue.

Experiments
When you have strong logical reasons to believe that your interventions will lead to desired results and you want to validate this
belief, you can conduct an experiment. Many programs evaluate
their effectiveness by looking at whether participants are better
off after the program than they were before it. On its face, this
approach seems to be a valid way to evaluate impact, and it pro-

vides a simple and easy way to learn about performance.

But there are two important problems with the before-and-after, or pretest/posttest approach. The main problem is that you won't know if the changes you find are a result of your program's work. Most social and environmental changes are very complex and are influenced by a large number of factors. Without examining these factors, you can't know what caused the change.

The best way to try to determine whether an intervention had the expected impact is through an experiment. In an experiment, some subjects receive or participate in an intervention while others do not. In other respects, the two groups of subjects are very similar. If you take this approach, you can see whether both groups changed in a similar manner over the time period when you look at the differences between pre- and post-test results. If one group changed more than another, you can attribute the difference to the intervention the group received.

Randomized control trials, or RCTs, have become the gold standard in providing evidence that a program works. RCTs have two major requirements. First, they use a control group that does not receive the intervention for comparison with the treatment group. This group serves as a "counterfactual"—it provides a picture of what would have happened without any intervention. Many factors can affect impacts, so it is difficult to tell whether impacts resulted from the intervention or something else, such as changes in economic, social, or natural conditions that affected beneficiaries. A control group subjected to the same factors lets you identify which changes resulted from the intervention.

Second, subjects must be randomly assigned to treatments. If subjects select which group they are in, results can be unreliable—for example, some may decide that they want to attend a drug treatment program while others decide not to participate. If more attendees than nonattendees stop using drugs during the study, it might be because the treatment program was effective, but it might be because those who decided to attend were more motivated to stop using drugs in the first place. By randomly assigning who gets the treatment and who does not, you can be more confident that changes are the result of the program and not some other variable.

While RCTs have advantages over other methods in that they can provide reliable evidence regarding an intervention's impact, they are useful only in very limited circumstances. In order for the RCT to produce useful information, the treatment, by itself, must be realistically capable of resulting in significant and measurable changes in impact. For the best chance of this happening, everything else that might affect the outcomes must remain as stable as possible. The control clients, who aren't getting the benefit of the program, will need to be assessed at both the beginning and the end of the study, which can be a challenge. More difficult still is to track clients who were in the group that received the treatment but dropped out during the course of the experiment. Surveying only clients that stayed in the study may lead to an overly positive evaluation of the treatment and its effects.

Another aspect of RCTs that can make them really difficult to use is that they require very strict control over the entire course of the intervention. As far as possible, all clients should get exactly the same treatment, so staff cannot be flexible in adjusting to changing circumstances individual client needs and must follow tightly scripted protocols when dealing with clients. The organization cannot change the treatment in the middle of the program. Even if a better approach for serving the clients is discovered, the program can't be changed until the experiment is finished—sometimes months or years later. It's also important to make sure that the control clients do not get any treatment, even from another organization, throughout the entire period.

Running an RCT is therefore appropriate only when the treatment is mature and well defined, and when the human participants are stable throughout the treatment. If anything does change during the course of the experiment, or if the treatment can't be randomly assigned, there are some ways to adjust the results through various design and statistical methods.

That said, when an intervention is stable and well defined, and clients can be randomly assigned to a treatment or control group, an RCT can often be conducted with very little effort. The organization will need to randomly assign clients to groups, gather baseline information, provide the intervention, and measure results at the end. If changes in outcomes for the group that received the intervention are measurably different from the outcomes for the group that did not, the organization can be confident that these changes resulted from the products or services provided. This provides evidence that its investments have resulted in significant social impacts.

Proof of impact can be very valuable to funders and other stakeholders. The Edna McConnell Clark Foundation, for example, stresses evidence-based investment and asks donees to provide convincing quantitative measurement of effectiveness of the programs it funds for transforming the lives of low-income youth. The foundation favors RCTs for evaluating interventions. Although RCTs can be costly for donees, the foundation supports the capacity building needed to get high levels of proof on social impacts.

Conducting a randomized control trial can be valuable to the organization and to other organizations pursuing similar social changes. Once it has been established that an intervention does result in desirable changes, the organization can use the treatment in similar circumstances without needing to repeat the measures or analysis. The organization can be fairly sure that the same outcomes will result if the circumstances are similar. In addition, the organization can communicate these outcomes more broadly once the treatment has been validated. This will provide a protocol for other organizations that care about the same social change and as a result will increase the organization's leverage in helping beneficiaries.

Action Agenda

1. Identify barriers that keep you from measuring impacts, such as difficulty, cost, and the possibility of misleading or dysfunctional measures.

2. Decide which constructs you want to measure and carefully define them.

3. Think about why you're measuring impact: for learning, for action, or for accountability.

4. Make sure that you choose measures that are actionable, manageable, and comparable.

5. Consider which approaches you'll use for monitoring and evaluation: developmental, formative, and/or summative.

6. Make sure that your data are representative and valid; consider using statistics and visualization for understanding impacts.

7. Consider randomized control trials if you can use them in a stable, tightly controlled setting.

8

Measurement Approaches

It is easy to become confident of program success even before any research on measurement begins. Day-to-day involvement and observations of activities in the field—seeing patients being vaccinated, full recycling bins, or a well-executed opera—can make it appear that the project is effective. Decision makers evaluate success, and they modify programs based on these evaluations. They often believe that success is so obvious that devoting resources to measurement to prove success to an outside funder or other stakeholder would be a waste of resources. But it's hard to write a success story if the program actually fails.

The Social Impact Creation Cycle outlines the steps to take to create social impact. In this chapter, we review some of the most commonly used approaches to measure that impact. This review is not comprehensive—there are hundreds of measurement approaches to choose from. But it will provide you with a good foundation for understanding the basic measurement strategies available and the situations for which each approach is most useful, along with sources for additional information.

The foundation of a good measurement system is a clearly articulated model that links actions to impacts. When direct measurement of impacts isn't feasible, we must substitute logic for measurement, and that logic must be sound. Without a clear understanding of the impacts you hope to achieve and the logical chain of events that will lead to those impacts, you'll find it difficult to devise a measurement system that can effectively measure or manage impacts.

Measurement approaches can be used for a variety of purposes:

- Project selection
- Monitoring during projects
- Evaluation after project completion
- Overall assessment of organizational impact

In our work with organizations, we have found that many have not yet thought carefully about the objectives they were trying to achieve and the actions they would need to take to create them. Others have difficulty deciding which impacts they want to achieve and how to measure them. Many organizations are unsure which measurement approaches they should use. The problem facing these organizations is not a lack of technical resources. Many effective approaches for evaluating impact are available to them; the Foundation Center, a leading knowledge bank for the social sector, has developed an online database, Tools and Resources for Assessing Social Impact (TRASI), that contains over 150 impact measurement tools, methods, and best practices categorized in a variety of ways to make it easy to identify tools that meet specific needs.[1]

Nevertheless, most organizations are unsure how to choose the best approach for their needs. And even those organizations considered by their peers to be the best at impact assessment believe they can do better. Though the choice is difficult, demand for greater focus on measurement is increasing rapidly, and organizations need to be prepared. Bill Gates recently said, "I have been struck by how important measurement is to improving the human condition. You can achieve incredible progress if you set a clear goal and find a measure that will drive progress toward that goal."[2]

Michael Bloomberg's foundation also places a high value on measurement. Its tagline is "results that can be measured and change that can be felt."[3] Organizations today need to focus more effort on measurement than they have in the past—not only because donors and other stakeholders are demanding it but because many excellent methods are now available, and better measurement can significantly improve performance and increase social impact.

Classification of Measurement Methods

Measurement approaches can be divided into four basic categories: trained judgment, qualitative research, quantification, and monetization. Table 8 lists these methods along with representative techniques for each category and examples of organizations that have effectively used these approaches.

- *Trained judgment.* Discussions and observations of programs by experienced professionals.
- *Qualitative research.* Systematic, in-depth research on social impacts that can include site visits, structured interviews, and focus groups.
- *Quantification.* Data and reports in numerical form. These can include direct measurements as well as survey responses.
- *Monetization.* Quantitative evaluation that converts some or all of the measured impact into monetary values.

Each method has strengths and weaknesses, and the choice of method should be driven by the measurement goals of the organization. Many organizations use multiple approaches to serve a variety of purposes, or to triangulate for greater understanding of performance.

Trained Judgment

Many of the current reports of success found on social purpose organization websites are assessments by experienced observers. These can be developed on the basis of discussions with beneficia-

Table 8 Current Approaches to Social Impact Measurement

Approach	Techniques	Organizations
Trained judgment	Discussions Observations Expert analysis	GlobalGiving
Qualitative research	Structured interviews Field visits	Knight Foundation Geneva Global Unilever Indonesia
Quantification	Surveys Direct measurements Cost analysis	Acumen Fund

Monetization	Benefit-cost analysis
	Social return on
	  investment
		Robin Hood Foundation
		Washington State Insti-
		  tute for Public Policy
		Newmont Ghana Gold
		  Ltd.

ries like clients, customers, or patients, or they can be developed from observations by professionals on the ground. But not all assessments are equally valid. Assessments can be based on logically grounded judgments and careful triangulation of perspectives, or they can be based on ad hoc discussions and examples from random events.

Ideally, assessments use evidence-based judgments based on field workers' observations and supported by reports by head office personnel or independent observers. These professionals may provide verification by going into the field and talking with program participants or observing programs in action. Verification fieldwork provides greater confidence that resources are being spent efficiently and effectively. For social impacts that cannot feasibly be measured, such as the impacts of programs that promote peace, trained judgment and expertise are essential for evaluating the logical relationships between the organization's activities and the desired outcomes.

Case Study: GlobalGiving Storytelling Project

GlobalGiving Foundation, a US-based nonprofit that connects social entrepreneurs and nonprofits with funders, launched its Storytelling Project to build a better community feedback loop directly from the stakeholders. The project collected 57,191 stories from community members in Uganda and Kenya by asking one simple question: "Tell us about a time when a person or an organization tried to change something in your community." The answers were totally open-ended and thus not easily compared across organizations. But donors and organizational leaders learned a great deal about beneficiary perceptions of program success. When used by trained professionals, such stories can provide valuable evidence regarding challenges and successes.

Source: GlobalGiving Foundation (2013) "Storytelling Project: Turning Anecdotes into Useful Data."

For many organizations, trained judgment marks the extent of measuring and reporting efforts, both internally and externally. Depending on the nature of the impacts and purpose of the measurements, trained judgment can be valuable and reliable, particularly when backed by well-developed logical support. However, in many cases this approach is insufficient for a full and in-depth understanding of performance. For those organizations that want or need to provide more systematic evidence of success, trained judgment can provide a base level of measurement and reporting. Additional research that includes qualitative or quantitative methods can then be used to supplement the trained judgments.

Qualitative Research

After operating in the field for some time, an organization's operating processes and results may become more routinized. In these circumstances, many organizations proceed to design systematic research to assess their social impacts. Sometimes this is done to provide confidence regarding overall success; at other times, the goal is to investigate the particular inputs, processes, outputs, and outcomes that are most likely to increase success. The push for

**Case Study: John S. and James L. Knight Foundation:
Qualitative Research**

The John S. and James L. Knight Foundation assesses its grants by using qualitative research. In its review of the MIT Center for Future Civic Media (C4), which received a four-year, $5 million grant, the Knight Foundation conducted thirty interviews, two surveys of the students and external partners, reviews of grant documents, investigations of selected projects, and research on selected peer institutions. The interview and survey questions were specifically designed for students, staff, and outsiders. The final report was a detailed qualitative analysis of C4 with case studies of several stakeholders.

Source: Palfrey and Bracy (2011) *Review of the MIT Center for Future Civic Media*.

more clarity and proof can come not only from an organization's leaders but also from existing and potential donors or investors. The process of developing a clear mission, theory of change, and logic model for a program or an organization will often suggest tests of various alternative approaches to the organization's work. The tests are intended to gain a better understanding of activities that could in turn lead to greater impacts.

One way to obtain additional evidence is through qualitative research. Rather than relying on observations and judgments by trained professionals, the organization establishes a systematic program of investigation. Internal staff may take charge of this work, but that is often a challenge for most organizations because they lack the expertise and human and financial resources necessary to conduct valid qualitative research. An independent external investigation is therefore desirable in some cases.

High-quality qualitative research demands systematic formulation of the research design and testing of the hypotheses that relate directly to the logic model. The logic model carefully articulates causal relationships leading from actions to impacts, and the research program should be designed to test some or all of those relationships. The research design describes and then executes a program for collection and analysis of data that provides evidence of the success (or lack of success) of the program. It may also provide guidance on the individual inputs, processes, outputs, and outcomes that need to change to lead to the desired impacts. The research may rely on focus groups, field interviews, in-depth case studies, or other qualitative methods. In contrast to trained judgment, qualitative methods rely on objectively validated and systematic documentation and analysis.

Quantification

Increasingly, social service nonprofits as well as donors and other investors are requesting quantification of results rather than trained judgments or qualitative research. Often this requirement takes the form of measurement and reporting of outputs rather than actual measurements of impact. As a result, organizations are increasingly quantifying things like average number of participants, numbers of dollars spent per participant, and number of products or services successfully delivered. They might gather data on the number of school lunches made, the number served, the number eaten, or the nutritional content of the lunches eaten. Some organizations go beyond measuring outputs and measure outcomes—the effects of the outputs on the beneficiaries. These organizations might measure how the school lunches changed the behavior of the children at school, behavior at home, school attendance, and so forth.

What an organization should measure depends on the purpose of the measurement and on the organization's impact goals and logic model. If, for example, more nutritious lunches are provided as a way to reduce childhood obesity, the organization could measure obesity directly. To get quantitative information, the weights of children could be taken or approximated by observers. If the goal was to improve health, results could be measured by the number of sick days taken or by observing how many minutes children are active on the playground each day.

Measures can take the form of raw scores, percentages of improvement, or comparisons with some reference point such as

Case Study: Geneva Global: Qualitative + Quantitative Research + Trained Judgment

Geneva Global is a philanthropic consulting firm that helps donors choose among international giving opportunities and provides independent assessment of alternatives. Its evaluation uses quantitative ratings and scores along with qualitative and narrative descriptions of progress. The results report consists of two quantitative sections—rating of performance and expected versus actual life change—and two qualitative sections—narrative analysis and recommendation for the next phase.

The quantitative sections enable a comparison between different programs that is essential to Geneva Global as it evaluates international programs across issue areas. The qualitative sections provide a detailed picture of the programs and serve as a source for supporting trained judgment. Geneva Global visits each project at least once a year. The site visit is not only a way to maintain the quality of projects, it also articulates the enthusiasm and expectations of Geneva Global.

Source: Geneva Global (2007) *Benequity Solutions: Monitoring Handbook.*

Case Study: Unilever Indonesia: Qualitative + Quantitative Research

Unilever Indonesia (UI) is the thirteenth-largest company in Indonesia. Its social impacts are generated from macroeconomic impacts, employment, the value chain from supply to distribution, and wide impacts in the community, including influence on government and the business community. Macroeconomic impacts come from employment generation, public-sector investment, higher productivity, and macroeconomic stability. Employment impacts stem from how people gain income and skills and can therefore improve their lives in a sustainable way. The value chain consists of supplier companies, raw materials producers, and low-income consumers.

UI and Oxfam examined activities along UI's value chain. The team gathered data on an agricultural product from UI's published and internal documents, other published sources, and emails and verbal communications, primarily from UI staff. The study used objective data and did not aggregate impacts. For example, the number of workers and their salaries were presented as employment impacts following a qualitative description of how UI positively affects its workers' lives that did not monetize these benefits.

Source: Clay (2005) *Exploring the Links between International Business and Poverty Reduction: A Case Study of Unilever in Indonesia.*

prior performance, targets, or the performance of others. Sometimes it is desirable to use quantitative measures to compare programs across an organization, either in terms of their cost effectiveness or their impacts.[4] This is difficult for projects in similar sectors but even more difficult for programs in different sectors.

One established technique of quantification is cost-effectiveness analysis (CEA).[5] This approach calculates the ratio of cost to a nonmonetary measure of inputs, outputs, or outcomes. These analyses commonly take the form of costs per unit of output or impact. For example, an organization might measure cost per employee placed or cost per life saved. The William and Flora Hewlett Foundation, one of the largest private foundations in the US, devised a CEA-based evaluation method called Expected Return, where the expected return equals the theoretical benefit times the probability of success times the philanthropy's contribution to the initiative. The resulting figure is divided by the expected costs invested. The usefulness of the Expected Return number depends on the quality of the estimates plugged into the formula, so the foundation makes careful assessments of costs, risks, and other key factors.[6]

Acumen Fund, a nonprofit global venture fund, uses a method it developed called BACO (from "best available charitable option") to capture the net cost per unit of social impact. The BACO ratio compares the expected impacts of the potential investment to impacts that would have been returned had the money been invested in the best charitable alternative. The ratio determines whether the investment is more effective than existing alternatives.[7] It can be difficult to find an appropriate BACO when no charitable program exists, yet the method does provide investment managers with information useful for making comparisons and decisions.

Monetization

Cost/benefit analysis, which ascribes monetary values to both market and nonmarket impacts, has been used extensively in the economics literature, in government, and in the evaluation of many social programs by expert evaluators. It assigns a monetary value to the measured outcomes, and subtracts the costs incurred to achieve them to produce a net social benefit (or cost) in monetary terms. Challenges do exist in trying to assign appropriate values, and assumptions must be made clear, but there are many good examples of monetization and good reasons to consider this approach.

Market impacts might include increased productivity, increased tax revenues from new jobs and spending, reduction in costs, and increased earnings. Nonmarket impacts might include additional years of life resulting from improved health, increased happiness due to counseling programs, or greater recreational benefits resulting from environmental improvements. Many programs create both market and nonmarket benefits. For example, job creation programs can lead to both increased tax revenues and reduced costs for welfare payments. They can also create increased family stability and happiness. Environmental improvement programs can create reduced cleanup costs along with increased quality of life and life span for residents.

Both market and nonmarket impacts can be measured and monetized. Though some measures lack objectivity and precision, they can still be relevant to evaluations and decisions. Most organizations have decided to forgo monetization because they don't know how to do it, they believe that it is too expensive to do, or they believe it is too imprecise to be reliable. As long as you understand the nature of the assumptions that underlie monetization, the approach can be valuable. And if assumptions are questioned, it is possible to see how changes in assumptions can influence the results. When assumptions and their ramifications are made apparent, methods can often be improved over time.

The monetary values of nonmarket social impacts are never zero. Social changes do have monetary consequences, whether or not we can measure them. Even when measurements are rough, they can be relevant to the evaluation of social programs and to

Case Studies: Monetization

Robin Hood Foundation aims to alleviate poverty in New York City. It defines its poverty-fighting impact as increased earnings and increased quality of life. For each project, Robin Hood Foundation lists its direct and induced outcomes and the probabilities of each of the outcomes. It then searches academic literature to relate the outcomes to increased earnings, or increased standard of living, as in health-related programs. The foundation accounts for the time value of money by discounting future benefits and costs. It also estimates the percentage of its influence on the project, the "Robin Hood factor," to get the final measure of benefit. This value is then divided by the total cost of the grant and produces the benefit-cost ratio.

Washington State Institute for Public Policy (WSIPP) is a nonpartisan government research institute that provides information for legislative decision-making. For each project, the institute computes the monetary benefits and costs produced for program participants, taxpayers, and others. The institute assigns monetary values in a consistent way so that policy makers can compare different programs. The conclusions are tested for riskiness by analyzing how the bottom line varies with changes in assumptions and estimates.

Source: Weinstein and Lamy (2009) *Measuring Success: How Robin Hood Estimates the Impact of Grants*; Ebrahim and Ross (2010) *The Robin Hood Foundation*; Aos et al. (2011) *Return on Investment: Evidence-Based Options to Improve State Outcomes*.

the improvement of decisions and social impact. In addition to its extensive use by governments and companies, monetization has been used successfully by nonprofits and foundations.

Social Return on Investment

Social return on investment (SROI) is one well-known monetization technique. The Roberts Enterprise Development Fund (REDF), a US venture philanthropy, pioneered the SROI approach. The objective of SROI is to evaluate the returns that could be generated by social investments. SROI is conceptually similar to return on investment (ROI), which is regularly used to evaluate financial returns expected from or realized by business investment. There are many different ways to calculate SROI, but in general the metric is calculated by dividing the impact returned from a project by the money invested. The greater the SROI, the more impact generated from every dollar invested. REDF's SROI framework originally had six key metrics: enterprise value, social purpose value, blended value, enterprise index of return, social purpose index of return, and blended index of return.[8] Each one of the values was calculated and discounted on a ten-year period.

Figure 19 SROI Work Flow
Source: Adapted from SROI Network (2005) *A Framework for Approaches to SROI Analysis;* Nicholls (2009) *A Guide to Social Return on Investment.*

Though REDF has modified its approach for measuring jobs creation, quality of life improvement, and reduced public costs,[9] other organizations are currently using versions of SROI that they have adapted to their own needs.[10] However, the general work flow used for the SROI approach remains similar. Figure 19 shows the steps for implementing SROI analyses.[11]

Jewish Vocational Service (JVS) is a US-based nonprofit that focuses on creating employment. In 2012, JVS calculated its SROI using this formula:

$$SROI = \frac{\text{Number of Clients Enrolled} * \text{Earning Difference}}{\text{Program Cost}}$$

For the earning difference metric in the numerator, JVS uses the projected income of the beneficiaries. SROI can be calculated for earnings over a one-, two-, five-, or ten-year period after the intervention.[12]

PUMA, the global footwear company that is part of luxury brand retailer PPR, places an economic valuation on environmental impacts. In 2011, it released its Environmental Profit and Loss

Account, which reported a negative social impact of over $150 million in 2010. PUMA measured its impacts in land use, water use, greenhouse gases, air pollution, and waste using the operational data from its own environmental management departments. PUMA uses the results to raise awareness of its social responsibility and step forward to reduce its negative impacts by examining the supply chain, innovating environmentally friendly products, and strengthening government relationships.[13]

SROI Case Study: Newmont Ghana Gold Ltd.

Newmont Ghana Gold Ltd. (NGGL), an operating region of Newmont Mining Corp., one of the largest gold companies in the world, has evaluated the socioeconomic impacts of a gold mine in Ghana. The team included both qualitative and monetized evaluations and generated an estimate of the mine's influence on employment, tax revenues, household incomes, Ghana's balance of payments, and supplier profits. The team also conducted interviews to evaluate NGGL's relationship with the local community and other stakeholders in Ghana.

The full range of NGGL's socioeconomic impacts include:

- Macroeconomic impacts (contributions to Ghana's GDP, balance of payments, and foreign capital investment).
- Socioeconomic impacts and linkages (contributions to value-added, employment, government revenues, education and skill development, and infrastructure).
- Community impacts (resettlement, reduction of available farmland, community development, changes in community and social structures, attraction of migrant workers, and community health).
- Environmental impacts (air pollution, water pollution, landscape modification and restoration, and deforestation and loss of biodiversity).

A broad set of direct, indirect, and induced impacts is included. NGGL's economic impact is the sum of its direct impact, the impacts of its suppliers, and the impacts of all household consumption decisions.

Source: Kapstein and Kim (2011) *The Socio-Economic Impact of Newmont Ghana*.

The choices of which impacts to measure and how to measure them are critical to reporting and improving social impacts. For-profit companies, governments, foundations, and NGOs have been using a variety of approaches to measure their impacts, and have effectively used trained judgment, qualitative research, quantification, and monetization. A large number of tools and resources are available for helping organizations implement particular impact measures.

By providing measurement basics in chapter 7 and a survey of some of the best practices in different types of measurement approaches in chapter 8, we have laid the groundwork for developing your own approach to measurement. Chapter 9 will help guide you through that process.

Action Agenda

1. Review tested approaches to impact measurement to determine the best fit for your needs.
2. Use trained judgment where you have a great deal of expertise, whether or not you also have formal measures.
3. Use qualitative research for deep understanding of issues and stakeholders, and for developing theories about the best methods for addressing these issues.
4. Use quantification when you want to perform numerical and graphical analyses and statistical tests, or when you have many subjects or variables to investigate.
5. Use monetization when you would like to use monetary values in your resource allocation decisions and when you want to compare disparate projects or programs.

9

Measuring Your Impact

You've laid the foundation for understanding and improving your social impacts. You've defined your social impact goals, and you've clarified your understanding of the chain of actions and results needed to achieve those goals. You've bought in to the idea that measuring impacts will help you learn and progress, and you've reviewed the basic approaches that organizations use to measure their impacts. Now you're ready to develop your own system for measuring impacts. It's time to stop hoping that you're making an impact, and it's time to stop guessing which investments have been most effective.

The easiest way to develop your impact measurement system is to start from the beginning. No matter what you're currently measuring and how you're using those metrics to manage your work, we're asking you to let go of your existing approaches and assumptions and start your thinking process with a clean slate. In the end, you'll keep some elements from your current system and add some new ones. If you start by considering a full range of possibilities, you won't be constrained by choices you've made in the past or by attempts to recoup the value of your sunk costs. Table 9 summarizes the steps you'll work through in developing or refining your impact measurement system. We'll walk you

through the activities involved in each step and give you extra
guidance where it's needed.

Table 9 Developing a Performance Measurement System

Step 1: Prepare the measurement foundation.
- Link planned actions to desired results.
- Inventory the full range of your impacts.

Step 2: Consider how you'll use the results.
- Decide whether the system will be used for control or understanding.
- Consider the purpose your measure will serve: learning, action, and/ or accountability.

Step 3: Identify key impacts and metrics.
- Identify your most significant impacts.
- Decide which primary and secondary impacts you need to monitor.
- Select metrics for each of the impacts you've chosen to measure.

Step 4: Develop your measurement system.
- Align the system with your organization's strategy.
- Gather data according to a plan.
- Analyze the data you collect.
- Communicate results to stakeholders.
- Take action to improve impacts.

Prepare the Measurement Foundation

Starting with a strong foundation helps ensure that your measurement system produces valid and useful information. The first step
is to review the logic model or results chain that links your activities and results in a causal model. For many organizations, this
is the most difficult part of the measurement process. But it is
essential that the desired impacts are perfectly clear, so that the
measurement system can be designed to provide the information
needed to achieve these impacts. The mission and logic model
were discussed in detail in chapter 6, and are summarized here.

Link Planned Actions to Desired Results

Your mission statement defines the social purpose of your organization or intervention and the social changes you want to bring
about through your investments. Your primary interest may be in

maximizing your organization's positive social impacts or minimizing its negative impacts. Your logic model lays out a clear path for creating those changes, as shown in Figure 20.

The logic through which your investment creates an impact should define the inputs you invest, the actions you pursue, and the outputs you provide to your beneficiaries. But if your model is to measure impact effectively, it should be very clear about how the outputs you produce will change the outcomes for your beneficiaries, and how those outcomes will result in the social impacts you desire. The outcomes and impacts specified in your logic model will be the focus of your impact measurement system.

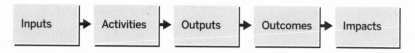

Figure 20 Logic Model

Inventory Your Full Impacts

When you develop a measurement system, you'll want to make sure that you are aware of the many ways in which your organization generates impacts, and you'll need to determine which of these are significant enough that you should include them in your measurement system. Your measurement system will include the primary, targeted impacts that you have laid out in your logic model. In addition to these core impacts, you'll need to examine the full range of positive and negative impacts you'll create for your beneficiaries and other stakeholders. As discussed in detail in chapter 5, you can affect stakeholders through:

- *Products and services.* Benefits to customers, impacts beyond customers, use and safety, and disposal.
- *Operations.* The supply chain, infrastructure, product design, human resource practices, and production.
- *Passive investments.* Mission-related investments, program-related investments, and socially responsible investments.

Along with the impacts created through these three areas, your work will also create second-order impacts—changes that come about as a result of your direct impacts. Your beneficiaries will be affected by both primary and secondary impacts, and other stakeholders will be affected by both types of impacts as well.

When your work has direct or indirect beneficiaries, it is essential to bring them in to make sure their interests are aligned with your goals and to explore risks associated with the planned changes. It's also critical that you have buy-in from the beneficiaries. Even if they agree with the need for change, they may not believe that outside intervention is the solution. In addition, you may need to find out if they will follow through on any requirements your project places on them, including providing feedback on the success of the program.[1] Keystone Accountability, a nonprofit consulting firm that strives to improve the effectiveness of charitable organizations, focuses on constituent voice. It provides guidance to help organizations learn from their constituents. Constituents share their critical views on programs and organizations use this input to support better collaboration and implement solutions more effectively.

In addition to beneficiaries, many other stakeholders will affect or be affected by your change. You should research both their interests in and potential responses to your intervention. Stakeholders include supply-chain partners, investors, regulators, local authorities, and community members. Competitors can also be stakeholders, because your organization's ability to attract lower-than-market-rate funding may undercut and damage local for-profit competitors.

Secondary impacts for the beneficiaries can be positive impacts, such as an increase in social status that accompanies a decrease in poverty. They can also be negative, such as strained family relationships that result from economic changes. Other stakeholders can be affected by the primary and secondary impacts as well. For example, if the income of a parent increases, the economic well-being of children in the household also increases. The increased consumption by the family could also impact local businesses from which they make purchases. Developing a thorough understanding of your full impacts will provide information useful for designing a system for managing key impacts.

Consider How You'll Use the Results

Once you have laid the foundation by identifying the impacts that will be measured by your system, you'll want to consider how you'll use the results. As discussed in chapter 7, any measurement effort will have costs, and you'll need to be selective in your choice of measurement. By thinking about the actions you'll take once you have results, and how those actions will ultimately affect your ability to improve impacts, you'll be positioned to make better choices when designing your measurement systems in organizations.

Measuring for Management

Providing information about impacts and what creates them is the most important aspect of measurement and can be a key driver in accomplishing the mission. Nevertheless, measuring impact is a subjective process, and measures can never fully represent the impacts they are intended to map. It's important, therefore, to be very intentional about the use of these measures. There are two basic ways for using measurement systems in organizations:

- Using measures for control
- Using measures for understanding

Control. Using measures to control behavior through a system that monitors and rewards individual performance can have unintended consequences. These consequences can undermine the very impact the organization is trying to create.

When rewards are based on metrics, programs are likely to be managed on the basis of those metrics, rather than on improving outcomes. For example, when program ratio (program spending divided by total expenses) is set as the basis for evaluating performance and making grant and donation decisions, decision makers commonly manage or manipulate this measure through a variety of mechanisms, such as reclassifying general expenses as program-related expenses.

Even large, extremely effective organizations make this mistake. Such distortions are not just based on overhead measures—measures of social impact can also be manipulated. An organization might, for example, announce that they will bring clean water to 1 million people in five years. After making this promise, managers then realize that to meet it, they will have to focus efforts on beneficiaries who are close to areas where water is already available because serving more remote clients would be more difficult and expensive. By focusing on easy-to-serve clients, the organization might meet its goal, but the impacts may be much less significant than if the organization had focused on reaching a smaller number of clients whose needs were greater.

Although there can be definite benefits to using measures to control performance, care should always be taken to ensure that measures don't have dysfunctional consequences. Impacts often result from the actions of many different people and may be beyond the control of any one manager or group. Rewarding managers based on results they can't control can be problematic. Alternatively, this approach can be beneficial if it encourages individuals and groups to work together and with a variety of other stakeholders to obtain the resources needed to drive results. Potential consequences should be considered when using impact measurements for control.

Understanding. Using measures to gain understanding is an essential goal of any performance metrics system and the primary purpose of measurement in the Social Impact Creation Cycle. It's never too early to begin asking the question of whether you're making an impact. You don't need to wait until your program is operational to set your measurement plans in motion. The best impact measurements are embedded throughout the life of an investment. Some impact evaluation can start even earlier, as the program is being designed. For example, you can run simulations to predict which outcomes would likely result from various designs, or you can test the intervention on a small sample to determine whether the desired impact can feasibly be expected to result from the program.

In addition, some assessments require identification of a control group. The control group includes subjects who are similar to the program's beneficiaries but who will not receive any intervention or investment. This group provides us with a *counterfactual*—a marker for what would have happened to our beneficiaries if they had not received our assistance. By comparing beneficiaries who received our intervention with those who didn't, we create evidence about whether our program was actually responsible for the results measured.

Measuring for Understanding

Understanding social impacts is a central concern of all social purpose organizations, which should be identified before a program is implemented. Impact measurement can play a key role in this effort in a variety of ways. As we discussed in chapter 7, there are many reasons we might wish to measure impacts:

- *Measure for learning:* to understand performance and to test assumptions.
- *Measure for action:* to guide behavior and communicate values.
- *Measure for accountability:* to report performance and build relationships.

Good measurement systems can shed light on the results and effectiveness of programs and on the many factors associated with success. Even well-established organizations can learn through measurement. For example, measurement can be used to compare the effectiveness of programs across populations or geographic regions in order to identify differences that influence impacts.

The majority of organizations don't measure impacts and instead use outputs—the products and services they provide—as proxies for impacts. But effective measurement can help organizations develop a better understanding of their impacts. In addition, measurement can be used to evaluate the links between elements in the logic chain and hypothesized relationships about how investments lead to outcomes and impacts.

Beyond basic learning about the logic model and results, measurement can be used to guide action and make changes in plans in order to improve impact. This is the most important function of any measurement system designed to improve organizational performance and increase impacts. The Bill & Melinda Gates Foundation promotes actionable measurement, which emphasizes the purpose of the measurement—to inform decisions and improve strategies. To get results that can improve impact, actionable measurement focuses on a limited number of questions and prioritizes the intended audiences. By focusing its measurement in this way, the foundation is able to use results information to revise targets as well as strategies.[2]

Measurement can be an effective tool to communicate which areas of performance in the organization are considered most important. Measurement can also be used to communicate performance to both internal and external stakeholders that have invested in the organization. The processes involved in developing and interpreting measures can help stakeholders develop a common understanding of the organization's challenges and accomplishments.

Measurement can also be used for accountability, and can help the organization report evidence about performance to a variety of stakeholders. Organizations that receive funding through grants are often required to measure specific aspects of performance that are of interest to the granting agency. Other investors might also require this kind of accountability. Some organizations treat this as simply a reporting exercise, and never use the information for their own internal purposes. Yet by using this information as a basis for developing shared understanding with its investors, the organization can strengthen relationships and shared purposes with these investors.

Identify Key Impacts and Metrics

Deciding which impacts to measure requires that you ask the right questions. To begin, you'll identify your most significant impacts, decide which information is most essential for managing your organization's performance, and then decide which metrics you'll use to measure them.

Asking the Right Questions about Impacts

Asking the right questions about your impact begins with the end in mind. The questions that motivated your investments and grounded your logic model were questions like What social problem do I want to solve? and What actions can I take to solve it? Now that you've answered those questions and designed your interventions, you're ready to ask whether your plan is working. Am I making an impact? is the ultimate question that drives impact measurements and keeps investors up at night.

Once you have inventoried your full range of impacts, you can begin to decide which are of most significance. If you have a sound logic model, you'll be very clear on the impacts you want to achieve. Understanding your ultimate impacts is fundamental to your organization's existence. To decide what to measure, you should ask questions like these that focus on those impacts:

- "What do we most need to understand about our impacts?"
- "What information would convince us that we've been successful?"
- "What information would be most helpful for guiding actions or revising strategy?"
- "What other key performance indicators could tell us how we're doing?"

In many cases, even when measuring impacts is straightfor-
ward, changes are only detectable after a long period of time. To
make timely course corrections and to improve impact management, it's useful to identify those indicators that will give you the
most useful predictive information about your performance:

- A school might measure the number of students who have
  passed proficiency exams and enrolled in secondary school.
- A heart hospital might want to know the survival rate of
  patients and the time it takes them to resume normal activities.
- A seller of efficient cookstoves might want to know the
  amount of fuel used and the level of satisfaction with the
  stoves.

The measures listed here might be considered output or outcome
measures. They serve as key intermediate steps between actions
and impacts. The factors most critical to successful impact creation should be included in the organization's measurement plan.

Some organizations measure primarily outputs because output data are easier to collect and manage, and provide immediate signals on program performance. If the logical relationships
between outcomes and impacts are well grounded or evidenced,
outcome information can be used in lieu of impacts for many
purposes. Pacific Community Ventures is a US-based nonprofit
organization that creates jobs in low-income areas through business advising, capital, and research. The organization measures
its primary social impact by evaluating outcome data on the reach
of its projects—for example, how many jobs were created. It has
sufficient logical and empirical support to believe that a person's
quality of life is improved by securing stable employment.[3]

It is useful to bear in mind that no metrics are perfect—they are
always proxies for the real phenomena they represent, and they
must be interpreted with that fact in mind. But as your measurement system evolves, you can continually revise and improve your

metrics, as well as the means by which you gather and use them. As a result, your measurements will become increasingly useful to support making decisions and guiding strategy.

Measures for Primary and Secondary Impacts

Measuring impacts begins with identifying the broad changes you wish to make. The metrics you use will show changes in

- An *absolute level*, such as tons of CO_2 emitted
- A *percentage*, such as the percentage of children who have learned to read
- A *ratio*, such as crop yield compared to the amount of fertilizer used

These numbers can then be compared with a standard that will provide the context for interpreting them. You can compare:

- Actual results to targeted results
- Results in one period to results in another
- Your results to the results of comparable organizations or to industry benchmarks

Figure 21 provides examples of impact areas and sample metrics for each area.

Many organizations pursue impacts that are difficult to measure. More guidance is being provided every day, as organizations grapple with measuring elusive outcomes and impacts. Table 10 shows examples of measures in six categories in which many social purpose organizations work.

In addition to the primary impacts your project has on intended beneficiaries, you'll also want to measure secondary positive and negative impacts on beneficiaries and other stakeholders. This is essential for organizations that want a complete picture of the impacts they are creating. A foundation, for example, may fund antismoking programs for teens who reduce their rates of smoking relative to their peers. Measuring only primary impacts would result in a picture of success. But what if this organization encouraged kids to eat snacks when they get the urge to smoke, which resulted in rapid weight gain for those in the program? What if comparing the dangers of smoking to marijuana use reduced the teenagers' anxieties about safety and resulted in increased marijuana use? Or what if the foundation's sizable endowment was invested in tobacco companies that help create the very problem the foundation seeks to address?

Social purpose organizations need to measure a variety of impacts to get the whole picture of the impact they are making.

Figure 21 Sample Impact Measures

Sample Measures

Environment
- Metric tons of CO_2 emitted
- Kilograms of hazardous waste treated
- Hectares reforested
- Kilometers of land preserved
- Hectares of native species planted
- kWh of sustainably sourced energy used
- ppm insecticide in runoff
- Liters of wastewater produced
- Number of protected wildlife per hectare

Community
- Perceptions of safety and security
- Crime rate
- Number of social connections
- Number of community meetings attended
- Number of government interactions
- Perceived influence of local government
- Corruption rating
- Number of people with access to transportation
- Number of people with access to latrines

Health
- Quality adjusted life years
- Number of people suffering illness
- Number of school days missed due to illness
- Number of deaths
- Average years of life expectancy
- Number of return hospital procedures
- Number of health-seeking behaviors
- Number of abuse cases
- Rate of infant mortality
- Visits to clinics per year
- Weight of newborns
- Number of smokers
- Circumference of child's upper arm

Economic
- Perceptions of safety and security
- Crime rate
- Number of social connections
- Number of community meetings attended
- Number of government interactions
- Perceived influence of local government
- Corruption rating
- Number of people with access to transportation
- Number of people with access to latrines

Table 10 Sample Metrics for Common Problem-Solving Methods

Innovation
- Number of successful innovations
- Number of innovations accepted by stakeholders
- Number of innovations that have contributed to social impact
- Number of innovations that have been adopted by other organizations

Service Delivery
- Percent reduction in the magnitude of a problem
- Percent of beneficiaries that have integrated the product or service into daily life
- Percent increase in the well-being of beneficiaries
- Number of adoptions of a service delivery model by social enterprises or government agencies

Capacity Building
- Percent increase in clients' meeting organizational goals
- Percent increase in efficiency of business processes
- Percent improvement in effectiveness of management structures and policies
- Percent increase in the quality of facilities and resources

Research
- Percent of projects with reliable evidence about impact drivers
- Number of contributions to professional or academic literature
- Number of viable new products or processes developed
- Number of patents and research grants awarded

Advocacy
- Number of policies adopted
- Percent increase in stakeholder support for position
- Number of changes in social conditions as a result of advocacy
- Percent increase in the strength of relationships with powerful partners

Infrastructure
- Number of organizations that use services offered to the network
- Number of organizations aligned toward common goals
- Percent improvement in cross-network benchmarks
- Number of network members that contribute and download online resources

If you lay a strong foundation by which to create impact and understand stakeholder interests related to those impacts, you'll be well positioned to decide which impacts are most critical to measure.

Why include only the most critical impacts and not all of them? Measurement can be expensive. Resources are required to gather measurements as well as to interpret them. The argument is often made that measurement draws resources from other needs and thereby reduces the impacts the organization can create. But if impacts and other key performance indicators are not being measured, the organization can't be sure it's making an impact in the first place. If measuring impacts is too costly, the process should be streamlined and revised to capture only the information most essential for managing and increasing impacts. In deciding what to measure, it's useful to consider the nature of the impacts. Social impacts can vary in:

- Desirability, ranging from positive to negative
- Scope, ranging from small to large-scale effects
- Intensity, ranging from very low to severe
- Direction, ranging from mutually enforcing to counterbalancing
- Duration, ranging from short term to permanent

Selecting Metrics

Metrics are intended to represent something in the real world. Kilowatt-hours of energy used can be used to represent CO_2 emissions, and blood pressure can be used to represent heart health. Some things are easy to measure, while others are more difficult. Choosing measures for self-confidence, relationship quality, or aesthetics, for example, requires a great deal of care. Measures for evaluating the effectiveness of advocacy or early-stage research can be even more difficult.

Many organizations recognize this problem and provide extensive lists of sample metrics that can fit various situations. The Impact Reporting and Investment Standards (IRIS) metrics are becoming well known in the nonprofit sector, and Global Reporting Index (GRI) indicators are widely used by for-profit corporations. Socially responsible investment funds also use ratings to rank companies. The proprietary MSCI ESG scores, built on the well-known KLD ratings, is one example. Table 11 lists a sample of some of the many sources for indicators.

Table 11 Sources for Indicators/Metrics

Primary Impacts and Key Performance Indicators	Secondary Impacts	Enterprise Ratings
• IRIS • Toxic materials ratings • SPTF microfinance	• GRI • International Labour Organization • Human Rights Watch • World Health Organization	• MSCI ESG (KLD) • S&I 100 • FTSE4Good

These impact indicators can be used alone, or can be combined with expense measures and other performance indicators, as discussed in chapter 8. Cost/benefit analysis, for example, compares the values of the impact indicators with the costs invested to produce those impacts. Methods that monetize social impacts, such as the social return on investment approach, use impact metrics, converted to monetary units, as the measure of returns for comparing returns to investments.

With so many indicators to choose from, it can be difficult to decide which are the most important. Here are some potential factors to consider:

- The number of people affected and the magnitude of positive and negative effects for those people.
- The duration and irreversibility of an impact, as well as the possible cumulative effects.
- The likelihood that an impact will have second-order effects and the nature of those effects.
- The level of controversy surrounding an impact and the potential effect of that conflict on future policy decisions.

When results of your organization's actions are associated with any of these factors, key indicators relating to those factors can be useful for both managing impacts and accounting for those impacts to key stakeholders.

Case Studies

Industree Crafts

Industree Crafts, a hybrid social enterprise that supports livelihoods of rural craft producers and agricultural workers in India, collects both qualitative and quantitative output indicators. Each indicator is connected to the enterprise activities and then connected to Industree's three major objectives—environmental and social sustainability, producers' access and market linkage, and advocacy to encourage the general public to purchase rural crafts. In this way, all measurements are clearly linked to Industree's mission to reduce rural poverty through helping people develop more productive livelihoods.

One of Industree's objectives is building awareness and appreciation for sustainable consumption among the public. To achieve this goal, Industree has worked to build its brand among customers and promoted rural sustainable crafts. It collects quantitative outputs like the number of customers reached by newsletters and the number of advocacy drives conducted. In addition, it collects and analyzes qualitative outputs like the content of newsletters and customers' responses to advocacy drives.

VillageReach

VillageReach is a US nonprofit that works on improving access to medical care. Its Chipatalach pa Foni (CCPF) project uses telephone hotlines and text messaging to provide health services. For this project, focus groups were used to gather data about the impacts of these services. VillageReach found that the project:

- Improved healthy behaviors such as breastfeeding and infant nutrition.
- Increased participation in antenatal and postnatal medical appointments.
- Increased the time and money as a result of forgoing travel to distant health clinics or paying fees to traditional healers.

VillageReach continually evaluates the impacts of its projects in order to refine those projects and inform new ones.

Source: VillageReach, "Evaluating the Social Impact of Our Work—CCPF Malawi," Http:// villagereach.org/2013/04/19/evaluating-the-social-impact-of-our-work-ccpf-malawi/.

Developing Your Measurement System

The final step in measuring social impact is developing the performance measurement system. In the previous steps, you decided what you will measure and how you will use those measures. In this step, you'll consider how the system you have defined can be implemented and put into use. We focus here only on the impact measurement system, but realize that organizations have systems in place for measuring financial and operational performance as well. Although the impact measurement system often focuses on high-level, long-term changes, it should be integrated as much as possible with other systems. Systems should work together and complement each other.

Implementing the social impact measurement system follows a path similar to other systems, except that the strategic nature of this system requires that you take special care throughout implementation. Figure 22 shows the sequence of steps in developing and implementing an impact measurement system.

Alignment

Alignment between organizational and measurement system goals is the key to implementing a system. Alignment begins with an understanding of how the actions of each individual, organizational unit, or program contribute to the organization's abil-

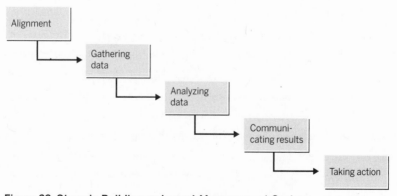

Figure 22 Steps in Building an Impact Measurement System

ity to make an impact. The people who lead these groups must believe in the value of the system, and they must also agree on key performance indicators. In a large organization, the overall performance measures may differ from those of individual units, but all of these measures and the strategic direction they support must be in alignment.

Many organizations have two or more sets of indicators to measure and report to funders and other stakeholders. Some organizations have shared measurement requirements associated with work on joint projects. In either case, it is best to find common ground among the partners and to determine whether the information required for external purposes can also be useful in managing social impact. If the organization has a strong belief in the validity of its own logic model and performance measures, it should make the effort to convey that to external parties. When external parties are in alignment on these critical items, they may be willing to adjust reporting requirements to accept measures that are mutually beneficial.

Gathering Data

A plan for gathering the data that will be used for impact reporting should ensure that the data are complete and reliable. The plan should lay out procedures for collecting data relating to each metric, including how and when data will be collected and from which internal or external sources. The plan should also prescribe how data will be validated before they are entered into the system. Data should be collected as close as possible to the source. Time and distance delays tend to decrease the quality of the data, as does the use of second parties for responses. Participants in data collection should be aware of the ramifications of incorrect or incomplete data, as well as of the problems that can result from biased samples. Careful supervision, quality control, and data cleaning can help ensure that the impact results are based on reliable evidence.

Analyzing Data

Data analysis procedures must be carefully designed and well tested. Whether you're employing information technology experts or creating your measurement system in a spreadsheet, it's important to review and test the system to ensure that results are complete and reliable. But much more is needed to ensure that the data are useful to the recipients. While numerous measures can be gathered and analyzed to meet a variety of needs, impact information should focus on the items deemed most valuable and actionable to the user of that information.

To make the data useful, analysis will typically compare performance to one or more benchmarks—for example, baseline data, past performance, average performance, targets and budgets, and industry or competitor performance. This provides context for interpreting results. This effort can be a double-edged sword, however. Changes in goals, processes, or metrics will limit historical comparability. However, sticking with measures that don't provide the most accurate and useful information is also problematic. Organizations need to balance priorities to maximize learning and impact.

Users might also be allowed access to raw data. With this access, they can answer ad hoc questions and make projections by manipulating data in real time, allowing them to customize the data to suit their own needs. Depending on the nature and sensitivity of the data, the data can also be shared with key stakeholders, who can perform their own analyses. Enterprise systems and desktop spreadsheet packages with features like graphing functions and pivot tables are available to many decision-makers. They enable dynamic analysis of data in ways that can greatly expand the organization's ability to meet decision-making needs.

Communicating Results

Communication of results can make or break a performance measurement system. Performance reports aren't useful unless they are used. They must contain information that is relevant and understandable, and that information must be discussed and used on a regular basis.[4]

First, the content of the reports must be accurate and relevant. Reports must provide information that is both trusted by and useful to the recipients, and the information must be relevant for making decisions or solving problems. But even with the best metrics, many reports go unused due to the effort required to make sense of them. If your reports are designed to require users to do much scanning, comparing, and mental arithmetic, they might well decide that the cost of using the reports outweighs the benefits.

The format of the reports matters, and when reports are uncluttered and well organized, readers are more likely to find and use the important information. Charts, graphs, and other kinds of visualization are increasingly available in standard software packages. These tools can convey content in a way that makes comparisons easy and highlights important patterns, making the information much more meaningful to the user. Thoughtful design is especially important for external stakeholders, who have less time and context for deciphering reports. Currently, many external reports include success stories and photographs that are designed to build a good marketing image. But stakeholders increasingly seek a more complete reporting on project and organizational performance.

Another important part of communication is the manner in which an organization discusses and uses information internally. If no one talks about impact information, its perceived importance will be low, and it will soon be ignored. This is the fate of many impact reports that are created for specific purposes, such as to secure or prove effective use of funding. Although thinking through the logic model and defining impact metrics are valuable in their own right, the full value of the measurement system is realized only when people use this information to drive results. Thus, effective communication relies on both the accessibility of the information and the ability to convey the importance and value of the information to those who can benefit from it. The Bill & Melinda Gates Foundation uses an interactive website called Insight, where staff and management can regularly report information on grants and strategy execution and learn from others' experiences.[5]

Investors often require third-party evaluations to verify performance reports. Some external evaluators take a hands-off approach, while others combine impact validation studies with consulting services. For example, Shujog, a Singapore-based social enterprise, provides assistance in designing and implementing performance measurement systems to help client organizations achieve their impact goals.

Taking Action

Finally, the information system must support the organization in taking action to improve impacts. In general, impact measurement systems produce two types of information, diagnostic and strategic. *Diagnostic information* is information that shows standard performance metrics and highlights results that are out of line with expectations. These reports are designed to help spot trends and variations as quickly as possible so that decision makers can take action to solve problems or to study and encourage activities associated with positive deviations. Responsibility for recognizing these problems and planning for remediation should be clearly defined. Specifying the person or group in charge, the process to follow, and the recommended time frames can all help ensure that a problem or opportunity will be diagnosed and contribute to organizational learning and improvement.

Strategic information has longer-term implications. Often, this information is very high level and describes large trends in the organization's performance as well as that of a sector or industry. The information should be useful for future planning—for example, by providing insights into key aspects of strategy, such as which interventions worked, in which locations, for which beneficiaries, and under what conditions.

It is not just the content of reports that makes them useful, but the way they are used to drive action. When used effectively, results information can serve an interactive role in the organization. This requires a regular schedule for meeting and discussing the results, their potential causes, potential areas for improvement, and future opportunities. The discussions must include managers at the highest levels of the organization, and they must be viewed as a means by which leaders can redefine strategy to drive greater social impact.

When using impact measures for diagnostic or strategic purposes, the action you take will depend on how results are interpreted. When there are variations between the impacts you expected and your actual results, there are three main sources to investigate:

- The relationships in the logic model
- The execution of the model
- The effectiveness of the measurements

All of these must be well defined and successful if impact results are to meet expectations.

The relationships you expect between the elements in your logic model should be grounded in strong logic and evidence. Before investing in an intervention, you need sound reasons to believe that it will create the desired results. The relationships in your model can be supported by expert judgment, a well-supported theory, and/or empirical evidence. Results that differ from expectations may suggest that one or more links in the chain of logic are weak. If any unforeseen changes have occurred, either within the organization or in critical elements in its environment, it might be necessary to revise action plans to accommodate them. Alternatively, you may need to make changes in expectations.

Each step in your logic chain must also be executed effectively. Policies, procedures, and guidelines, supported by training, supervision, and rewards, guide behavior and ensure that plans are executed effectively. If you are convinced that the logic that links actions to results is sound but the results are not those you expected, it is likely that at some point the execution of your program has deviated from your plans.

Discussing the shortfall with those involved in executing the plan can help identify issues. Problems with resources, training, guidance, information, and a host of other strategic and operational issues can lead to execution failures. While impact measures won't necessarily help pinpoint specific problems, they can provide the general information you need to begin investigating and remedying the problem.

Finally, your measurement design must be valid and properly implemented. An accurate understanding of the impact you're making requires effective measurement. If your measurement system is problematic—for example, because your metrics are poor proxies for the phenomena they represent—you are likely to find performance results that are not representative of actual impacts.

People involved in gathering and using these measures and those closest to the outcomes and impacts are good sources when you are investigating potential problems with the metrics and measurement processes. Developing effective metrics is an ongoing process, so identifying problems as they occur can provide the means by which you can make measurements more effective over time.

At a basic level, performance reporting systems appear to be similar—they contain the same basic components and are used for similar purposes. However, the way these systems are developed and used varies greatly, and savvy organizations use performance measurement systems as one of their most valuable tools in creating impact. Regardless of how well designed the initial performance measurement system is, it will not remain static. Measurement systems generally continue to improve over time as results are investigated and used. In addition, the environment within which the system operates continually changes, and the system will need to evolve to remain effective. Thus, you'll cycle back through the steps again and again as you refine and improve your organization's approach to creating positive impacts.

Impact Measurement: How It Works in Practice

School for Life (S4L, a fictitious company) works in impoverished regions where jobs are scarce and people earn their livings by subsistence farming or trading. S4L provides entrepreneurship workbooks, teacher training, and ongoing support to private schools. S4L's project uses a student-centered pedagogy in which young students take leadership roles in developing and executing projects. S4L's mission is to empower children with the organizational and entrepreneurial skills that will enable them to build secure livelihoods.[6]

S4L has decided to develop its first impact measurement system, and it begins by selecting a small number of measures that are important to its success. The elements of S4L's logic model and sample measures for each element are listed below.

Primary Impacts

Inputs	Processes	Outputs	Outcomes	Impacts
Entrepreneurship workbook	Production of workbooks	Workbooks provided	Students engaged	Students start businesses
Funds from workbook sales	*Sales of the program*	*Teacher training delivered*	High-quality instruction	Students feel empowered to pursue diverse livelihoods
Donations	Supervisory activities	Supervision provided	*Students have new knowledge and skills*	*Students use course skills in their occupations*

S4L selects four key measures to include in its initial system:

- *Sales of the program.* Program sales are essential to increasing the number of students who receive training.

- *Teacher training delivered.* S4L can use teacher ratings to determine if its own training methods are effective.
- *Students have new knowledge and skills.* The final project requires development of a microenterprise. Higher scores indicate that students can create a quality business.
- *Students use course skills in their occupations.* If students report using their new skills, it's likely that the training helped them change their livelihood strategies.

In addition to these primary impact goals, S4L recognizes that its activities can create positive and negative impacts for a variety of stakeholders. The organization meets with constituents to identify the following impacts.

Secondary Impacts

Families	Teachers	School Administrators	Community Businesses
Less help available while child attends classes	Pedagogical training spills over to other subjects	*Changes in school attendance*	Community businesses suffer from new competition
Empowered children leave village	Teachers create entrepreneurial ventures to diversify income	Students are successful at school	Community has access to new goods and services
Families adopt entrepreneurial concepts to improve their businesses	Teachers are dissatisfied with new work demands	Parents and community members are more engaged with school	Pool of qualified labor increases

S4L decides to include one of these measures in its system: *changes in school attendance.* High attendance suggests that parents and students find the program valuable. The measure is also important because the schools' financial success relies on attendance. Next, S4L determines metrics for each of the five selected measures and a plan for gathering data on each measurement indicator:

Data Gathering Plan

Indicator	Metric	Baseline	Target	Data Sources	Frequency
Sales of the program	Number of schools using the program	14 schools	25 schools by year end	Signed sales contracts	Monthly
Teacher training delivered	Average teacher rating	6.5 out of 10	8 out of 10 by year end	S4L evaluates each teacher at the end of teacher training	At the end of each teacher training session
Students have new knowledge and skills	Average student score on final project	58% last year	80% this year	S4L assessment of each student's final project	Yearly
Students use course skills in their occupations	Percent of students surveyed using skills 6 months and 12 months after graduation	20% after 6 months 50% after 1 year	50% after 6 months 70% after 1 year	Structured interviews with alumni 1/2 year and 1 year after graduation	Each semester
School attendance increases	Average attendance	78%	85%	Gathered by administrators from attendance records	Reported weekly to S4L

The S4L example shows how simple it can be to develop a basic but powerful system of measurement and reporting. By identifying important aspects of the logic model and thinking about what matters to stakeholders, S4L was able to identify a handful of key metrics that can help it understand and improve impacts. Over time, S4L can continue to revise and improve this system as it learns about the effectiveness of its strategy, its execution of that strategy, and its impacts.

Action Agenda

1. Decide which impacts are most important and the information needed to manage those impacts.
2. Decide how you'll use information about impacts and their drivers.
3. Decide which metrics will best represent your significant impacts.
4. Develop your impact measurement system.

Part 5
How Can You Increase Impact?

10

Social Impact Measurement Maturity

Ultimately, the goal of performance measurement is to increase your impact. The most effective way to do this is through careful measurement and management of your organization's projects. If your social impact measurement system is mature, it can provide you with a better understanding of how you are investing your resources and the specific results they are producing. And it can provide the information you need for careful and dynamic management of activities that is responsive to outcomes, needs, and changes in the environment. In this chapter, we introduce a five-level model that you can use to describe and evaluate your current social impact measurement system and to generate ideas about how you could improve that system.

Our model, shown in Figure 23, uses a stepwise or maturity-stage format that highlights the characteristics of impact management systems. The model has five categories, which represent general profiles of organizational capability, though your organization may find it has characteristics of two or more levels. Organizations usually move through the levels as they become more experienced in evaluating impact and in using this information to make decisions. Each level encompasses the capabilities of all the categories below that level.

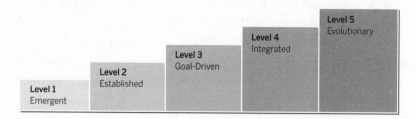

Figure 23 Social Impact Maturity Measurement Model

- *Emergent systems* support internal decisions by tracking funds raised and expenses.
- *Established systems* monitor the quantity and quality of products and services delivered to beneficiaries. If your organization has a well-established system that doesn't include impact measures, it is probably at this level.
- *Goal-driven systems* ensure that the logic model is functioning as planned. These systems measure, either directly or indirectly, the social impact created.
- *Integrated systems* embed performance metrics into managerial processes. Measurement becomes an integral aspect of day-to-day decision-making so that social impact can be achieved.
- *Evolutionary systems* support learning. In these systems, performance results are used to drive resource allocations and to revise strategies to ensure continuous improvement in social impacts.

The model can be helpful for understanding where your organization ranks on various aspects of measurement maturity and where you might improve your system. Systems should be designed to evolve as the organization grows. Performance measurement systems are thus most effective when they are integrated with the growth and development of the organization. As you move through the steps of the social impact creation cycle, you will likely make corresponding changes to your performance measurement system.

The highest level in the maturity model represents a strategic form of impact-driven management that is perhaps more an ideal to strive toward than a reality. Based on our experience, only a small fraction of social purpose organizations achieve this level, but the vast majority are recognizing the importance of measurement and taking steps that move them toward more effective management of their impact performance.

Dimensions of Impact Measurement and Management Maturity

Each level in the model describes three characteristics of systems at that level: the purpose of the performance measurement system, the metrics likely to be incorporated into the system, and the relationship between the system and the organization's strategy.

Purpose

The first dimension reflects the purpose for which a performance management and measurement system is used. Organizations at the early stages of performance measurement use their systems primarily for managing the day-to-day operations of the organization or for accountability to regulators and donors. Organizations with mature measurement systems invest in metrics as part of a program to continuously improve social performance and transform the organization to pursue changing opportunities.

Metrics

The second dimension addresses the types of metrics gathered by archetypical firms at each level. Organizations with immature measurement systems lack clear systems of measurement and capture metrics on an ad hoc basis. Organizations at the highest levels systematically gather a metrics for assessing a full range of social impacts that reflect the evolving strategic interests of the organization and its stakeholders.

Strategy

The third dimension explores the relationship between the impact measurement system and the design of the organization's strategies and business models. At the lower levels, where organizations generally lack formalized measurement of impact, positive impacts are presumed rather than evidenced, and strategies are typically designed on this basis. At higher levels of maturity, when rigorous evidence-based measures have been established, organizations embed these measurements into decision-making processes such as performance or cost/benefit evaluations and ultimately use knowledge of impact and its drivers to shape the organization and its strategies.

Social Impact Measurement System Maturity Levels

Figure 23 depicts five maturity levels. Many organizations are not on the scale because they have not yet developed systems for measuring social impact; we refer to these as nascent organizations. Of the millions of registered nonprofits, perhaps the majority fall into this category. Nascent organizations haven't been systematic about defining and measuring impact. Founders and key officers of these organizations certainly hold mental models of the good their organizations seek to provide, but they have not formally identified or developed metrics to analyze the outcomes and impacts they desire.

This does not suggest that these organizations are not making an impact—their impacts may well be significant and positive. For example, a rapidly constructed center for contemplation and worship set up in a refugee camp may lack clear impact objectives, but it may nonetheless be highly valuable to its constituents.

Metrics for organizations with nascent systems often center on the actions and health of the organization rather than on its intended beneficiaries. Such metrics often include inputs such as the amount of funding or number of volunteers used to operate the organization. Nascent performance measurement systems therefore tend to focus on internal record-keeping and the financial survival of the organization. Metrics have little direct relationship to the organization's intended social impact or to the strategies pursued in creating it. Table 11 summarizes the characteristics of the measurement system at each level of maturity beyond this nascent stage.

Table 11 Characteristics of Social Impact Measurement Systems

Maturity Level	Metrics	Purpose of System	Relationship with Strategy
1 Emergent	Operational performance	Accountability	Presumed
2 Established	Inputs, processes, and outputs	Monitoring	Planned
3 Goal-Driven	Direct measures of social impact	Execution	Defined
4 Integrated	Impact sources and improvements	Improvement	Embedded
5 Evolutionary	Multiple facets of social issues	Transformation	Reciprocal

Level 1: Emergent

Purpose. Level 1 organizations have impact measurement systems that gather metrics on an ad hoc basis as a way to track progress on initiatives and programs. In addition to basic financial transaction tracking, organizations at this level are likely to gather metrics related to the work being done, such as the number of meals provided at a soup kitchen or the number of solar panels installed.

Metrics. The basic determinant of which metrics are gathered is the requirement for accountability to external funders. Organizations receiving grant money, for example, typically provide progress reports to grantors that include the metrics specified by the grantor. While these metrics may be useful in evaluating performance or impact, their primary purpose is to satisfy funding requirements. In most cases, when the organization seeks funding, it makes implicit or explicit claims about the impact that it will make through the investment. At the emergent level, however, impact is not measured directly unless that is mandated by funders or other key stakeholders.

Strategy. As with the metrics themselves, the systems for gathering the metrics are often prescribed by external parties. In these organizations, systems for collecting, analyzing, and reporting metrics are often attached to specific grants or programs rather than being instituted across the organization. These measurement systems evolve as the organizational activities shift toward the needs of each new program or initiative. As a result, the organization may be maintaining multiple reporting systems to satisfy different external funders or other decision makers.

Level 2: Established

We refer to Level 2 systems as "established" systems because they have been developed as a result of intentional design efforts and are in place and functioning as planned. Systems at this level are significantly different from emergent systems in that they are based on a clear understanding of the relationship of actions to impacts. Impacts in this model are explicit, not simply inferred or implied. The organization's mission is tied in some way to impact, and the organization has some form of theory of change or logic model that links its actions to the impacts it wants.

Purpose. Organizations at Level 2 generally have systems designed to meet the organization's own internal needs. Although they also satisfy the reporting demands of funders, a core characteristic of Level 2 performance measurement systems is that they provide information related to the organization's own desired activities and impacts. The basic purpose of measurement for organizations at Level 2 is to the monitor internal performance of the entire organization or of programs pursued by the organization. The system seeks to track and record the day-to-day activities and transactions of the organization. Through such tracking, the organization is able to monitor its actions and use of resources. In organizations that maintain detailed budgets, the actual activities can be compared against planned actions and variances can be analyzed.

Metrics. Metrics used by organizations with Level 2 systems tend to focus on the organization's inputs, processes, and, to some extent, outputs. An organization at this level is likely to track resources invested in its pursuit of program and organizational objectives as well as the processes it has adopted. Educational programs might, for example, track the number of schools they have contacted or the number of classrooms that have adopted a particular educational intervention. Organizations at this level may also track outputs, such as the number of intervention hours provided or the number of students who have received the intervention. The focus of these measures tends to be on the contributions of the organization toward addressing a problem rather than changes in social or environmental conditions.

Strategy. The relationship between strategy and measurement at this level is based on a clear plan. Level 2 organizations have well-defined theories of change or logic models that specify the desired social impacts as well as the strategies they will pursue to achieve these impacts. Relationships between the organization's actions and the intended impact are carefully planned, and well understood. While organizations at this level typically measure outcomes rather than impact, they have a well-developed understanding of the impacts they are seeking and, either explicitly or implicitly, use the outcome measures as proxies for actual social impact. Interventions that seek to reduce poverty, for example, might measure changes in access to health clinics or bank loans rather than changes in poverty directly.

Level 3: Goal-Driven

Organizations at Level 3 can truly be considered impact-driven organizations, and their measurement systems reflect this. Organizations that have well-developed logic frameworks or standardized protocols for gathering outcome or impact data fall into this level.

Purpose. The primary purpose of measurement systems at this level is to help organizations ensure that they can effectively execute their plans and achieve these goals. Organizations with goal-driven performance measurement systems are beginning to use their systems both to monitor social performance and to assess progress toward achieving desired social impact goals.

Metrics. These systems gather metrics that include the outcome-centered metrics of Level 2 but add two important components. First, they add targets for social impact. Like financial budgets, impact targets define the results that organizations seek to achieve during the course of a program or time period. Second, these systems gather impact measures, which can be compared against their goals. As we have discussed earlier, some impacts cannot be feasibly measured; in these cases, organizations use proxies.

Strategies. Level 3 organizations have strategies that clearly link actions with impacts, and they hold themselves accountable for achieving their impact targets. Organizations at this level may also have systems for reporting their impacts to donors or other key stakeholders. Transparent reporting in these systems serves not only to communicate performance to stakeholders but provides a strong external accountability mechanism. Randomized control trials, structured field interviews, and other rigorous evaluation methods often operate at this level. These evaluations are designed to determine whether the actions the organization is pursuing are in fact generating the desired impact. The organization has validation for its logic model once it is able to establish strong evidence for this relationship.

Level 4: Integrated
Level 4 systems take a more holistic view of overall impact and seek not only to promote execution of a plan but also facilitate modification of actions that can lead to enhancements in impact over time. In Level 4 organizations, performance measurements

are not conducted separately from operations or reported periodically. Instead, performance measurement is integrated into the
operation of the organization. Performance tracking is ongoing
and is used to make continual adjustments in resource allocations,
policies, and organizational processes.

Purpose. In Level 4 organizations, improvement of both impact
and the activities that generate impact is a central concern. Performance measures play an important and ongoing role in the
organization's internal management. Components of impact
measurements may be used to determine which donor pools to
pursue, how resources are allocated to programs, how major capital investments are made, or how individual staff performance is
evaluated and rewarded. Major decisions rely on the performance
measurement system for predicting and assessing the capacity for
these decisions to improve the impact of the organization.

Metrics. These systems use metrics that integrate impact measures
with other aspects of organizational management. Impact measurements are not simply conducted after a program or initiative
has concluded. Instead, they are used in an ongoing manner as
a way to determine if corrections are necessary to improve outcomes throughout the course of a project or period. Organizations at this level tend to measure social impact as one part of a
broader set of outcome measures in which targeted social impact
is evaluated in concert with economic performance and other
social indicators that may not be primary to the organization's
objectives, but that are nonetheless affected by the organization's
actions. Organizations at this level may have broad systems that
can accommodate a full range of consequences—unintended as
well as intended—and secondary as well as primary impacts.

Strategy. For Level 4 organizations, performance measurement
is embedded throughout the organization and is integral to both
development and evaluation of strategy. These organizations use

impact and related performance measures to evaluate both the execution of the organization's strategy and the strategy itself. Impact measures provide a way to determine whether the strategy is optimal, as well as important data for use in discussions of adjustments to organizational strategies. In these organizations, programs and resources are secured and invested with the express purpose of generating impact, and the relationships between inputs, processes, outputs, outcomes, and impacts are central to the design of organizational strategy.

Level 5: Evolutionary

While Level 4 performance management systems are designed to ensure that incremental strategic and operational adjustments lead to continual improvements in social performance, Level 5 systems seek nothing less than transformation of the organization.

Purpose. The purpose of these systems is learning. As in Level 4, the system provides information necessary for continuously improving performance. But systems at this level open the organization up to reconfiguration on the basis of what is learned. The system also tracks innovations that can lead to incremental or transformative improvements in how problems are addressed and how impacts are achieved. While strengthening performance using the current logic model is important, the organization also looks for opportunities to improve impact through other logics. For example, an organization seeking to reduce childhood obesity through healthier school lunches may recognize that students who contribute to school gardens are likelier to make healthier selections when those are available, and the organization may decide to allocate resources to gardens to make this happen.

Metrics. Metrics provided by systems at this level necessarily extend beyond those dictated by the logic model. In addition to inputs, processes, outputs, outcomes, and impacts, the organization has systems that gather information about new opportunities,

Case Study: The James Irvine Foundation

The James Irvine Foundation seeks to serve Californians by expanding opportunities for college and career success through youth programs, nurturing the state's cultural environment by supporting the arts, and enhancing democracy by supporting effective public policy decision-making. The foundation implements its Performance Assessment Framework to enable ongoing impact evaluation and improvement.

The foundation collects quantitative and qualitative information on its progress in both program impact and institutional effectiveness. To assess impact, it tracks data in program context, outcomes, results, learning, and program refinement. To evaluate its organizational effectiveness, it examines foundation leadership, constituent feedback, and financial health.

The Performance Assessment Framework calls for continuous learning. The foundation shares its performance publicly every year in reports that identify its short-term and medium-term objectives. It also creates feedback loops to use the evaluation results, because the ongoing evaluation and learning process among all stakeholders is essential to improvement.

Source: Canales and Rafter (2012) "Assessing One's Own Performance"; James Irvine Foundation (2011) *A Framework to Assess the Performance of The James Irvine Foundation: Evaluation Policies and Guidelines.*

new approaches, and potential collaborators and partners. Organizations at this level are likely to monitor not only the targeted impact indicator but a variety of other indicators in addition that might be related to the social issue of concern. Childhood obesity advocates might, for example, monitor the number of hours children spend online or the incomes of parents or guardians. Organizations at this level commonly share data and other resources broadly, both with stakeholders and with organizations working on similar problems or different aspects of the same problem.

Strategy. Performance management systems and strategy in these organizations are tightly coupled. As systems produce information about the organization's actions and the impacts produced by these actions, the effectiveness of strategies pursued is continuously reevaluated as well. Level 5 organizations use evidence-based approaches both to design and to evaluate their strategies, and they are continually seeking innovative processes, techniques, and models for improving social impact.

Toward Improved Measurement Maturity

Few organizations are able to operate at the highest level due to a variety of internal and external constraints. Many organizations are in continuous fund-raising mode and must focus a great deal of energy on obtaining funds and satisfying funders in order to survive. Others focus on effectively executing the actions they have laid out and on making adjustments and solving problems as they arise. Only organizations that have sufficient administrative and monetary resources have the leeway to deviate beyond planned activities and proven models toward true innovation.

Beyond Level 5: Issue-Focused Organizations

Most organizations can make only a small contribution to the massive social problems they seek to address. Organizations can choose among many potential routes to pursue social impact, and many of these will in turn expand their work beyond the organization itself. Organizations can collaborate or partner with other organizations, contribute to industry-level associations, and share knowledge and best practices or use influence to encourage other organizations to devote resources to the social issue. In this manner, they contribute to the ecosystem, which supports a range of organizations working in the same area.

Performance management systems in these organizations seek to promote achievement of broader social impact, and their focus encompasses the broad social issue in addition to their efforts to address specific aspects of the issue. These systems will monitor the organization's impact on the issue but will also monitor the impact of other organizations within and beyond that sector. In addition, these systems will monitor positive and negative social impacts beyond those targeted since they are affected by the organization and its constituents' activities.

Action Agenda

1. Decide what role you want your social impact measurement system to play and assess its current maturity level.
2. Determine which categories of metrics your system should include and develop the means for capturing the needed data.
3. Identify the purpose of your measurement system and decide how you can best use it for managing impacts.
4. Consider the role you want your system to play in guiding strategy and develop processes to support that role.
5. Monitor your system periodically to maintain or increase its maturity level.

11

Amplifying Your Impact

Increasing the efficiency and effectiveness of your organization is the key to maximizing impact from the resources at hand. With a clear understanding of the links between actions and impacts and a well-designed measurement program, you're on your way to meeting your impact goals and logging successes year after year. But what if that's not enough? Social and environmental problems will always be greater than our ability to address them. Once you've developed the ability to be consistently successful in creating social change, you may feel that it's time to take on bigger challenges.

For-profits or nonprofits operating in competitive markets have no choice of whether to strive for continual improvement and reinvention. As soon as they reach a level at which they're comfortably profitable, some other organization will attempt to copy or compete with them for customers and profits. However, many nonprofits lack the market pressure that requires diligent management to avoid losing competitive advantage. As long as funding sources are accessible, nonprofits can survive for decades without making significant gains in impact.

But that kind of stagnation is unfortunate, because by pushing beyond their current routines and constraints social purpose

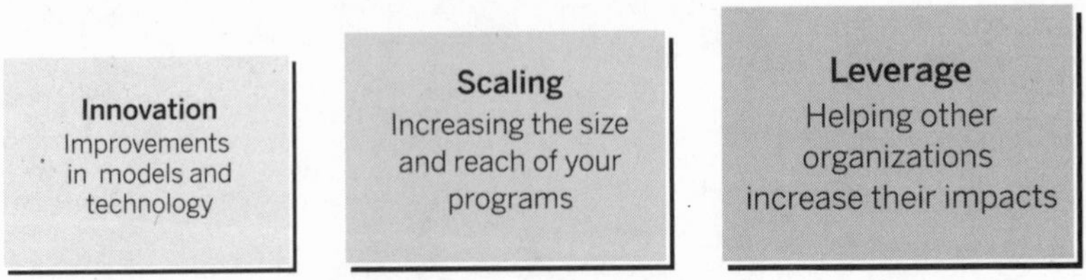

Figure 24 Three Pathways to Amplify Your Impact

organizations can amplify their social impacts and increase their contribution to creating the social changes they desire. Organizations can radically increase their impacts in three different ways, as shown in Figure 24: through innovation, through scaling successful approaches, and through leveraging impact by working with others.

Innovation

Innovation is essential to achieving large-scale progress in any type of social purpose organization. Fine-tuning programs to increase quality and efficiency can be highly effective, but it will never produce the disruptive changes needed to tackle huge social challenges. Likewise, incremental improvements are rarely enough to accommodate the major shifts commonly faced by social purpose organizations. Changes in political, economic, natural, or sociological circumstances can stimulate an organization to make significant changes to maintain its effectiveness—changes that are sometimes necessary to ensure the organization's very survival.

Because of the potential transformational impact of new ideas, a large and growing number of individual donors and foundations support innovation as a core component of their mission. Ashoka, for example, seeks out and funds social innovations and social entrepreneurs. Jeff Skoll, former president of eBay, has been a major supporter of innovation in the social sector and has been joined by funders such as Sergey Brin, the cofounder of Google, and Anne Wojcicki, founder of 23andMe. The Laura and John Arnold Foundation supports projects with the potential for transformational change. They take an entrepreneurial approach, seeking out big, risky opportunities that have the potential to develop and spread valuable innovations. The Social Innovation Fund, an initiative of the Corporation for National and Community Service, a US federal agency, provides funding to support community organizations with innovative approaches to problems such as lack of economic opportunity. It also provides a platform for sharing program successes to help ensure their broad adoption.

Agile organizations continually scan their external environments for threats and opportunities, and they develop strategies for addressing changes by shoring up weaknesses and building new strengths. Innovations can come in many forms, typically as business model innovations or innovations in technology.

Business model innovations are changes in the way an organization operates and structures itself to create and deliver value to its customers. An organization can expand or modify its target market to make its services available to new sets of customers or beneficiaries. It can revise its value proposition by providing new or expanded benefits to its customers. And it can make changes in its supply chain, improving quality or efficiency in securing needed supplies.

VisionSpring is known for its business model innovations. VisionSpring has expanded its target market for reading glasses and other services in twenty-six developing countries to include people who previously lacked access as a result of their remote locations and meager incomes. It has also revised its business model, training locals living in remote areas to be "vision entrepreneurs." These entrepreneurs travel from village to village, transforming the supply chain to allow delivery of products directly to consumers rather than forcing them to travel to clinics in district centers.

Technology innovations are operational changes that affect the products and services produced by an organization or the manner in which those outputs are produced. Innovations in processes can affect the way the organization performs any activity, while innovations in enabling technologies like machinery or information technology can spawn changes throughout the organization.

Vestergaard Frandsen's LifeStraw is an example of an innovative product designed to combat the problem of lack of access to safe drinking water. It is a small cylindrical device that functions like a straw, but it uses a filter to purify the water as the user is drinking it. PATH, an international nonprofit organization, focuses on process innovation. In addition to developing low-cost health solutions, PATH has increased its performance through innovations such as digitizing patient health records. Changes in enabling technologies like access to online video calls have enabled new forms of telemedicine and helped healthcare organizations provide high-quality care in underserved regions.

All social purpose organizations must evolve continually to make the most of the resources available and to deal with the ever-changing nature of the problems they seek to address. Making game-changing innovations can greatly enhance the social impacts of these organizations. But not every organization needs to develop novel products, services, or processes on its own. The social sector abounds with excellent business models and technologies, and innovations are being announced every day. Unfortunately, many excellent innovations never spread, and as a result organizations spend scarce resources reinventing the wheel. For most organizations, innovating in-house isn't optimal or even necessary. Adopting innovations that have been developed, tested, and used successfully by others can lead to improvements in performance and impacts.

Social purpose organizations can become aware of these innovations through systematic efforts to scan their environments. Creative solutions to most of the problems identified by these organizations likely already exist. And new opportunities that haven't been considered can also be identified through scanning. Regularly reading trade publications and web postings to identify opportunities is one way to find out about these innovations. Net-

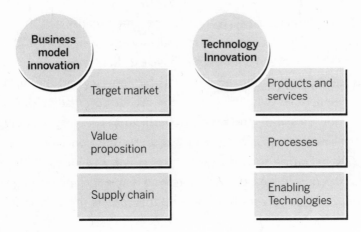

Figure 25 Sources of Innovation

working and participating in industry-level organizations are others. By developing strong relationships, an organization can better sort through the vast amount of information available and learn about innovations that its peers have found useful.

Numerous organizations have been created to spread innovations and promote effective practices for organizations of all types. Grantmakers for Effective Organizations, for example, is a coalition of more than 400 grant-making organizations that provides conferences, peer-to-peer learning, and networking opportunities to enable knowledge sharing in the nonprofit sector.

Scaling

The second pathway for amplifying impact is through scale.[1] Scaling typically refers to the rapid growth of an organization and its programs. As with purely commercial enterprises, social purpose organizations can take advantage of many economies of scale as they grow. Operating and support functions can expand to serve larger problems or constituencies without requiring a corresponding increase in investment. Large organizations may also have access to other resources unavailable to smaller organizations, such as greater influence with policy makers and greater access to investor groups or highly specialized employees.

The current social sector landscape is marked by vast numbers of tiny nonprofits that lack specialization among staff and programs. These organizations may have excellent means for producing social impact, but the size of these impacts and the number of beneficiaries who receive them are quite small. Using one common measure—the ratio of overhead to total expenditures—many small organizations spend more money on administering the organization than on serving their constituencies. Although this is a common starting point among many entrepreneurial ventures, the best way to move beyond this state is through scale.

Scaling Approaches

Without the market discipline associated with tightly managing costs in order to attract customers and investors, many organizations remain stuck at a size that is not optimal from a resource management perspective. As a group, such organizations are able to direct fewer resources to social problems than they would after achieving greater scale. At scale, not only are the total impacts greater, but the amount of impact provided by each unit of resources consumed is higher in most cases.Organizations tend to scale in one or more of the following ways:

Organic growth. An organization continues to pursue its established theory of change and to scale through increased investment, which results in delivery of a higher level of output. This enables the organization to serve a greater number of clients using the methods and approaches it has found to be successful in the past.

Under the organic growth model, the organization can also expand its mission by pursuing new markets. It can develop and provide additional products and services or modify operations to accommodate new approaches to achieving impact. And it can expand its target customer base to include segments whose needs or access requirements are different from those of current customers.

Franchising. Rather than grow through its own investment, the organization can systemically expand its process chain and license rights to use its methods in franchises. With a franchising model, an outside party replicates the approach used by the organization. The franchisee generally provides its own funding and staff but uses valuable intellectual property of the host organization, such as the processes, policies, trademarks, and networks it has developed and proven successful.

Franchising enables the organization to scale up more rapidly than could be achieved through organic growth. This makes it possible for the host organization to serve a larger number of clients and produce more social change without greatly expanding the level of invested resources, staff, or products and services, and it allows those that have funds but lack some operational resources to make an impact as well.

Mergers and acquisitions. Under this approach, two or more organizations combine rather than growing or replicating the processes used by one organization. In some cases, the primary purpose is to combine like organizations that may be competing for investors, staff, or clients in order to achieve economies of scale. In others, the organizations have different strengths and the combined organization has a fuller range of capabilities.

Partnerships. Organizations can collaborate on projects to enhance their effectiveness by partnering to bring together different but complementary capabilities. One organization may have expertise in producing durable products for subsistence marketplaces, while its partner has distribution channels or political ties in a target market. These combinations can help ensure that the organizations aren't simply repeating practices that have emerged over time. Instead, they can help combine the best ideas and abilities of all the parties in a way that multiplies value and rapidly increases the organizations' capacity to produce social change.

Scaling Levers

Regardless of the growth model pursued by the organization, there are many qualities that can make it easier for the organization to scale. Here we refine them down to three fundamental levers that are essential for maintaining the quality of the products and services an organization produces and the organization's effectiveness in creating impact as it grows:

- *Product lever.* A state-of-the-art product or service that is highly effective in creating the desired social change.
- *Process lever.* Processes that are so well designed and defined that they can be easily replicated and adjusted to use in new contexts.
- *Passion lever.* Commitment of staff and other stakeholders to pushing the organization forward and working to continually create better solutions.

Table 12 shows the characteristics of each lever that contribute to effective scaling. Organizations seeking scale can use these characteristics as benchmarks to evaluate their own potential for growth. As Table 12 shows, having a high-quality product or service is not sufficient to achieve scale, even if adequate funding for growth is available. There should be evidence that the product contributes to creating social impact in its current form before the organization scales up.

In the for-profit world, many organizations use process as the critical lever in their scaling programs. Rules, procedures, and policies are established, tested, and optimized, and then are replicated as the organization grows. This lever can be particularly effective for social purpose organizations with tight budgets. Following a proven model tends to keep costs and uncertainty low during the scaling process.

In the nonprofit world, many organizations are excellent at employing the passion lever. Founders and top management are typically strong champions for a cause, and many nonprofits are effective in keeping staff, funders, and other stakeholders engaged in working passionately for creating meaningful change.

Table 12 Scaling Levers: The 3P Model

Program	Process	Passion
Effectiveness: The program is highly effective in meeting impact objectives	Efficiency: Efficient processes minimize costs of delivery	Engagement: Participants believe in and support the mission
Alignment: The program is aligned with the needs and resources of the market	Support: Guidance is provided for operational and administrative support	Empowerment: Staff are empowered as program owners
Integration: The program addresses psychological and sociological dimensions	Accountability: Continuous monitoring, evaluation, and process improvement	Flexibility: The program and processes can be adjusted to changing circumstances

Our work with highly effective organizations suggests that the best approaches to scale make use of all three levers. Organizations following this path carefully manage each of the three levers so that they can maintain the highest possible impact at the lowest possible cost as they scale.

Leverage

The third way to increase social impact is by leveraging assets beyond the boundaries of the organization—and this may be the most powerful method of all.[2] An organization with an effective strategy, model, or process can scale its impact exponentially by sharing proven innovations with other organizations. While an organization's direct impact will always be limited by the scale it is able to achieve in its own operations, its indirect impact is virtually unlimited. Most organizations can greatly amplify their impacts by leveraging resources through sharing and cooperation with other organizations.

Any asset, practice, or capability can potentially be shared with other organizations working toward the same cause. Making valuable resources available to others can often be a way to achieve greater impacts at very low cost. For example, a small organization providing education may share its school buildings with organizations that provide health information and other services to the same communities. A large organization can fund research on an intervention's effectiveness that can help all of the organizations using that intervention to improve their work.

David M. Rubenstein, a US billionaire financier who works to pass on his fund-raising skills to social purpose organizations, chairs or co-chairs six fund-raising campaigns, including campaigns at Harvard University and the University of Chicago. He does this in order to leverage more financial resources for the social sector beyond the amounts he could donate personally. In India, Dasra works to improve a wide range of capacities in social sector firms. Dasra has created and hosted network forums, education programs, collaborative giving, and research programs to equip Indian philanthropists with better knowledge, funding opportunities, and capabilities and to prepare nonprofits to use funds effectively. Through this work, Dasra works to spread the use of effective philanthropic organizations and approaches.

The people we interviewed for this book were all widely recognized for their expertise in both their own industries and in the social sector. Each one was doing excellent work to leverage knowledge and other resources. All were active participants in discussions and organizations focused on how to best address social problems. All were continually innovating, and they were willing to share those innovations with others working in the sector through informal conversations, meetings, presentations, and written publications. And all were willing to share their precious time helping us to pursue our own social impact goals.

Yet despite the tremendous intellectual and material resources devoted to such activities, only a tiny fraction of the organizations we interviewed were attempting to systematically assess the

impacts of these leveraging activities. While they carefully monitored their direct social impacts, they didn't attempt to monitor
the many contributions they were making toward social impact
goals through the work of others.

We encourage those organizations and we encourage you to
approach leverage more programmatically. We believe that if
organzations begin tracking these activities and the impacts they
help create, they will be better positioned to manage and increase
those impacts. Leveraging can be accomplished in many ways.
Organizations can share:

- *Results.* Information about their impacts along with their own
  diagnosis of why their efforts succeeded or failed.
- *Data.* Data and metrics of all kinds, such as composite demographic information about clients, information about actions
  and outcomes, and information about performance. These
  can be shared with other organizations or contributed to an
  industry-level database.
- *Best practices.* Processes and policies the organization has
  developed that have contributed to its success.
- *Innovations.* Advances in business models and technologies
  that can be given or licensed to others.
- *Advocacy.* Participation in advocacy organizations and initiatives.
- *Reputation.* A goodwill asset that can be used to raise the profile and credibility of other organizations and causes, or can
  be used to garner support or participation in a cause.
- *Networks.* Conduits for sharing resources and for spreading
  knowledge or for participating in collective impact initiatives.

These resources and capabilities can be used by others to amplify
total social impacts.. Figure 26 illustrates how ideas can be spread
to larger and larger groups of organizations to amplify impact.

Leverage at the *industry level* means sharing resources with
your peers and contributing to ecosystem services that support

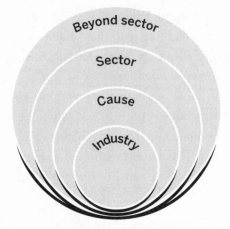

Figure 26 Leveraging Impact Beyond Your Organization

your industry. Microfinance institutions have been a model for industry-level leverage. Organizations contribute to industrywide conferences; databases of papers documenting research, innovations, and best practices; and trade organizations that report key operational and financial metrics and advocate for changing usury laws and other banking regulations. The industry has scaled more than tenfold in a decade, and these collaborative activities contributed greatly to that success. The industry has also come together to analyze and act upon failures, and a Social Performance Task Force has prescribed impact metrics that are now shared in the industry's benchmarking databases.

Leverage at the *cause level* involves engaging other organizations that are working on the same cause, but from a different perspective or using different intervention methods. Organizations that work on reducing childhood obesity may focus on education, food marketing, safe play areas, or a number of other factors. If these organizations work together toward a common agenda, they can find areas where their work overlaps or is mutually enforcing, and they can use their knowledge and data to develop a more complete understanding of the problem they wish to address.

Corporations have made great strides in working at the cause level to leverage impact. The GreenXchange is a collaboration among for-profit corporations to share rights to patents for environmentally friendly innovations. Nike, a US-based sports and apparel company, developed a type of shoe rubber that reduced toxins by 96 percent compared with previously used materials. This technology was included in GreenXchange so that other companies could get their own environmentally friendly products to market much more quickly. To date, Nike has placed more than 400 patents in the GreenXchange.[3]

Leverage at the sector level involves sharing assets with social-sector organizations pursuing different causes but still in need of basic operational, management, and strategic tools to improve their effectiveness. One well-known example of an innovation that has been shared is the social return on investment (SROI) framework. REDF, also known as the Roberts Enterprise Development Fund, first developed the SROI framework as a tool for measuring the organization's impact on employing homeless people in California. Since then the tool has been widely used and adapted by organizations worldwide and has influenced the thinking of the entire social sector. The organization continues to refine its impact measurement approaches, and allocates a percentage of managers' heavily sought-after time to meet with outside organizations to share its impact measurement innovations. REDF's work has helped shift the entire sector away from a paradigm of receiving donations and providing services to a paradigm of carefully investing resources in order to maximize social returns.

The highest level is leverage beyond the sector, typically to government agencies and corporations that can employ the assets of the social sector. Social impact bonds are an example of this category. They are instruments through which social organizations loan money to government agencies to fund interventions, and the loans are repaid if these interventions are successful. Social Finance launched the first social impact bond fund in 2010. This innovation has proven promising. Goldman Sachs subsequently created a $10 million social impact bond and has announced the launch of a $250 million social impact fund for such initiatives.[4]

Low-cost product and service designs developed for use in impoverished regions have spilled over into commercial markets. Small, efficient foot stoves, for example, were developed for use in areas in which firewood is scarce and respiratory issues are prevalent. These technologies have been adapted to regions that don't have these issues but are instead concerned about the environmental damage caused by traditional cooking methods.

Every effective organization has opportunities to amplify impacts. Although few may have excess resources to devote toward this goal, amplifying impacts may in fact be a more effective investment than serving a few more clients or completing one more project. By sharing and pooling resources, organizations and investors can make far greater impacts on the causes they care about than they could alone. By creating processes for amplifying impact and by monitoring the results of those activities, organizations can become more aware of the impacts they create beyond their own walls and can devote more effort toward activities that have proven to be effective.

Action Agenda

1. Decide whether you're ready to amplify your impact and choose your best strategy—through innovation, scaling, or leveraging your resources.
2. Regularly scan your external and internal environments for opportunities to create innovative business models or technologies.
3. Identify assets you can use for scaling up your organization and impacts: quality products or services, well-designed processes, and/or passionate people.
4. Determine which of your resources can be leveraged through other organizations: your results, data, best practices, innovations, advocacy work, reputation, or networks.

12

Call to Action

Investing in impact is not easy, but the world needs you. The social and environmental issues we face today are tremendous. But investors like you are making great strides in many areas, and there has never been more interest in solving the big problems. Tackling the challenges that lie ahead will require all of us to invest our scarce resources in the most strategic and effective ways possible.

You've already chosen to devote your time, money, and other precious resources to help others by promoting positive social and environmental changes. And now you're making the decision to manage your investments in new ways to create the maximum possible benefits. We've all heard about well-meant projects that have languished or failed, and none of us wants to waste resources or fall short of the promises we've made to our beneficiaries and ourselves. With good intentions, deep thinking, and careful management, every investor can create better outcomes.

The time is right to focus on impact. Virtually all stakeholders involved with social impact—investors, regulators, community members, trade partners, and beneficiaries—are more interested than ever in making sure that these investments make a difference. While this puts pressure on investors to deliver, it also leads to a

Figure 28 The Social Impact Creation Cycle

great deal more attention toward providing support and resources that can help deliver impact.

This book is one of those resources. It can serve as a guide for investors at all stages of the social impact creation journey. And it can be used by those who don't have specific impact goals, but want to be good social and environmental citizens. The book has been organized around the concept of a simple cycle that can be used to plan and execute each stage of investing in social impact. If you want to get the most impact from your investment, this basic cycle can provide a wealth of ideas for how to do that.

This cycle, and the ideas included in the book, emerged from a variety of sources. We interviewed leaders who were identified by their peers as the best-of-the-best in measuring social impact. We interviewed some of the world's leading companies in CSR and sustainability. We conducted an extensive search of writings by industry professionals and academic analysts. And we drew on our own backgrounds as business professors and consultants.

At the end of this chapter, you'll find a summary of the key ideas from the book. There are a lot of ideas packed into each chapter, and we hope you've found some that resonate with you and that you'll commit to using in order to improve your impact.

But now we're going to make our final pitch and ask you to take some bold actions. Here are a few essential things you can do if you want to make a bigger impact on the world:

Investors....

Choose investments thoughtfully. Think about what you care about and what resources you have to invest. Then choose high-potential investments that are a good fit for you.

Pay attention to impact. Demand transparency from the organizations you invest in. Make sure that your investment isn't wasted, but contributes to making a meaningful impact.

Organizations....

Use a logic model. This is the best way to ensure that your efforts make a difference. Make sure you are clear about the impact you want to make and that you have a solid plan for making it happen.

Measure. Instincts aren't always correct. Develop a system that comes as close as possible to measuring the impacts you want to create. Then talk frequently about results so that you can use them to keep getting better.

Share your knowledge. Others can learn from you, copy your success, and benefit from your connections. The more you help them out, the more you'll learn, and the more they can contribute to making the changes you care about. Use your power to make this happen.

Readers...

To evaluate your current performance in each element of the Social Impact Creation Cycle, read through the summary on the following page and then ask yourself the questions at the end of each chapter. You can also take the Social Impact Self-Assessment. The link to the self-assessment and a brief description follow this chapter. The assessment includes questions relating to key practices discussed in this book. Whether you're an investor, an investee, or both, the self-assessment will help you take a snapshot of the status of your impact creation profile right now and provide you with guidance for improving your areas of weakness so that you can create more impact in the future.

Finally, share your success stories with us. We'll post stories on our website, www.measuringsocialimpacts.com, along with other information about creating social impacts. By posting your success stories (and failures, too!), you can amplify your impacts by sharing what you've learned with others working hard to maximize their impacts. Let us know which ideas sparked your imagination and put you on a course for making positive changes. And let us know how you measured and improved your impacts!

Summary: Measuring and Improving Social Impacts

Investors, Values, and Resources (Chapter 2)
Creating social impacts is a process that begins well before investments are made. Investors need to inventory their interests, resources, values, and beliefs before they begin investing. Values determine which impacts we want and how important it is to maximize them. Understanding our values provides the foundation for making effective social investments.

Target Problems (Chapter 3)
Your social mission should be built on those social and environmental changes you value most, and the problem-solving approaches you'd like to use to make those changes: research, service delivery, advocacy, or some other approach. An inventory of your unique skills and resources will help you determine where your investment can create the greatest social change.

Investment Structures and Investor Roles (Chapter 4)
Decide how you'd prefer to structure your investment—for example, through equity, a loan, or a grant. Decide whether a non-

profit, social enterprise, or another type of organization can best achieve your impact goals. Consider how deeply you want to be involved—whether you'll work directly in a social purpose organization, serve as a board member or advisor, or contribute in another capacity. Then evaluate each investment option to ensure alignment with your mission.

Understanding Impacts (Chapter 5)

Identify and understand your organization's primary impacts. For nonprofits and social enterprises, these usually come through products and services, while for companies they usually come as a result of operations. But all organizations make impacts in both areas. Investments such as endowments also create impacts. Manage all three to maximize your impact.

Logic Models: Linking Actions to Impacts (Chapter 6)

Recognize that there are very few controls in place to ensure that impact investments really make a difference. Be very clear about the impact mission and goals. Then make sure you have a sound theory of which actions will create the impacts, and a logic model that explains how this will be done. Make sure your plans are aligned with the interests of your beneficiaries.

Measurement: Are Impacts Really Happening? (Chapter 7)

You'll need good measures to know whether you're making an impact. Although measurement is difficult and costly, at a minimum you should think through what impacts you'd like to measure if you could. Use measurement and evaluation to manage operations and impact evaluation to measure impacts. You can use a combination of investigation, analytics, and experiments to learn about impacts.

Measurement Approaches (Chapter 8)

Decide what kind of measurement approach will best suit your needs: trained judgment, qualitative research, quantitative research, and/or monetization. Become familiar with the many tested measurement approaches so you can use them as needed.

Impact Assessment and Metrics (Chapter 9)

Decide which impacts are most critical to driving your decisions and measuring your success. Identify indicators for the systematic changes you want to measure and determine how you'll use the results. Develop a system for gathering and using these metrics to improve your impact.

Maturity: Measurement as a Feedback Loop (Chapter 10)

Evaluate the maturity of your social impact measurement system. Consider changes you could make to move upward toward developing strategy and driving transformational change.

Amplifying Impacts (Chapter 11)

Beyond organic growth, think about ways to amplify your organization's impact. These include innovating, scaling, and leveraging your knowledge and assets by collaborating with other organizations working toward social change.

Social Impact Self-Assessment

To help you evaluate your progress on the social impact creation journey, we have created a Social Impact Self-Assessment companion product, which can be found at

www.bkconnection.com/socialimpact-sa

The assessment allows you to think about impacts from the perspective of both the investors who contribute money and energy and the operating organizations that directly create the impact. If you're taking the assessment as a way to better understand your investors or if you are an investor, the assessment will help you understand investment goals, priorities, resources, as well as how investors select causes and investment opportunities. If you're taking the assessment to better understand organizations that are working directly to create social impact, the assessment will help you identify the desired impacts and processes for creating them, and will help you determine the preferred characteristics for a system that can measure impacts and help improve them.

You can work through the assessment on your own, either one time or at multiple points as you work toward creating greater impacts. You can ask a group of your organizational peers or board members to take the assessment, and then use your results to understand differences in perspectives and goals as well as to increase alignment within the group. If you're an investor, you can share your assessment results with your investees, and if you're an operator, you can share your results with investors. Making assessment part of your learning about impact will be useful for ensuring that you're maximizing the value of both the resources invested and the impacts generated to make the greatest possible changes in the social issues that matter to you. Bulk-order discounts are also available for organizational programs.

Notes

Chapter 1 *The Social Impact Creation Cycle*

1 J.P.Morgan (2013) "Perspectives on Progress: The Impact Investor Survey."

2 Preston (2010) "Some 70% of Grant Makers Say Foundations Have Few Measures to Test Their Effectiveness."

3 Center for Global Development (2006) *When Will We Ever Learn? Improving Lives Through Impact Evaluation*, p. 17.

Chapter 2 *Understanding the Investor*

1 *The Chronicle of Philanthropy* (2013) "How America's Biggest Companies Give."

2 Walmart Foundation (2013) "Walmart Giving in Last Fiscal Year Exceeds $1 Billion for the First Time," www.foundation.walmart.com.

3 The Giving Pledge (2012), www.givingpledge.org.

4 Raikes (2011) *Progress and Partnerships*.

5 National Park Service (2013) "Giving Statistics"; National Park Service (2009) "The Center On Philanthropy Panel Study."

6 Swartz (2013) "Tech's New Entrepreneurial Approach to Philanthropy."

7 GIVING USA (2012) *The Annual Report on Philanthropy for the Year 2011*.

8 Salamon, Sokolowski, and Geller (2012) *Nonprofit Economic Data Bulletin No. 39. Holding the Fort: Nonprofit Employment during a Decade of Turmoil.*

9 "Volunteering and Civic Life in America 2012," www.volunteeringinamerica.gov/.

10 Tierney and Fleischman (2011) *Give Smart: Philanthropy That Gets Results.*

11 For more on donors' giving behaviors, see Karlan, List, and Shafir (2010), and Small, Loewenstein, and Slovic (2006).

12 Another list of returns that philanthropists value can be found in Bronfman and Solomon (2010) *The Art of Giving: Where the Soul Meets a Business Plan*, pp. 46–47.

13 UBS and INSEAD (2011) "UBS-INSEAD Study on Family Philanthropy in Asia."

14 India Knowledge@Wharton (2013) "Philanthropy in India Is Taking Its Own Route."

15 Frank (2012) "Impact Investing: What Exactly Is New?"

16 El-Naggar (2013) "In Lieu of Money, Toyota Donates Efficiency to New York Charity," *New York Times*, July 26.

17 Huffington Post (2013) "Food Waste: Half of All Food Ends Up Thrown Away."

Chapter 3 *Understanding the Problem*

1 Porter and Kramer (2002) "The Competitive Advantage of Corporate Philanthropy."

2 McCormick (2010) "Changing: To Make Greater Change."

3 Rodin and MacPherson (2012) "Shared Outcomes."

4 See http://mahb.stanford.edu/endorse-the-message-to-world-leaders/complete-list-of-endorsers/.

5 Preskill and Beer (2012) *Evaluating Social Innovation*.

6 Cynthia Chua et al. (2011) "Beyond the Margin: Redirecting Asia's Capitalism."

7 More discussion on advocacy can be found in chapter 3 of Crutchfield, Kania, and Kramer (2011) *Do More Than Give*. Though assessing advocacy can be challenging, readers may want to review Barkhorn, Huttner, and Blau (2013) "Assessing Advocacy"; and Teles and Schmitt (2011) "The Elusive Craft of Evaluating Advocacy."

8 Markets for Good (2012) *Upgrading the Information Infrastructure for Social Change*.

9 Orenstein (2013) "Our Feel-Good War on Breast Cancer."

10 Crutchfield, Kania, and Kramer discussed six practices of catalytic philanthropy in their book *Do More Than Give* (2011).

11 Kramer (2009) "Catalytic Philanthropy."

Chapter 4 *Understanding the Investment Options*

1 Form 990 is required for tax-exempt organizations by the Internal Revenue Service. It discloses the financial information of such organizations.

2 A more complete list of financial instruments used in the impact invest-

ment industry can be found in an impact investor survey, Saltuk et al. (2013) "Perspectives on Progress: The Impact Investor Survey."

3 Annino (2013) "For-Profit Philanthropy: Has Its Time Come?"

4 Additional discussion on social bonds can be found in McKinsey & Co. (2012) "From Potential to Action: Bringing Social Impact Bonds to the U.S."; Knowledge@Wharton (2012) "Social Finance's Tracy Paland-jian on the Next Generation of Responsible Investing"; Callanan and Law (2012) "Will Social Impact Bonds Work in the United States?"; and Bugg-Levine, Kogut, and Kulatilaka (2012) "A New Approach to Funding Social Enterprises."

5 Alden (2013) "Goldman Sachs to Finance Early Education Program."

6 Cohen and Sahlman (2013) "Social Impact Investing Will Be the New Venture Capital."

7 Nonprofit Finance Fund, and The White House (2012) *Pay for Success: Investing in What Works.*

8 Gose (2013) "Kresge Seeks to Do More Without Spending More."

9 For more information on Root Capital's rural finance model, please see its website: www.rootcapital.org/our-approach.

10 For a more thorough discussion on impact investment, please see the important work by Bugg-Levine and Emerson (2011) *Impact Investing: Transforming How We Make Money While Making a Difference.*

11 Monitor Institute (2009) *Investing for Social & Environmental Impact: A Design for Catalyzing an Emerging Industry.*

12 Saltuk et al. (2013) "Perspectives on Progress: Impact Investor Survey."

13 Bannick and Hallstein (2012) "Learning from Silicon Valley."

14 Annino (2013) "For-Profit Philanthropy: Has Its Time Come?"

15 For more discussion on social enterprises, see Bromberger (2011) "A New Type of Hybrid"; Bugg-Levine and Emerson (2011) *Impact Investing: Transforming How We Make Money While Making a Difference.*

16 From the email newsletter from Bridges Ventures by Philip Newbor-ough, June 13, 2013.

17 Social Enterprise UK (2012) *Social Enterprise and Youth Policy Paper.*

18 Karnani (2013) "Mandatory CSR in India: A Bad Proposal."

19 Thornley and Colby, Federal Reserve Bank of San Francisco (2010) *Building Scale in Community Impact Investing through Nonfinancial Performance Measurement.*

20 From Melissa Berman, president and chief executive of Rockefeller Philanthropy Advisors (2010) "Philanthropy Becoming New Status Symbol For Wealthy," *New York Times,* August 11.

21 See also McCray (2011) *Is Grantmaking Getting Smarter? A National Study of Philanthropic Practice.*

Chapter 5 *How Social Impacts Are Created*

1 Credit Suisse and the Schwab Foundation for Social Entrepreneurship (2012) *Investing for Impact: How Social Entrepreneurship Is Redefining the Meaning of Return*. Acumen Fund has invested in many social businesses that provide affordable products and services to the poor in developing countries. Some of its programs are described in Jacqueline Novogratz (2011) "Making a Case for Patient Capital."

2 Herrera (2013) "Questioning the TOMS Shoes Model for Social Enterprise."

3 Epstein, Buhovac, and Yuthas (2009) *Managing Social, Environmental, and Financial Performance Simultaneously: What Can We Learn from Corporate Best Practices?*

4 From Industree's third Social Audit Certification.

5 Garrigo (2011) "Corporate Responsibility at Chevron."

6 GrantMakers in Health (2011) *Guide to Impact Investing.*

7 Cooch and Kramer (2007). More discussion on PRI and MRI can be found in Brest and Harvey (2008) *Money Well Spent: A Strategic Plan for Smart Philanthropy*, chapter 8.

Chapter 6 *Linking Actions to Impacts*

1 Idealware (2012) *The State of Nonprofit Data.*

2 HOPE Consulting (2010) *Money for Good: The US Market for Impact Investments and Charitable Gifts from Individual Donors and Investors.*

3 Saul (2011) "The End of Fundraising: Raise More Money by Selling Your Impact."

4 Scharpnick (2013) "Can You Sum Up Your Charity's Work in One Simple Tag Line?"

5 Starr (2012) "The Eight-Word Mission Statement."

6 This paragraph draws from Starr (2012) "The Eight-Word Mission Statement."

7 Mento (2013) "Why $1 Billion to Aid the Sick Did Little Good"; Mento (2013) "Grant Makers Open Up about Failed Projects in Hopes Others Can Learn from Them"; Showstack and Wolfe (2012) *RWJF Retrospective Series: Chronic Care Programs.*

8 You can look up the definition of theory of change in Mathison, ed. (2005) *Encyclopedia of Evaluation*; and Rossi and Freeman (1985) *Evaluation: A Systematic Approach.* See chapter 6 in Peter Frumkin's *Strategic Giving: The Art and Science of Philanthropy* (2006) for a theory of change in detail; and Paul Brest for a discussion of different stages of theories of change and different views toward a theory of change in "The Power of Theories of Change" (2010).

9 Bill & Melinda Gates Foundation (2011) *The Strategy Lifecycle: A Guide.*

10 Harris (2005) "An Introduction to Theory of Change."

11 Kail (2012) "Using 'Theory of Change' to Measure Your Charity's Impact: A New Approach Is Helping Charities Prioritize Activities and Plan for the Future."

12 PATH (2012) "PATH: A Catalyst for Global Health."

13 See also the definition of logic models and their elements in Mathison, ed. (2005) *Encyclopedia of Evaluation;* and Rossi and Freeman (1985) *Evaluation: A Systematic Approach.* Frumkin's *Strategic Giving: The Art and Science of Philanthropy* (2006) discusses logic models in detail in chapter 6.

14 More discussion on logic models can be found in W. K. Kellogg Foundation (2004) *Logic Model Development Guide.*

15 This section draws largely from Mercy Corps (2005) *Design, Monitoring and Evaluation Guidebook.*

16 Twersky, Buchanan, and Threlfall (2013) "Listening to Those Who Matter Most, the Beneficiaries."

Chapter 7 *Measurement Basics*

1 Idealware (2012) "The State of Nonprofit Data."

2 Preston (2010) "Some 70 Percent of Grant Makers Say Foundations Have Few Measures to Test Their Effectiveness."

3 Wallace (2012) "Database Indexes Nonprofit Research."

4 Jodi Nelson, director of strategy, measurement, and evaluation at the Bill & Melinda Gates Foundation, argues that the assessments for different programs should not be accumulated or compared because success is measured in different ways in different fields; Forti (2012) "Actionable Measurement at the Gates Foundation," April 29.

5 United States Government Accountability Office (2003) *Youth Illicit Drug Use Prevention: DARE Long-Term Evaluations and Federal Efforts to Identify Effective Programs.*

6 J.P. Morgan (2013) "Perspectives on Progress: The Impact Investor Survey."

7 More discussion of monitoring and evaluation can be found in Twersky and Lindblom (2012) *Evaluation Principles and Practice.*

8 Grantmakers for Effective Organizations (2011) "How Do We Approach Impact and Evaluation in the Context of Scale?" Another common classification distinguishes between formative evaluation, process evaluation, and summative evaluation. For further descriptions, see Mathison, ed. (2005) *Encyclopedia of Evaluation;* and Rossi and Freeman (1985) *Evaluation: A Systematic Approach.*

9 For more on developmental evaluation, see Gamble (2008) *A Developmental Evaluation Primer.*

10 More discussion of James Irvine Foundation's method is available in The James Irvine Foundation (2011) *A Framework to Assess the Performance of The James Irvine Foundation*; and Canales and Rafter (2012) "Assessing One's Own Performance."

Chapter 8 *Measurement Approaches*

1 TRASI (http://trasi.foundationcenter.org/) provides more than 150 social impact cases and the site can be searched by the purpose of measurement, type of organization, sector, and measurement focus.

2 Gates (2013) "Bill Gates: My Plan to Fix the World's Biggest Problems."

3 Preston (2013) "Bloomberg Philanthropies Unveils Web Site and Priorities."

4 Discussion of various evaluation methods can be found in Brest and Harvey (2008) *Money Well Spent: A Strategic Plan for Smart Philanthropy*, chapter 10.

5 More discussion on cost-effective analysis can be found at Tuan (2008) *Measuring and/or Estimating Social Value Creation: Insights into Eight Integrated Cost Approaches*.

6 Tuan (2008) "Profiles of Eight Integrated Cost Approaches to Measuring and/or Estimating Social Value Creation"; Brest (2012). "Risky Business."

7 Acumen Fund Metrics Team (2007) *The Best Available Charitable Option*.

8 Roberts Foundation (2001) *SROI Methodology*.

9 For more on RDEF's current evaluation approach, see Twersky and BTW Consultants (2002) "An Information OASIS"; Gair (2002) *A Report from the Good Ship SROI*; Gair (2009) *SROI Act II: A Call to Action for Next-Generation SROI*.

10 SROI Network (2005) *A Framework for Approaches to SROI Analysis*.

11 More discussion on SROI can be found in Tuan (2008) *Measuring and/or Estimating Social Value Creation: Insights into Eight Integrated Cost Approaches*.

12 Cooney and Lynch-Cerullo (2012) *Social Return on Investment: A Case Study of JVS*.

13 For more on PUMA, see PUMA (2011) "PUMA Completes First Environmental Profit and Loss Account Which Values Impacts at €145 Million"; and PUMA (2011) "Environmental Key Performance Indicators Methodology."

Chapter 9 *Measuring Your Impact*

1 For a useful discussion of constituent voice and ownership, see Forti (2012) "Measurement That Benefits the Measured."

2 Twersky, Nelson, and Ratcliffe (2010) *A Guide to Actionable Measurement*.

3 Sirull (2009) "Measurement Matters: Maximizing Total Return on Responsible Investments In Private Equity"; Rosenzweig, Clark, Long, and Olsen (2003) *Double Bottom Line Project Report: Assessing Social Impact in Double Bottom Lines Ventures (Methods Catalog)*.

4 More on principles of reporting can be found in New Philanthropy Capital et al. (2012) *Principles of Good Impact Reporting for Charities and Social Enterprises*.

5 For more information on the Gates Foundation's Strategy Lifecycle and Insight, see Bill & Melinda Gates Foundation (2011) *The Strategy Lifecycle: A Guide*.

6 Working with the assistance of authors Marc Epstein and Kristi Yuthas, Escuela Nueva, a Colombian nonprofit, has developed entrepreneurship training courses for primary age children like the ones described here and is preparing to pilot-test them.

Chapter 11 *Amplifying Your Impact*

1 Much of the content of this section is drawn from Epstein and Yuthas (2012) "Scaling Effective Education for the Poor in Developing Countries: A Report from the Field."

2 See Frumkin (2006) *Strategic Giving: The Art and Science of Philanthropy,* chapter 6, for a discussion of leverage in detail. Another worthwhile resource is Grant, McLeod, and Crutchfield (2007) "Creating High-Impact Nonprofits."

3 AHA! (2010) "Nike's Lorrie Vogel: 'No Finish Line for Sustainable Product Innovation.'"

4 See Lydia DePillis, *Washington Post,* "Wonkblog," November 5, 2013, www.washingtonpost.com/blogs/wonkblog/wp/2013/11/05/goldman-sachs-thinks-it-can-make-money-by-being-a-do-gooder/.

Bibliography

Absolute Return for Kids. *Annual Review 2010*. London: ARK, 2011.

———. *Annual Report 2011*. London: ARK, 2012.

Abt Associates Inc. *Measuring Social Performance*. Cambridge, MA: Abt Associates, 1973.

Acumen Fund. *A Bold New Way of Tackling Poverty That Works: Ten-Year Report*. New York: Acuman Fund, 2011.

Acumen Fund Metrics Team. *The Best Available Charitable Option*. New York: Acumen Fund, 2007.

AHA! "Nike's Lorrie Vogel: 'No Finish Line for Sustainable Product Innovation.'" *Opportunity Green*, September 15, 2010.

Alden, William. "Goldman Sachs to Finance Early Education Program." *New York Times*, July 12, 2013.

Alliance. "Interview: Paul Brest, Jed Everson, Katherina Rosqueta, Brian Trelstad, and Michael Weinstein." Alliancemagazine.org, April 1, 2009.

Ambuja Cement Foundation. *Sustainability: Annual Report 2011–2012*. Kolkatta: Ambuja Cement Foundation, 2012.

Annino, Patricia M. "For-Profit Philanthropy: Has Its Time Come?" *CPA2Biz*, March 25, 2013.

Aos, Steve, et al. *Return on Investment: Evidence-Based Options to Improve State Outcomes*. Olympia, WA: Washington State Institute for Public Policy, 2011.

———. *Return on Investment: Evidence-Based Options to Improve Statewide Outcomes: Technical Appendix I, Detailed Tables*. Olympia, WA: Washington State Institute for Public Policy, 2011.

———. *Return on Investment: Evidence-Based Options to Improve Statewide Outcomes: Technical Appendix II, Methods and User-Manual*. Olympia, WA: Washington State Institute for Public Policy, 2011.

Arabella Advisors. *Use Your Investments: Generating Impact and Returns in Chicago*. Washington, DC: Arabella Advisors, 2012.

———. *Use Your Investments: Generating Impact and Returns in New York*. Washington, DC: Arabella Advisors, 2012.. Washington, DC: Arabella Advisors, 2012.

———. *Use Your Investments: Generating Impact and Returns in San Francisco*. Washington, DC: Arabella Advisors, 2012.

———. *Use Your Investments: Generating Impact and Returns in Washington D.C.* Washington, DC: Arabella Advisors, 2012.

Arnold, Frank S. "Regs Require Value-of-Life Calculations." *Environmental Forum*.

———. "Can't Do Cost-Benefit Without It." *Environmental Forum* (November/December 2001).

Arosio, Marco. *Impact Investing in Emerging Markets*. Singapore: Responsible Research, 2011.

Arrillaga-Andreessen, Laura. *Giving 2.0*. San Francisco: Jossey-Bass, 2012.

Aureos Capital. "Emerging Markets: Building High-Growth Businesses." Aureos, www.aureos.com, accessed January 9, 2012.

Balfour, Doug. "Ten Principles of International Giving." *Global Philanthropy*, June 7, 2011.

Banerjee, A.V., and Esther Duflo. *Poor Economics: A Radical Rethinking of the Way to Fight Global Poverty*. New York: PublicAffairs, 2011.

Bannick, Matt, and Paula Goldman. "Priming the Pump: The Case for a Sector-Based Approach to Impact Investing." Redwood City, CA: Omidyar Network, 2012.

Bannick, Matt, and Eric Hallstein. "Learning from Silicon Valley." In *Advancing Evaluation Practices in Philanthropy*, sponsored Supplement to *Stanford Social Innovation Review* 10, no. 3 (Summer 2012): 8–11.

Barker, Memphis. "Bill Gates, Impact Evaluation, and Why Anxiety Is a Catalyst for More Effective Social Change." *The Independent* (London), January 29, 2013.

Barkhorn, Ivan, Nathan Huttner, and Jason Blau. "Assessing Advocacy." *Stanford Social Innovation Review* 11, no. 2 (Spring 2013): 58–64.

Baron, Jon. "Increasing Government Effectiveness Through Rigorous Evidence about 'What Works.'" coalition4evidence.org, June 28, 2012.

Batavia, Hima, Justin Chakma, Hassan Masum, and Peter Singer. "Market-Minded Development." *Stanford Social Innovation Review* 9, no. 1 (Winter 2011): 66–71.

Baxter. "Baxter Recognized Suppliers Through e-Impact Program." www.sustainability.baxter.com, accessed March 2, 2012.

———. "Priorities and Goals." www.sustainability.baxter.com, accessed March 2, 2012.

Beloff, Beth R., Earl R. Beaver, and Heidi Massin. "Assessing Societal Costs Associated with Environmental Impacts." *Environmental Quality Management* 10, no. 2 (Winter 2000): 67–82.

Berkman, Jacob. "Donors Are Settling for a 'Bronze Standard' for Measuring Charities." *Chronicle of Philanthropy*, June 14, 2011.

Bernstein, Margaret, and *The Plain Dealer*. "Nonprofits Can Transform Society But First They Must Transform Themselves: Margaret Bernstein." www.cleveland.com/bernstein/index.ssf/2012/05/nonprofits_can_transform_socie.html, May 26, 2012.

Bettinger, Eric P., Bridget Terry Long, Philip Oreopoulos, and Lisa Sanbonmatsu. *The Role of Simplification and Information in College Decisions: Results from the H&R Block FAFSA Experiment*. Cambridge, MA: National Bureau of Economic Research, 2009.

Bhattacharya, C. B., and S. Sen. "Doing Better at Doing Good: When, Why, and How Consumers Respond to Corporate Social Initiatives." *California Management Review* 47, no. 1 (2004): 9–16.

Bill & Melinda Gates Foundation. *The Strategy Lifecycle: A Guide.* Seattle: Bill & Melinda Gates Foundation, 2011.

Bing, Eric G., and Marc J. Epstein. *Pharmacy on a Bicycle: Innovative Solutions for Global Health and Poverty.* San Francisco: Berrett-Koehler, 2013.

Birchall, Jonathan. "Wal-Mart Overhauls Its Charity Spending." *Financial Times,* March 3, 2008.

Bishop, Matthew, and M. Green. *Philanthrocapitalism: How Giving Can Save the World.* New York: Bloomsbury Press, 2009.

Bleiberg, Rob, et al. *$650 Million Ain't What It Used to Be (A): The Meyer Memorial Trust Considers Mission Related Investing.* Boston: Harvard Business School, 2010.

———. *$650 Million Ain't What It Used to Be (B): The Meyer Memorial Trust Considers Mission Related Investing.* Boston: Harvard Business School, 2010.

Bloom, Paul N., and J. Gregory Dees. "Cultivate Your Ecosystem." *Stanford Social Innovation Review* 6, no. 1 (Winter 2008): 47–53.

Bornstein, David. "The Power of Nursing." Opinionator, *New York Times,* May 16, 2012.

———. "The Dawn of the Evidence-Based Budget." Opinionator, *New York Times,* May 30, 2013.

Bradley, Bill, Paul Jansen, and Les Silverman. "The Nonprofit Sector's $100 Billion Opportunity." *Harvard Business Review* 81, no. 5 (2003): 94–103.

Brandenburg, Margot. "Impact Investing's Three Measurement Tools." *Stanford Social Innovation Review,* October 3, 2012.

Brest, Paul. "The Power of Theories of Change." *Stanford Social Innovation Review* 8, no. 2 (Spring 2010): 47–51 .

———. "A Decade of Outcome-Oriented Philanthropy." *Stanford Social Innovation Review,* 10, no. 2 (Spring 2012): 42–47.

———. "Risky Business." *Advancing Evaluation Practices in Philanthropy,* supplement to *Stanford Social Innovation Review* 10, no. 3 (Summer 2012): 16–19.

———. "Laura Arrillaga-Andreessen's Gift to Philanthropy." *Stanford Social Innovation Review,* June 19, 2013.

Brest, Paul, and Hal Harvey. *Money Well Spent: A Strategic Plan for Smart Philanthropy.* New York: Bloomberg Press, 2008.

Brest, Paul, Hal Harvey, and Kelvin Low. "Calculated Impact." *Stanford Social Innovation Review* 7, no. 1 (Winter 2009): 50–56.

Bridges Ventures. *2011 Impact Report.* London: Bridges Ventures, 2012.

———. *Ten-Year Report: A Decade of Investing for Impact and Sustainable Growth.* London: Bridges Ventures, 2013.

Brock, Andrea, Ellie Buteau, and An-Li Herring. *Room for Improvement: Foundations' Support of Nonprofit Performance Assessment.* Cambridge, MA: Center of Effective Philanthropy, 2012.

Bromberger, Allen R. "A New Type of Hybrid." *Stanford Social Innovation Review* 9, no. 2 (Spring 2011): 49–53.

Bronfman, Charles, and J. Solomon. *The Art of Giving: Where the Soul Meets a Business Plan.* San Francisco: Jossey-Bass, 2010.

Bruch, Heike, and Frank Walter. "The Keys to Rethinking Corporate Philanthropy." *MIT Sloan Management Review* 47, no. 1 (2005): 51.

Bryant, Adam. "When Humility and Audacity Go Hand in Hand." *New York Times,* September 29, 2012.

Bryson, John M. "What to Do When Stakeholders Matter: Stakeholder Identification and Analysis Techniques." *Public Management Review* 6, no. 1 (2004): 21–53.

Bryson, John M., and Roering, W. D. "Initiation of Strategic Planning by Governments." *Public Administration Review* 48, no. 6 (1988): 995–1004.

Bugg-Levine, Antony, and Jed Emerson. *Impact Investing: Transforming How We Make Money While Making a Difference.* San Francisco: Jossey-Bass, 2011.

Bugg-Levine, Antony, Bruce Kogut, and Nalin Kulatilaka. "A New Approach to Funding Social Enterprises." *Harvard Business Review* (January/February 2012): 2–7.

Cagney, Penelope. "New Organizations Pose Challenges for Nonprofit Consultants." *Chronicle of Philanthropy,* August 29, 2011.

Callanan, Laura, and Jonathan Law. "Will Social Impact Bonds Work in the United States?" *McKinsey on Society,* March 2012.

Campbell Soup Company. *2011 Update of the Corporate Social Responsibility Report.* Camden, NJ: Campbell Soup Company, 2011.

Canales, James E., and Kevin Rafter. "Assessing One's Own Performance." *Advancing Evaluation Practices in Philanthropy,* supplement to *Stanford Social Innovation Review* 10, no. 3 (Summer 2012): 20–23.

Carson, Emmett D. "Redefining Community Foundations." *Stanford Social Innovation Review* 11, no. 1 (Winter 2013): 21–22.

Case, Jean. "Fearless Focus: Mario Morino of VPP." Case Foundation, May 30, 2012, http://casefoundation.org/blog/fearless-focus-mario-morino-vpp.

Center for Effective Philanthropy. *Indicators of Effectiveness: Understanding and Improving Foundation Performance.* Boston: Center for Effective Philanthropy, 2002.

———. "New Report Dispels the Myth of Nonprofit Complacency." September 12, 2012.

Center for Global Development. *When Will We Ever Learn? Improving Lives Through Impact Evaluation.* Report of the Evaluation Gap Working Group. Washington, DC: Center for Global Development, 2006.

Center for the Advancement of Social Entrepreneurship. *Duke's Fuqua School of Business Launches Initiative on Impact Investing.* Durham, NC: Duke University, 2011.

Chen, David W. "Goldman to Invest in City Jail Program, Profiting if Recidivism Falls Sharply." *New York Times,* August 2, 2012.

Children's Investment Fund Foundation. *Performance Measurement and Effectiveness: On the Path to Transformative Change for Children.* London: Children's Investment Fund Foundation, 2011.

Chronicle of Philanthropy. "Calif. Latest State to OK Socially Focused 'Benefit Corporations.'" October 13, 2011.

———. "Ore. Law Ends Tax Breaks for Charities with High Overhead." June 18, 2013.

———. "Business Bellwether Delaware Approves Benefit Corporations." July 18, 2013.

———. "How America's Biggest Companies Give." July 22, 2013.

Chua, Cynthia, et al. *Beyond the Margin: Redirecting Asia's Capitalism.* Hong Kong and Beijing: Advantage Ventures, 2011.

Clark, Catherine H., Matthew H. Allen, Bonny Moellenbrock, and Chinwe Onyeagoro. *Accelerating Impact Enterprises: How to Lock, Stock, and Anchor Impact Enterprises for Maximum Impact.* Durham, NC: SJF Institute and Duke University's Fuqua School of Business, May 2013.

Clark, Catherine H.; Jed Emerson, and Ben Thornley. "A Market Emerges: The Six Dynamics of Impact Investing." *The Impact Investor.* Pacific Community Ventures, Inc., ImpactAssets, and Duke University's Fuqua School of Business, October 2012.

Clay, Jason. *Exploring the Links Between International Business and Poverty Reduction: A Case Study of Unilever in Indonesia.* Eynsham, UK: Information Press, 2005.

Clinton, Bill. *Giving: How Each of Us Can Change the World.* New York: Knopf, 2007.

Coalition for Evidence-Based Policy. *Rigorous Program Evaluations on a Budget: How Low-Cost Randomized Controlled Trials Are Possible in Many Areas of Social Policy.* Washington, DC: Coalition for Evidence-Based Policy, 2012.

———. *H&R Block College Financial Aid Application Assistance.* Top Tier Evidence Initiative. Washington, DC: Coalition for Evidence-Based Policy, 2012.

Coastal Enterprises, Inc. *Measuring Impact in Practice: Reflections and Recommendations from Coastal Enterprises, Inc.'s Experience.* Wiscasset, ME: Coastal Enterprises, 2006.

Cochrane, Gene Jr. *Advancing Evaluation: Conversations with Philanthropic Leaders on Strategic Evaluation, Issue 2.* FSG (2010), www.fsg.org/nl/evaluation/eval_culture/index.html.

Cohen, Sir Ronald, and William A. Sahlman. "Social Impact Investing Will Be the New Venture Capital." *Harvard Business Review,* January 17, 2013.

Colby, David. "Wise Distributions: Moving Beyond the Giving Pledge." *Huff Post Impact,* December 21, 2010.

———. "Looking for Impact in Some of the Wrong Places." *Grantmakers for Effective Organizations,* May 12, 2011.

———. "The Challenge and Potential of Transparency." *Grantmakers for Effective Organizations,* June 7, 2011.

Colby, David, Nancy W. Fishman, and Sarah G. Pickell. "Achieving Foundation Accountability and Transparency: Lessons from the Robert Wood Johnson Foundation's Scorecard." *Foundation Review* 3, no. 1 (2011): 70–80.

Colby, David, and Sarah G. Pickell. "Investing for Good: Measuring Nonfinancial Performance." *Community Development Investment Review* 6, no. 1 (December 2010): 64–68.

Colby, Susan, Nan Stone, and Paul Carttar. "Zeroing In on Impact." *Stanford Social Innovation Review* 2, no. 2 (Fall 2004): 24–33.

Cooch, Sarah, and Mark Kramer. *Compounding Impact: Mission Investing by U.S. Foundations.* Boston: FSG, 2007.

Cooney, Kate, and Kristin Lynch-Cerullo. *Social Return on Investment: A Case Study of JVS.* San Francisco: Jewish Vocational Service, 2012.

Cooney, Scott. "Impact Investing Goes Mainstream: Morgan Stanley Jumps on Board." TriplePundit.com, May 15, 2012.

Corporation for National and Community Service. "Volunteering and Civic Life in America 2012." Washington, DC: CNCS, December 2012, www.volunteeringinamerica.gov.

Coughlin, Chrissy. "Campbell's Soup's Dave Stangis on the Evolution of Sustainability." GreenBiz.com, August 31, 2011.

Credit Suisse and Schwab Foundation for Social Entrepreneurship. *Investing for Impact: How Social Entrepreneurship Is Redefining the Meaning of Return.* Geneva: Schwab Foundation, 2012.

Crutchfield, L. R., and Heather McLeod Grant. *Forces for Good: The Six Practices of High-Impact Nonprofits.* San Francisco: Jossey-Bass, 2008.

Crutchfield, L. R., J. V. Kania, and M. R. Kramer. *Do More Than Give.* San Francisco: Jossey-Bass, 2011.

Dagher, Veronica. "Bridging the Gap Between Charity, Business." *Wall Street Journal,* December 26, 2012.

Dalberg Global Development Advisors. "Impact Investing in West Africa." San Francisco: Dalberg, 2011.

Dartmouth Biomedical Libraries. "Evidence-Based Medicine (EBM) Resources," www.dartmouth.edu/~biomed/resources.htmld/guides/ebm_resources.shtml, assessed June 17, 2012.

Dasra and Godrej. *Making the Grade: Improving Mumbai's Public Schools.* Mumbai: Dasra, 2012.

Dasra and Omidyar Network. *Measure Up: Landscaping the State of Impact Assessment Practices Amongst Corporate and Family Foundations in India.* Mumbai: Dasra, 2012.

Dolnick, Sam. "Pennsylvania Study Finds Halfway Houses Don't Reduce Recidivism." *New York Times,* March 24, 2013.

Donovan, Doug. "White House Hosts Innovation Forum for Philanthropists." *Chronicle of Philanthropy,* September 21, 2012.

Dumaine, Brian. "Built to Last." *Fortune,* August 13, 2012.

Earth Capital Partners. *Approach to Sustainability Development.* London: Earth Capital Partners, 2010.

Ebrahim, Alnoor, and V. Kasturi Rangan. *Acumen Fund: Measurement in Impact Investing (A).* Boston: Harvard Business School, 2010.

Ebrahim, Alnoor, and Catherine Ross. *The Robin Hood Foundation.* Boston: Harvard Business School, 2010.

Eckhart-Queenan, Jeri, and Matt Forti. *Measurement as Learning: What Nonprofit CEOs, Board Members, and Philanthropists Need to Know to Keep Improving.* Boston: Bridgespan Group, 2011.

Economist. "The Patient Capitalist: Jacqueline Novogratz Wants to Transform the World's Approach to Development." May 21, 2009.

———. "B Corps—Firms with Benefits: A New Sort of Caring, Sharing Company Gathers Momentum." January 7, 2012.

EdelGive Foundation. *Annual Report 2011–2012.* Mumbai: EdelGive Foundation, 2012.

Edna McConnell Clark Foundation. *2010 Annual Report.* New York: Edna McConnell Clark Foundation, 2011.

Edwards, Michael. "Should a Charity Be Like a Business?" New York: Dow Jones, 2011.

El-Naggar, Mona. "In Lieu of Money, Toyota Donates Efficiency to New York Charity." *New York Times,* July 26, 2013.

Emerson, Jed. "But Does It Work? How Best to Assess Program Performance." *Stanford Social Innovation Review* 7, no. 1 (Winter 2009): 29–30.

———. *Beyond Good Versus Evil: Hedge Fund Investing, Capital Markets and the Sustainability Challenge.* BlendedValue.org, 2009, www.blendedvalue.org/beyond-good-versus-evil-hedge-fund-investing-capital-markets-and-the-sustainability-challenge/.

———. "The Blended Value Proposition: Integrating Social and Financial Returns." *California Management Review* 45, no. 4 (Summer 2003): 35–51.

Endeavor Global. "Our Model." www.Endeavor.Org/Model/Ourmodel, accessed February 5, 2013.

Epstein, Marc J. *Measuring Corporate Environmental Performance: Best Practices for Costing and Managing an Effective Environmental Strategy.* New York: McGraw-Hill, 1996.

———. *Making Sustainability Work: Best Practices in Managing and Measuring Corporate Social, Environmental, and Economic Impacts.* San Francisco: Berrett-Koehler, 2008.

———. "Implementing Corporate Sustainability: Measuring and Managing Social and Environmental Impacts." *Strategic Finance* 88, no. 1 (January 2008): 25–31.

Epstein, Marc J., and Adriana Rejc Buhovac. *Performance Measurement of Not-For-Profit Organizations.* New York: American Institute of Certified Public Accountants, Inc.; Mississauga, Ont.: Society of Management Accountants of Canada, 2009.

Epstein, Marc J., Adriana Rejc Buhovac, and Kristi Yuthas. *Managing Social, Environmental, and Financial Performance Simultaneously: What Can We Learn from Corporate Best Practices?* Montvale, NJ: Foundation for Applied Research, 2009.

———. "Implementing Sustainability: The Role of Leadership and Organizational Culture." *Strategic Finance* 91, no. 10 (2010): 41–47.

Epstein, Marc. J., and Christopher A. Crane. "Alleviating Global Poverty through Microfinance: Factors and Measures of Financial, Economic, and Social Performance," in V. Kasturi Rangan, John A. Quelch, Gustavo Herrero, and Brooke Barton, eds., *Business Solutions for the Global Poor: Creating Social and Economic Value.* San Francisco: Jossey-Bass, 2007, pp. 321–34.

Epstein, Marc J., Eric G. Flamholtz, and John J. McDonough. *Corporate Social Performance: The Measurement of Product and Service Contributions.* New York: National Association of Accountants, 1977.

Epstein, Marc J., and Jean-François Manzoni. "Implementing Corporate Strategy: From Tableaux de Bord to Balanced Scorecards." *European Management Journal* 16, no. 2 (April 1998): 190–203.

Epstein, Marc J., and Robert A. Westbrook. "Linking Actions to Profits in Strategic Decision Making." *MIT Sloan Management Review* 42, no. 3 (Spring 2001): 39–49.

Epstein, Marc J., and Sally K. Widener. "Facilitating Sustainable Development Decisions: Measuring Stakeholder Reactions." *Business Strategy and the Environment* 20, no. 2 (2011): 107–23.

———. "Identification and Use of Sustainability Performance Measures in Decision-Making." *Journal of Corporate Citizenship* 40 (February 2011): 43–73.

Epstein, Marc J., and Priscilla S. Wisner. "Using a Balanced Scorecard to Implement Sustainability." *Environmental Quality Management* 11, no. 2 (2001): 1–10.

———. "Good Neighbors: Implementing Social and Environmental Strategies with the BSC." *Balanced Scorecard Report* 3, no. 3 (May/June 2001): 3–6.

———. "Increasing Corporate Accountability: The External Disclosure of Balanced Scorecard Measures." *Balanced Scorecard Report* 3, no. 4 (July/August 2001).

Epstein, Marc J., and S. David Young. "'Greening' with EVA." *Management Accounting* (January 1999): 45–49.

Epstein, Marc J., and Kristi Yuthas. "Scaling Effective Education for the Poor in Developing Countries: A Report from the Field." *Journal of Public Policy & Marketing* 31, no. 1 (Spring 2012): 102–14.

European Venture Philanthropy Association. *Strategies for Foundations: When, Why and How to Use Venture Philanthropy.* Brussels: EVPA Knowledge Center, 2010.

———. *A Guide to Venture Philanthropy: For Venture Capital and Private Equity Investors.* Brussels: EVPA Knowledge Center, 2011.

———. *A Practical Guide to Impact Measurement (First Draft).* Brussels: EVPA Knowledge Center, 2012.

———. "What is VP?" Brussels: EVPA Knowledge Centre, 2012. evpa.eu.com/knowledge-centre/what-is-vp/. Accessed July 13, 2012.

Evenett, Rupert, and Karl H. Richter. "Making Good in Social Impact Investment: Opportunities in an Emerging Asset Class." *The Social Investment Business* and *TheCityUK* (October 2011): 17–23.

Flandez, Raymund. "Peer Pressure Makes Donors Give More Than Planned." *Chronicle of Philanthropy*, March 2013, http://philanthropy.com/article/Peer-Pressure-Makes-Donors/138055/.

Forbes. "When Measuring Social Impact, We Need to Move Beyond Counting." July 15, 2013.

Forti, Matthew. "Now, What Exactly Should We Measure?" www.bridgespan.org, accessed July 7, 2011.

———. "Don't Let Conventional Measurement Wisdom Fragment Your Impact." *Stanford Social Innovation Review,* August 22, 2011.

———. "Six Theory of Change Pitfalls to Avoid." *Stanford Social Innovation Review,* May 23, 2012.

———. "Measurement That Benefits the Measured." *Stanford Social Innovation Review,* June 25, 2012.

———. "Actionable Measurement at the Gates Foundation." *Stanford Social Innovation Review,* August 29, 2012.

Forti, Matthew, and Michaela Kerrissey. "Measuring to Scale What Works at the YMCA." *Stanford Social Innovation Review,* December 5, 2012.

Forti, Matthew, and Colin Murphy. "What Obama's Campaign Can Teach Nonprofits about Measurement: Five Measurement Practices That Obama's Campaign and High-Performing Nonprofits Have in Common." *Stanford Social Innovation Review*, January 22, 2013.

Frank, Roger. "Impact Investing: What Exactly Is New?" *Stanford Social Innovation Review* 10, no. 1 (Winter 2012).

Fremont-Smith, M. R. *Governing Nonprofit Organizations: Federal and State Law and Regulation.* Cambridge, MA: Belknap Press of Harvard University Press, 2004.

Friend, J. K., and A. Hickling. *Planning Under Pressure: The Strategic Choice Approach,* 2nd edn. Oxford: Heinemann, 1997.

Fruchterman, Jim. "For Love or Lucre." *Stanford Social Innovation Review* 9, no. 2 (Spring 2011): 42–47.

Frumkin, Peter. *Strategic Giving: The Art and Science of Philanthropy.* Chicago: University of Chicago Press, 2006.

FSG. "Fix That Fits: What Is the Right Evaluation for Social Innovation?" *Forbes India*, November 28, 2012.

Gair, Cynthia. *A Report from the Good Ship SROI.* San Francisco: Roberts Foundation, 2002.

———. *SROI Act II: A Call to Action for Next-Generation SROI.* San Francisco: Roberts Foundation, 2009.

Gamble, Jamie A. *A Developmental Evaluation Primer.* Montreal: J. W. McConnell Family Foundation, 2006.

Garrigo, Silvia M. "Corporate Responsibility at Chevron." *Utah Environmental Law Review* 31, no. 1 (2011): 129–33.

Gates, Bill. "The Way We Give." *Fortune,* January 22, 2007.

———. "Bill Gates: My Plan to Fix the World's Biggest Problems." *Wall Street Journal,* January 25, 2013.

Gelfand, Sarah. "Why IRIS?" *Stanford Social Innovation Review,* October 10, 2012.

Geneva Global. *Benequity Solutions: Monitoring Handbook,* ver. 1.0. London: Geneva Global, 2007.

———. *Geneva Global's Solutions: Due Diligence Handbook,* ver. 2.0. London: Geneva Global, 2007.

———. *Geneva Global Brand Table.* London: Geneva Global, 2010.

———. "FAQ: Frequently Asked Questions." London: Geneva Global, 2012.

Gertler, Paul J., Sebastian Martinez, Patrick Premand, Laura B. Rawlings, and Christel M. J. Vermeersch. *Impact Evaluation in Practice.* Washington, DC: World Bank Publications, 2010.

Giudice, Phil, and Kevin Bolduc. *Assessment Performance at the Robert Wood Johnson Foundation: A Case Study.* Cambridge, MA: Center for Effective Philanthropy, 2004.

Giving Pledge, LLC. *The Giving Pledge,* http://Givingpledge.Org/#Bill+_Gates, accessed April 4, 2012

Giving USA. *The Annual Report on Philanthropy for the Year 2011.* Chicago: Giving USA, 2012.

GiveWell. "VillageReach Update (2011–2012)." Givewell.org, www.givewell.org/international/charities/villagereach/updates/2011-2012, accessed March 26, 2012.

GlobalGiving Foundation. "Storytelling Project: Turning Anecdotes into Useful Data." Globalgiving.org, www.globalgiving.org/stories/, accessed June 25, 2013.

Global Impact Investing Network. *Data Driven: A Performance Analysis for the Impact Investing Industry.* New York: GIIN and IRIS, 2011.

———. *Impact-based Incentive Structures: Aligning Fund Manager Compensation with Social and Environmental Performance.* New York: GIIN, 2011.

———. "GIIN Launches Public IRIS User Registry." GIIN, www.theglin.org, September 9, 2012.

———. "Investor Spotlight: Michael Milken." GIIN, www.theglin.org, March 28, 2013.

———. "Small and Growing Business Metrics (from ANDE)." GIIN, http://iris.theglin.org, accessed June 16, 2013.

Global Impact Investing Rating System. "Update on B Lab and GIIRS Research Project." CASE at Duke, www.caseatduke.org.

———. *Impact Investing: Challenges and Opportunities to Scale (2011 Progress Report).* Wayne, PA: Global Impact Investing Rating System, 2012.

———. "Company Rating Report." GIIRS, http://giirs.org/storage/documents/CompanyReports/sample_company_report.pdf, accessed July 4, 2013.

Global Reporting Initiative. *Sustainability Reporting Guidelines & NGO Sector Supplement,* ver. 3.0/NGOSS final version. Amsterdam: Global Reporting Initiative, 2011.

———. *G4 Sector Disclosures: Financial Services.* Amsterdam: Global Reporting Initiative, 2013.

Godeke, Steven, et al. *Solutions for Impact Investors: From Strategy to Implementation.* New York: Rockefeller Philanthropy Advisors, 2009.

Goldseker, Sharna, and Michael Moody. "Young Wealthy Donors Bring Tastes for Risk, Hands-on Involvement to Philanthropy." *Chronicle of Philanthropy,* May 19, 2013.

Gose, Ben. "Kresge Seeks to Do More Without Spending More." *Chronicle of Philanthropy,* March 24, 2013.

Grace, K. S., and Alan L. Wendroff. *High-Impact Philanthropy: How Donors, Boards, and Nonprofit Organizations Can Transform Communities.* New York: Wiley, 2001.

Grant, Heather McLeod, and Leslie R. Crutchfield. "Creating High-Impact Nonprofits." *Stanford Social Innovation Review* 5, no. 4 (Fall 2007): 32–41.

Grantmakers for Effective Organizations. "Assessing the Impact." *General Operating Support* 2, 2008. Washington, DC: Grantmakers for Effective Organizations, 2008.

———. *Evaluation in Philanthropy: Perspectives from the Field.* Washington, DC: Grantmakers for Effective Organizations, 2009.

———. "How Do We Approach Impact and Evaluation in the Context of Scale?" in *A Learning Initiative of Scaling What Works.* Washington, DC: Grantmakers for Effective Organizations, 2011.

———. "How Does Financial Sustainability Relate to Growth—And What Can Grantmakers Do to Support It?" in *A Learning Initiative of Scaling What Works.* Washington, DC: Grantmakers for Effective Organizations, 2011.

———. "How Can Grantmakers Support Readiness to Scale Impact?" in *A Learning Initiative of Scaling What Works.* Washington, DC: Grantmakers for Effective Organizations, 2011.

———. *Pathways to Grow Impact: Philanthropy's Role in the Journey.* Washington, DC: Grantmakers for Effective Organizations, 2013.

Grantmakers in Health. *Guide to Impact Investing.* Washington, DC: Grantmakers in Health, 2011.

Green, Elizabeth. "Study: $75M Teacher Pay Initiative Did Not Improve Achievement." GothamSchools.org., March 7, 2011.

Hammitt, James K. "Valuing Lifesaving: Is Contingent Valuation Useful?" *Risk in Perspective* 8, no. 3 (2000): 1–6.

Hanleybrown, Fay, John Kania, and Mark Kramer. "Channeling Change: Making Collective Impact Work." *Stanford Social Innovation Review,* January 26, 2012.

Harji, Karim, and Edward T. Jackson. *Accelerating Impact: Achievements, Challenges and What's Next in Building the Impact Investing Industry.* Ottawa: E. T. Jackson and Associates Ltd., 2012.

Harris, Erin. "An Introduction to Theory of Change." *Evaluation Exchange* 11, no. 2 (2005): 12.

Heath, Thomas. "Carlyle Group's David Rubenstein Practices 'Patriotic Philanthropy.'" *Washington Post,* June 30, 2013.

Herman, R. P. *The HIP Investor: Make Bigger Profits by Building a Better World.* Hoboken, NJ: Wiley, 2010.

Herrera, Adriana. "Questioning the TOMS Shoes Model for Social Enterprise." *New York Times,* March 19, 2013.

Herrero, Sonia. *Integrated Monitoring: A Practical Manual for Organizations That Want to Achieve Results.* Berlin: inProgress UG, 2012.

HOPE Consulting. *Money for Good: The US Market for Impact Investments and Charitable Gifts from Individual Donors and Investors.* San Francisco: HOPE Consulting, 2010.

———. *Money for Good II: Driving Dollars to the Highest-Performance Nonprofits.* San Francisco: HOPE Consulting, 2011.

Hornsby, Adrian, and Gabi Blumberg. *The Good Investor: A Book of Best Impact Practice.* London: Investing for Good, 2013.

Hudson, Sophie. "Communicating Impact: The Next Challenge." *The Guardian,* August 31, 2012.

Huffington Post. "Food Waste: Half of All Food Ends up Thrown Away," January 10, 2013.

Hundley, Kris, and Kendall Taggart. "Above the Law: America's Worst Charities." *CNN,* June 13, 2013.

Hunter, David E. K. "Daniel and the Rhinoceros." *Evaluation and Program Planning* 29, no. 2 (2006): 180–85.

———. "Using a Theory of Change Approach to Build Organizational Strength, Capacity and Sustainability with Not-for-Profit Organizations in the Human Services Sector." *Evaluation and Program Planning* 29, no. 2 (2006): 193–200.

———. *Working Hard—and Working Well: A Practical Guide to Performance Management for Leaders Serving Children, Adults, and Families.* Hamden, CT: Hunter Consulting, 2013.

Idealware. *The State of Nonprofit Data.* Portland, OR: NTEN, 2012.

India Knowledge@Wharton. "Philanthropy in India Is Taking Its Own Route." *India Knowledge@Wharton,* March 21, 2013.

Industree Crafts. *Social Accounts – Cycle 2.* Bangalore: Industree, 2009.

———. *Social Accounts – Cycle 3 Fy 2011–12.* Bangalore: Industree, 2012.

InProgress. "Offering Support to Non-Profits." inprogressweb.com, accessed June 28, 2012.

Investing for Good. *Investing for Good Dictionary of Indicators.* London: Investing for Good, 2012.

IRIS. *Collecting and Reporting Poverty Data: Using the Progress out of Poverty Index Toolkit with the Impact Reporting and Investment Standards.* New York: IRIS, 2013.

Jagpal, Niki. *Criteria for Philanthropy at Its Best: Benchmarks to Assess and Enhance Grantmaker Impact.* Washington, DC: National Committee for Responsive Philanthropy, 2009.

James Irvine Foundation. *A Framework to Assess the Performance of the James Irvine Foundation. Evaluation Policies and Guidelines.* San Francisco: James Irvine Foundation, 2011.

Javits, Carla I. *REDF's Current Approach to SROI.* San Francisco: Roberts Foundation, 2008.

Jaworski, Kathi. "What Should Corporate America Do for Nonprofits?" *Nonprofit Quarterly,* June 25, 2012.

Jensen, Brennen. "Charities Get Change to Test Innovations and Win Prizes in Scholarly Experiment." *Chronicle of Philanthropy,* April 7, 2013.

Jethi, Pradeep. "What a Stock Exchange Could Do for Social Business." *The Guardian,* June 6, 2013.

Johnston, Katie. "Nonprofits Quantify Their Success." *Boston Globe,* August 15, 2012.

J.P. Morgan. "Perspectives on Progress: The Impact Investor Survey." *Global Social Finance,* January 7, 2013.

KaBOOM! "Why Play Matters," http://kaboom.org/take_action/play_research/why_play_matters/, accessed June 5, 2013.

Kail, Angela. "Using 'Theory of Change' to Measure Your Charity's Impact: A New Approach Is Helping Charities Prioritize Activities and Plan for the Future." *The Guardian,* April 19, 2012.

Kanani, Rahim. "An In-depth Interview with Sally Osberg, President and CEO of The Skoll Foundation." *Huffington Post,* March 22, 2011.

Kania, John, and Mark Kramer. "Collective Impact." *Stanford Social Innovation Review* 9, no. 1 (Winter 2011): 36–41.

Kanter, B., and Katie Delahaye Paine. *Measuring the Networked Nonprofit: Using Data to Change the World.* San Francisco: Jossey-Bass, 2012.

Kaplan, Robert S., and Allen S. Grossman. "The Emerging Capital Market for Non-profits: How Market Mechanisms from the Private Sector Could Energize the Nonprofit World." *Harvard Business Review,* October 2010, pp. 114, 116.

Kapstein, Ethan, and René Kim. *The Socio-Economic Impact of Newmont Ghana Gold Limited.* Haarlem: Stratcomm Africa, 2011.

Karlan, Dean, and Jacob Appel. *More Than Good Intentions: How a New Economics Is Helping to Solve Global Poverty.* New York: Penguin, 2011.

Karlan, Dean, John A. List, and Eldar Shafir. "Small Matches and Charitable Giving: Evidence from a Natural Field Experiment." *Journal of Public Economics* (November 2010): 344–50.

Karnani, Aneel. "Mandatory CSR in India: A Bad Proposal." *Stanford Social Innovation,* May 20, 2013.

Karoly, Lynn A. *Valuing Benefits in Benefit-Cost Studies of Social Programs.* Santa Monica, CA: RAND Corporation, 2008.

Katz, Russel. "FDA: Evidentiary Standards for Drug Development and Approval." *NeuroRx: Journal of the American Society for Experimental NeuroTherapeutics* 1 (June 2004): 307–16.

Kaufmann, Katherine, and Robert Searle. *The Annie E. Casey Foundation: Answering the Hard Question: "What Difference Are We Making?"* Boston: Bridgespan Group, 2007.

Kickul, Jill, Christine Janssen-Selvadurai, and Mark D. Griffiths. "A Blended Value Framework for Educating the Next Cadre of Social Entrepreneurs." *Academy of Management Learning & Education* 11, no. 3 (2012): 479–93.

KL Felicitas Foundation. "About Us." www.klfelicitasfoundation.org, accessed January 15, 2012.

———. "Impact Investing Strategy Overview." www.klfelicitasfoundation.org, accessed January 31, 2012.

Knickman, James R., and Kelly A. Hunt. "The Robert Wood Johnson Foundation's Approach to Evaluation," in *The Robert Wood Johnson Foundation Anthology: To Improve Health and Health Care,* vol. 11. San Francisco: Jossey-Bass, 2007.

Knowledge@Wharton. "Social Finance's Tracy Palandjian on the Next Generation of Responsible Investing." http://knowledge.wharton.upenn.edu, March 14, 2012.

———. "Social Impact Bonds: Can a Market Prescription Cure Social Ills?" http://knowledge.wharton.upenn.edu, September 12, 2012.

———. "B Lab's Bart Houlahan: Building More Socially Responsible Corporations." http://knowledge.wharton.upenn.edu, November 7, 2012.

———. "Impact Investing's Next Hurdle: Better Networking." http://knowledge.
wharton.upenn.edu, November 30, 2012.

Koh, Harvey, Ashish Karamchandani, and Robert Katz. "From Blueprint to Scale:
The Case for Philanthropy in Impact Investing." *Monitor*, April 2012.

Korn, Melissa. "How to Turn Your Generosity into Philanthropy." *Wall Street Journal*,
June 6, 2013.

Kramer, Mark R. *Measuring Innovation: Evaluation in the Field of Social Entrepreneurship*. Boston: FSG, 2005.

———. "Catalytic Philanthropy." *Stanford Social Innovation Review* 7, no. 4 (Fall 2009):
30–35.

Kramer, Mark R., and Sarah E. Cooch. "The Power of Strategic Mission Investing."
Stanford Social Innovation Review 5, no. 4 (Fall 2007): 43–51.

Kramer, Mark R., Rebecca Graves, Jason Hirschhorn, and Leigh Fiske (2007). *From
Insights to Action: New Directions in Foundation Evaluation*. Boston: FSG; Menlo
Park, CA: William and Flora Hewlett Foundation.

Kramer, Mark, Marcie Parkhurst, and Lalitha Vaidyanathan. *Breakthroughs in Shared
Measurement and Social Impact*. Boston: FSG Social Impact Advisors, 2009.

Kubzansky, Michael, Ansulie Cooper, and Victoria Barbary. *Promise and Progress:
Market-Based Solutions to Poverty in Africa*. Cambridge, MA: Monitor Group, 2011.

Lawrence, Steven, and Reina Mukai. *Key Facts on Mission Investing*. New York: Foundation Center, 2011.

Lee, Stephanie, Steve Aos, Elizabeth Drake, Annie Pennucci, Marna Miller, and Laurie Anderson. *Return on Investment: Evidence-Based Options to Improve Statewide Outcomes*. Olympia, WA: Washington State Institute for Public Policy, 2012.

———. *Return on Investment: Evidence-Based Options to Improve Statewide Outcomes:
Technical Appendix Methods and User-Manual*. Olympia, WA: Washington State
Institute for Public Policy, 2012.

Legatum Foundation. *Legatum Foundation Fund I: 2007–2010 Philanthropic Investment
Report*. Dubai: Legatum Foundation, 2011.

Lehr, David. *Microfranchising at the Base of the Pyramid*. New York: Acumen Fund,
2008.

Leonard, Herman B., Marc J. Epstein, and Wendy Smith. *Digital Divide Data: A Social
Enterprise in Action*. Boston: Harvard Business School, 2007.

Leonard, Herman B., Marc J. Epstein, and Melissa Tritter. *Opportunity International:
Measuring and Mission*. Boston: Harvard Business School, 2007.

———. *Absolute Return for Kids*. Boston: Harvard Business School, 2008.

Leonard, Herman B., Marc J. Epstein, and Laura Winig. *Playgrounds and Performance:
Results Management at KaBOOM! (A)*. Boston: Harvard Business School, 2005.

———. *Playgrounds and Performance: Results Management at KaBOOM! (B)*. Boston:
Harvard Business School, 2005.

———. *Playgrounds and Performance: Results Management at KaBOOM! (C)*. Boston:
Harvard Business School, 2005.

Lifsher, Marc. "Businesses Seek State's New 'Benefit Corporation' Status." *Los Ange-
les Times*, January 4, 2012.

Lilly Family School of Philanthropy. *The Center on Philanthropy Panel Study*. Bloomington, IN: Lilly Family School of Philanthropy, Indiana University, 2009.

Lim, Terence. *Measuring the Value of Corporate Philanthropy: Social Impact, Business
Benefits, and Investor Returns*. New York: Committee Encouraging Corporate Philanthropy, 2010.

Lingane, Alison, and Sara Olsen. "Guidelines for Social Return on Investment." *California Management Review* 46, no. 3 (Spring 2004): 116–35.

London, Ted. "Making Better Investment at the Base of the Pyramid." *Harvard Business Review*, May 2009.

Lopez, Rachel. "Giving to Charity Just to Avoid Tax? Make Sure Your Money Works as Hard as You Do." *Hindustan Times*, December 9, 2012.

Maas, Karen, and Kellie Liket. "Social Impact Measurement: Classification of Methods." In *Environmental Management Accounting and Supply Chain Management*, vol. 27 of *Eco-Efficiency in Industry and Science*. Dordrecht: Springer Science + Business Media BV, 2011.

Maclennan, Alison. "Should Charities Measure Efficiency?" *The Guardian*, April 26, 2012.

Mahmood, Mahboob, and Filipe Santos. *UBS-INSEAD Study on Family Philanthropy in Asia*. Zurich: UBS/Fontainebleau: INSEAD, 2011.

Mair, Vibeka. "Report on Impact Measurement Highlights Importance of the Story." www.civilsociety.co.uk, March 11, 2013.

Margulies, Paula. "Linda Rottenberg's High-Impact Endeavor." *Strategy+Business* 66 (Spring 2012).

Mark, M. M., Gary T. Henry, and George Julnes. *Evaluation: An Integrated Framework for Understanding, Guiding, and Improving Policies and Programs*. San Francisco: Jossey-Bass, 2000.

Markets for Good. *Upgrading the Information Infrastructure for Social Change*. N.p.: Markets for Good, 2012, www.marketsforgood.com.

Marquis, Christopher, Andrew Klaber, and Bobbi Thomason. *B Lab: Building a New Sector of the Economy*. Boston: Harvard Business School, 2010.

Massarsky, Cynthia W., and John F. Gillespie. *The State of Scaling Social Impact: Results of a National Study of Nonprofits*. New York: Growth Philanthropy Network, 2013.

Mathison, Sandra, ed. *Encyclopedia of Evaluation*. Thousand Oaks, CA: Sage Publications, 2005.

Mayne, John. *Addressing Attribution Through Contribution Analysis: Using Performance Measures Sensibly*. Ottawa: Auditor General of Canada, 1999.

McCormick, Steve. "Changing: To Make Greater Change." President's Corner; Gordon and Betty Moore Foundation, July 2, 2010, www.moore.org.

McCray, J. *Is Grantmaking Getting Smarter? A National Study of Philanthropic Practice*. Washington, DC: Grantmakers for Effective Organizations, 2011.

McCreless, Michael, and Brain Trelstad. "A GPS System for Social Impact." *Stanford Social Innovation Review* 10, no. 4 (Fall 2012): 21–22.

McGill, Larry. "Why Measuring Impact Remains an Elusive Goal." *Philantopic*, November 15, 2011.

McKinsey & Company. *Learning for Social Impact: What Foundations Can Do*. New York: McKinsey, 2010.

———. *From Potential to Action: Bringing Social Impact Bonds to the US*. New York: McKinsey, 2012.

McVeigh, Patrick. "Impact Investing Done Right: No Shortcuts to Social Change." *Triplepundit*, May 18, 2012.

McVeigh, Tracy. "World Poverty Is Shrinking Rapidly, New Index Reveals." *The Guardian*, March 16, 2013.

MDRC. "Lessons from Three Decades of Research." *MDRC.org*, accessed June 28, 2012.

Mento, Maria Di. "Affluent Donors Prefer Restricted Gifts." *Chronicle of Philanthropy*, September 18, 2012.

———. "Why $1 Billion to Aid the Sick Did Little Good." *Chronicle of Philanthropy*, June 16, 2013.

———. "Grant Makers Open Up about Failed Projects in Hopes Others Can Learn from Them." *Chronicle Of Philanthropy*, June 16, 2013.

Mercy Corps. *Design, Monitoring and Evaluation Guidebook*. Portland, OR: Mercy Corps, 2005.

Meyerson, Adam. "When Philanthropy Goes Wrong." *Wall Street Journal*, March 10, 2012.

Minhas, Shahryar, and Susan Parker. *Robert Wood Johnson Foundation: Frequent Check-ups Make for Healthier Funding Relationships*. Cambridge, MA: Center For Effective Philanthropy, 2011.

Mitchell, Jennifer. *Industry-Based Sustainability Standards to Guide Corporations and Investors on Material Issue for Disclosure in the Form 10-K*. San Francisco: Sustainability Accounting Standards Board, 2012.

Mitchell, R. K., B. R. Agle, and D. J. Wood. "Toward a Theory of Stakeholder Identification and Salience: Defining the Principle of Who and What Really Counts." *Academy of Management Review* 22, no. 4 (1997): 853–86.

Monitor Institute. *Investing for Social & Environmental Impact: A Design for Catalyzing an Emerging Industry*. San Francisco: Monitor Institute, 2009.

Morino, Mario. *Leap of Reason: Managing to Outcomes in an Era of Scarcity*. Washington, DC: Venture Philanthropy Partners, 2011.

———. "Relentless: Investing in Leaders Who Stop at Nothing in Pursuit of Greater Social Impact." Leapofreason.org, April 27, 2012.

Morra Imas, L. G., and Ray C. Gist. *The Road to Results: Designing and Conducting Effective Development Evaluations*. Washington, DC: World Bank, 2009.

National Council for Voluntary Organisations. *The Code of Good Impact Practice*. London: NCVO, 2013.

National Park Service. "Giving Statistics," www.Nps.Gov/Partnerships/Fundraising_Individuals_Statistics.Htm, accessed June 16, 2013.

Nee, Eric. "Impact Investing Grows Up." *Stanford Social Innovation Review*, November 14, 2012.

Newcomer, K. E. *Using Performance Measurement to Improve Public Nonprofit Programs*. San Francisco: Jossey-Bass, 1997.

New Philanthropy Capital. *Inspiring Impact: Working Together for a Bigger Impact in the UK Social Sector*. London: NPC, 2011.

———. *Mapping Outcomes for Social Investment*. London: NPC, SROI Network, Investing for Good, and Big Society Capital, Version 1.0, 2013.

New Philanthropy Capital et al. *Principles of Good Impact Reporting for Charities and Social Enterprises*. London: ACEVO, Charity Finance Group, Institute of Fundraising, NCVO, NPC, Small Charities Coalition, Social Enterprise UK, SROI Network, 2012.

Nicholls, Jeremy, et al. *A Guide to Social Return on Investment*. London: Cabinet Office, 2009.

Nidumolu, Ram, Kevin Kramer, and Jochen Zeitz. "Connecting Heart to Head." *Stanford Social Innovation Review* 10, no. 1 (Winter 2012).

Niggemann, Gesche, and Stefan Brägger. "Socially Responsible Investments (SRI)— Introducing Impact Investing." *Wealth Management Research*, August 11, 2011.

Nike, Inc. "III. Impact Areas: People & Culture," www.Nikeresponsibility.Com/ Report/Content/Chapter/People-And-Culture, accessed June 16, 2013.

Nonprofit Finance Fund and FSC. *Root Capital 2009–2013 Private Offering Memorandum*. New York: Nonprofit Finance Fund and FSC, 2013.

Nonprofit Finance Fund and The White House. *Pay for Success: Investing in What Works*. New York: Nonprofit Finance Fund, 2012.

Noonan, Kathleen, and Katherina Rosqueta. *"I'm Not Rockefeller": 33 High Net Worth Philanthropists Discuss Their Approach to Giving*. Philadelphia: Center for High Impact Philanthropy, 2008.

Northwest Area Foundation, Annie E. Casey Foundation, and Pacific Community Ventures. "Invest Northwest: Assessing Social Return in 2011." St. Paul, MN: Northwest Area Foundation, 2011.

Norton, Michel. "Social Franchising and Social Business." Paper presented at Graduate School of Business Research Seminar, University of Cape Town, 2010.

———. "Social Franchising: A Mechanism for Scaling Up to Meet Social Need." Paper presented at Graduate School of Business Research Seminar, University of Cape Town, 2011.

Novogratz, Jacqueline. "Making a Case for Patient Capital." *Bloomberg Businessweek*, October 24–30, 2011.

———. "If Not Now, When? Pakistan's Social Entrepreneurs Are Making a Difference." *Innovation*.

O'Donnell, Jayne. "BBB's Charity Ratings, Seal of Approval under Fire." *USA Today*, December 27, 2012.

Ógáin, Eibhlín Ní, Tris Lumley, and David Pritchard. *Making an Impact: Impact Measurement among Charities and Social Enterprises in the UK*. London: NPC, 2012.

Ógáin, Eibhlín Ní, Marina Svistak, and Lucy de Las Casas. *Blueprint for Shared Measurement: Developing, Designing and Implementing Shared Approaches to Impact Measurement*. London: NPC and Inspiring Impact, 2013.

Orenstein, Peggy. "Our Feel-Good War on Breast Cancer." *New York Times*, April 25, 2013.

Palfrey, John, and Catherine Bracy. *Review of the MIT Center for Future Civic Media*. Miami: Knight Foundation/Cambridge, MA: Center for Future Civic Media, 2011.

PATH. "Path: A Catalyst for Global Health," www.path.org.

Paton, Rob. *Managing and Measuring Social Enterprises*. Thousand Oaks, CA: Sage, 2003.

Penna, R. M. *The Nonprofit Outcomes Toolbox: A Complete Guide to Program Effectiveness, Performance Measurement, and Results*. Hoboken, NJ: Wiley, 2011.

Perlroth, Nicole. "Non-Profit Couch Surfing Raises Millions in Funding." *Forbes*, August 24, 2011.

Perry, Suzanne. "3 Major Charity Groups Ask Donors to Stop Focusing on Overhead Costs." *Chronicle of Philanthropy*, June 17, 2013.

Porter, Michael E. *Corporate Philanthropy: Taking The High Ground*. Boston: FSG, 2003.

Porter, Michael E., Greg Hills, Marc Pfitzer, Sonja Patscheke, and Elizabeth Hawkins.

Measuring Shared Value: How to Unlock Value by Linking Social and Business Results. Boston: FSG, 2012.

Porter, Michael E., and Mark R. Kramer. "Philanthropy's New Agenda: Creating Value." *Harvard Business Review* (November/December 1999): 121–30.

———. "The Competitive Advantage of Corporate Philanthropy." *Harvard Business Review* (December 2002): 5–16.

Pozen, Robert C., and Heather L. Kline. "7 Ways To Ensure Gifts for Medical Research Do More Good." *Chronicle of Philanthropy*, February 5, 2012.

Preskill, Hallie, and Tanya Beer. *Evaluating Social Innovation.* Boston: FSG/Center for Evaluation Innovation, 2012.

Preston, Caroline. "Some 70% of Grant Makers Say Foundations Have Few Measures to Test Their Effectiveness." *Chronicle of Philanthropy*, July 14, 2010.

———. "A Potential $15-Billion Windfall for Effective Nonprofits." *Chronicle of Philanthropy*, November 30, 2011.

———. "Who's Behind the Evaluation Curtain." *Chronicle of Philanthropy*, August 1, 2012.

———. "Nonprofits Are Dissatisfied with Foundations' Evaluation Efforts." *Chronicle of Philanthropy*, September 13, 2012.

———. "Bill Clinton Urges Donor to Think about Results from the Start." *Chronicle of Philanthropy*, September 24, 2012.

———. "Bloomberg Philanthropies Unveils Web Site and Priorities." *Chronicle of Philanthropy*, April 30, 2013.

———. "Applying for Grants Is Still a Burden, Say Fundraisers." *Chronicle of Philanthropy*, May 19, 2013.

PULSE Wiki. "3. Impact Reporting and Investment Standards (IRIS) Information." *Pulse Wiki,* accessed January 8, 2013.

PUMA. "PUMA Completes First Environmental Profit and Loss Account Which Values Impacts at €145 Million." Web. Munich, November 2011.

———. "Environmental Key Performance Indicators Methodology." Web. Munich, November, 2011.

———. "THE PUMAVision." http://about.puma.com/wp-content/themes/about-PUMA_theme/media/pdf/PUMAVision.pdf. Accessed June 16, 2013.

Raikes, Jeff. *Progress and Partnerships; 2010 Annual Report, CEO Letter. The Bill & Melinda Gates Foundation.* Seattle: Bill and Melinda Gates Foundation, 2011.

Ralser, Tom. *ROI for Nonprofits.* Hoboken, NJ: Wiley, 2007.

Rangan, V. Kasturi, Sarah Appleby, and Laura Moon. *The Promise of Impact Investing.* Boston: Harvard Business School, 2012.

Reddy, Nidhi, Lalitha Vaidyanathan, Katyayani Balasubramanian, Kavitha Gorapalli, and Sharad Sharma. *Catalytic Philanthropy in India: How India's Ultra-High-Net-Worth Philanthropists Are Helping Solve Large-Scale Social Problems.* Boston: FSG, 2012.

REDF. *SROI Reports: Overview and Guide.* San Francisco: REDF, 2000.

———. *SROI Methodology.* San Francisco: REDF, 2001.

Reed, Ehren, and Johanna Morariu. *State of Evaluation: Evaluation Practice and Capacity in the Nonprofit Sector.* Washington, DC: Innovation Network, 2010.

Reinhardt, Uwe E. "How Efficient Is Private Charity?" *New York Times,* January 14, 2011.

Reuters. "Philanthropy Becoming New Status Symbol for Wealthy." *New York Times*, August 11, 2010.

Rickey, Benedict, Tris Lumley, and Eibhlín Ní Ógáin. *Journey to Greater Impact: Six Charities That Learned to Measure Better.* London: New Philanthropy Capital, 2011.

Ridge, Javan B. *Evaluation Techniques: For Difficult to Measure Programs.* Bloomington, IN: Xlibris, 2010.

Riley, Jason L. "Was the $5 Billion Worth It?" *Wall Street Journal*, July 23, 2011.

Robert Wood Johnson Foundation. *Helping Americans Lead Healthier Lives and Get the Care They Need.* Princeton, NJ: Robert Wood Johnson Foundation, 2008

———. *Assessing Our Impact.* Princeton, NJ: Robert Wood Johnson Foundation, 2011.

———. *2011 Assessment Report.* Princeton, NJ: Robert Wood Johnson Foundation, 2011.

Rockefeller Philanthropy Advisors. *Your Philanthropy Roadmap.* New York: Rockefeller Philanthropy Advisors, n.d.

———. *The Giving Commitment: Knowing Your Motivations.* New York: Rockefeller Philanthropy Advisors, n.d.

———. *Assessing Impact.* New York: Rockefeller Philanthropy Advisors, n.d.

Rodin, Judith, and Nancy MacPherson. "Shared Outcomes" in *Advancing Evaluation Practices in Philanthropy*, sponsored supplement to *Stanford Social Innovation Review* 10, no. 3 (Summer 2012).

Root Cause. *Learning from Performance Measurement: Investing in What Works.* Cambridge, MA: Root Cause, 2010.

Rosenberg, Tina. "Putting Charities to the Test." Opinionator, *New York Times*, December 5, 2012.

Rosenzweig, William, Catherine Clark, David Long, and Sara Olsen. *Double Bottom Line Project Report: Assessing Social Impact in Double Bottom Lines Ventures (Methods Catalog).* Berkeley, CA: Center for Responsible Business, University of California, Berkeley, 2004.

Rossi, P. H., and H. E. Freeman. *Evaluation: A Systematic Approach.* Thousand Oaks, CA: Sage, 1985.

Salamon, Lester M., S. Wojciech Sokolowski, and Stephanie L. Gellen. *Holding The Fort: Nonprofit Employment during a Decade of Turmoil.* Nonprofit Economic Data Bulletin no. 39. Baltimore: Johns Hopkins University, 2012.

Salls, Manda. "Making Social Investment Accountable." *Harvard Business School Working Knowledge*, November 4, 2004.

Salman, Saba. "Impact Measurement Is Essential to Winning Public Service Contracts." *The Guardian*, January 24, 2013.

Salmon, Felix. "Philanthropy: You're Doing It Wrong." *Thomas Reuters*, December 26, 2012.

Samuelson, Judith. "All Business Should Have a Public Purpose, Not Just 'B-Corps.'" *Huff Post Business*, July 29, 2011.

Sasse, Craig M., and Ryan T. Trahan. *Rethinking the New Corporate Philanthropy.* Bloomington, IN: Indiana University, Kelley School of Business, 2006.

Saul, Jason. *The End of Fundraising: Raise More Money by Selling Your Impact.* San Francisco: Jossey-Bass, 2011.

Scharpnick, Matthew. "Can You Sum Up Your Charity's Work in One Simple Tag Line?" *Chronicle of Philanthropy*, January 17, 2013.

Scher, Eddie. "Sally Osberg at the Commonwealth Club, July 2010: Social Entrepreneurship and the Art of Motorcycle Maintenance." www.skollfoundation.org, 2010.

Schorr, Lisbeth B. "Broader Evidence for Bigger Impact." *Stanford Social Innovation Review* 10, no. 4 (Fall 2012),

Schrage, Michael. "The Real Reason Organizations Resist Analytics." *HBR Blog Network, Harvard Business Review*, January 29, 2013.

Serafrin, George, Paul M. Healy, and Aldo Sesia. *Oddo Securities: ESG Integration.* Boston: Harvard Business School, 2011.

Serwer, Andy. "The Legend of Robin Hood." *Fortune*, September 8, 2006.

Showstack, Jonathan, and Nicole Wolfe. *RWJF Retrospective Series: Chronic Care Programs.* Princeton, NJ: Robert Wood Johnson Foundation, 2012.

Sirull, Beth. "Measurement Matters: Maximizing Total Return on Responsible Investments in Private Equity." Paper presented at UN PRI Academic Conference, Ottawa, 2009.

Small, Deborah A., George Loewenstein, and Paul Slovic. "Sympathy and Callousness: The Impact of Deliberative Thought on Donations to Identifiable and Statistical Victims." *Organizational Behavior and Human Decision Processes* 102 (2007): 143–53.

Snibbe, Alana Conner. "Drowning in Data." *Stanford Social Innovation Review* 4, no. 3 (Fall 2006): 39–45.

Snyman, Eugene, Margaret Schlott, and Jessica Matthews. *Driving Change Through Mission-Related Investing: What Investors Need to Know.* Sydney: Cambridge Associates, 2011.

Social Enterprise UK. *Social Enterprise and Youth Policy Paper.* London: Social Enterprise UK, 2012.

Social Impact Exchange. "Philanthropy Group Launches Index of High-Impact Nonprofits." PR Newswire, November 25, 2012.

Social Investment Task Force. *Social Investment Manual: An Introduction for Social Entrepreneurs.* Geneva: Schwab Foundation for Social Entrepreneurship, 2011.

SROI Network. *A Framework for Approaches to SROI Analysis.* Haddington, Scotland: SROI Network, 2005.

Starr, Kevin. "Go Big or Go Home: One Foundation's Approach to Maximum Impact." *Stanford Social Innovation Review* 6, no. 4 (Fall 2008).

———. "The Eight-Word Mission Statement." *Stanford Social Innovation Review*, September 18, 2012.

Stern, Ken. *With Charity for All: Why Charities Are Failing and a Better Way to Give.* New York: Doubleday, 2013.

Strom, Stephanie. "To Help Donors Choose, Web Site Alters How It Sizes Up Charities." *New York Times*, November 26, 2010.

———. "Donors Weigh the Ideals of Meaningful Giving." *New York Times*, November 1, 2011.

———. "To Advance Their Cause, Foundations Buy Stocks." *New York Times*, November 24, 2011.

Sullivan, Paul. "Philanthropists Weigh the Returns of Doing Good." *New York Times*, September 28, 2012.

———. "Two Parts for Charitable Giving: From the Head or from the Heart." *New York Times*, June 28, 2013.

Swartz, Jon. "Tech's New Entrepreneurial Approach to Philanthropy." *USA Today,* February 11, 2013.

Teles, Steven, and Mark Schmitt. "The Elusive Craft of Evaluating Advocacy." *Stanford Social Innovation Review* 9, no. 3 (Summer 2011): 39–43.

Thornley, Ben. "Solidifying the Business Case for CDFI Nonfinancial Performance Measurement." *Community Development Investment Review* 7, no. 2 (2012): 53–59.

———. "An Impact Investing Milestone: The London Principles." *Huffington Post,* July 16, 2013.

Thornley, Ben, and Colby Dailey. "Building Scale in Community Impact Investing Through Nonfinancial Performance Measurement." *Community Development Investment Review* 6, no. 1 (2010): 1–46.

Thornley, Ben, David Wood, Katie Grace, and Sarah Sullivant. *Impact Investing: A Framework for Policy Design and Analysis.* San Francisco: Insight at Pacific Community Ventures/Cambridge, MA: Initiative for Responsible Investment at Harvard University, 2011.

Tides Foundation. *Impact Investing Field Scan: Landscape Overview and Group Profiles.* San Francisco: Tides Foundation, 2011.

Tierney, Thomas J., and Joel L. Fleishman. *Give Smart: Philanthropy That Gets Results.* New York: Publicaffairs, 2011.

Trelstad, Brian. "Simple Measures for Social Enterprise." *Innovations* 3, no. 3 (2008): 105–18.

Trelstad, Brian, and Robert Katz. "Mission, Margin, Mandate: Multiple Paths to Scale." *Innovations* 6, no. 3 (2011): 41–53.

Tuan, Melinda T. *Measuring and/or Estimating Social Value Creation: Insights into Eight Integrated Cost Approaches.* Seattle: Bill & Melinda Gates Foundation, 2008.

Tuan, Melinda, and Julia Jones. *SROI Reports: Overview and Guide.* San Francisco: Roberts Foundation, 2000.

Tulchin, Drew. *Microfinance's Double Bottom Line: Measuring Social Return for the Microfinance Industry.* Seattle: Social Enterprise Associates, 2003.

Tully, Kathryn. "Charity That Offers Fair Profit." *Financial Times,* July 28, 2007.

Twersky, Fay, and BTW Consultants. *An Information Oasis.* San Francisco: Roberts Foundation, 2002.

Twersky, Fay, Phil Buchanan, and Valerie Threlfall."Listening to Those Who Matter Most, the Beneficiaries." *Stanford Social Innovation Review* 11, no. 2 (Spring 2013): 41–45.

Twersky, Fay, and Karen Lindblom. *Evaluation Principles and Practices: An Internal Working Paper.* Menlo Park, CA: William and Flora Hewlett Foundation, 2012.

Twersky, Fay, Jodi Nelson, and Amy Ratcliffe. *A Guide to Actionable Measurement.* Seattle: Bill & Melinda Gates Foundation, 2010.

Ubiñas, Luis A. "A Focus on Culture," in *Advancing Evaluation Practices in Philanthropy,* sponsored supplement to *Stanford Social Innovation Review* 10, no. 3 (Summer 2012): 4–7.

Unilever Global. *Country Study: Indonesia.* Jakarta: Unilever Indonesia, 2012.

United Nations Global Compact and the Rockefeller Foundation. *A Framework for Action: Social Enterprise & Impact Investing.* New York: United Nations Global Compact, 2012.

US Government Accountability Office. *Performance Measurement and Evaluation: Definitions and Relationships.* GAO-05-739SP. Washington, DC: GAO, 2005.

———. *Designing Evaluations: 2012 Revision. GAO Applied Research and Methods*, GAO-12-208G. Washington, DC: GAO, 2012.

———. *Youth Illicit Drug Use Prevention: DARE Long-Term Evaluations and Federal Efforts to Identify Effective Programs*. GAO-03-172R. Washington, DC: GAO, 2013.

US Office of Management and Budget. "OMB Leadership Bios." www.whitehouse.gov.

VillageReach. "Evaluating the Social Impact of Our Work—CCPF Malawi," http://villagereach.org/2013/04/19/evaluating-the-social-impact-of-our-work-ccpf-malawi/.

Wales, Jane. "Framing the Issue," in *Advancing Evaluation Practices in Philanthropy*, sponsored supplement to *Stanford Social Innovation Review* 10, no. 3 (Summer 2012): 2–3.

Wallace, Nicole. "Roughly 1 in 7 Foundations Holds Mission Investments." *Chronicle of Philanthropy*, October 27, 2011.

———. "A Grant Maker Builds a Record of Helping Nonprofits Innovate." *Chronicle of Philanthropy*, May 27, 2012.

———. "Database Indexes Nonprofit Research." *Chronicle of Philanthropy*, December 2, 2012.

———. "Calif. Charity Measures Progress All Year to Fix Problems Early and Impress Donors: First Place for Youth's budget grew from $2-million to $11-million." *Innovation*, May 5, 2013

———. "A Foundation Risks All of Its Endowment on Creating Jobs." *Chronicle of Philanthropy*, May 19, 2013.

Wartzman, Rick. "Three Things Business Leaders Should Do to Help the Nonprofit Sector before It's Too Late." *Forbes*, June 19, 2012.

Watson, Tom. "Smashing the Startup Myth: You Don't 'Build a Team,' the Team Builds the Enterprise." *Forbes.com*, June 22, 2012.

Weinstein, M., and R. M. Bradburd. *The Robin Hood Rules for Smart Giving*. New York: Columbia University Press, 2013.

Weinstein, Michael M., with Cynthia Esposito Lamy. *Measuring Success: How Robin Hood Estimates the Impact of Grants*. New York: Robin Hood Foundation, 2009.

Weiss, Michael J., Howard S. Bloom, and Thomas Brock. *A Conceptual Framework for Studying the Sources of Variation in Program Effects*. New York: MDRC, 2013.

West, Mollie, and Andy Posner. "Defining Your Competitive Advantage." *Stanford Social Innovation Review*, January 23, 2013.

Wikipedia. "PULSE Impact Inventing Management Software." *Wikipedia*, accessed January 8, 2013.

William and Flora Hewlett Foundation and McKinsey & Company. *The Nonprofit Marketplace: Bridging the Information Gap in Philanthropy*. Menlo Park, CA: William and Flora Hewlett Foundation, 2008.

W. K. Kellogg Foundation. *Evaluation Handbook*. Battle Creek, MI: W. K. Kellogg Foundation, 2004.

———. *Logic Model Development Guide*. Battle Creek, MI: W. K. Kellogg Foundation, 2004.

Wolfe, Alexandra. "Over the Hedge." *Bloomberg Businessweek*, December 4, 2012.

Wolk, Andrew. "Social Impact Markets." *Stanford Social Innovation Review* 10, no. 1 (Winter 2012): 21–23.

Wolk, Andrew, Anand Dholakia, and Kelley Kreitz (2009). *Building a Performance Measurement System: Using Data to Accelerate Social Impact*. Cambridge, MA: Root Cause, 2009.

Woo, Stu. "Clarity, with Entrepreneurial Spin." *Wall Street Journal*, June 30, 2011.

World Economic Forum. *Blended Value Investing: Capital Opportunities for Social and Environmental Impact*. Geneva: World Economic Forum, 2006.

Zients, Jeffrey D. *Use of Evidence and Evaluation in the 2014 Budget*. M-12-14 Memorandum to the Heads of Executive Departments and Agencies. Washington, DC: Executive Office of the President, Office of Management and Budget, 2012.

Zunz, Oliver. *Philanthropy in America*. Princeton, NJ: Princeton University Press, 2012.

Index

About the Authors

Marc J. Epstein is Distinguished Research Professor of Management at Jones Graduate School of Business at Rice University in Houston, Texas. Prior to joining Rice, Dr. Epstein was a professor at Stanford Business School, Harvard Business School, and INSEAD (European Institute of Business Administration). In both aca-

demic research and managerial practice, Dr. Epstein is considered one of the global leaders in the areas of innovation, sustainability, governance, performance measurement, and accountability in both corporations and not-for-profit organizations.

Dr. Epstein has extensive academic and practical experience in the implementation of corporate strategies and the development of performance metrics for use in these implementations. He has extensive industry experience and has been a senior consultant to leading corporations and governments throughout the world for over twenty-five years. In many recent articles and books Epstein shows how the use of new strategic management systems can help companies focus strategy, link to performance metrics, and drive improved performance in organizations.

He has focused and published extensively on sustainability and corporate social responsibility for most of his career and was in at the beginning of the development of the corporate social audit and the measurement of corporate social, environmental, and economic impacts.

He is also currently working in developing countries in Africa, Asia, and South America on innovative and entrepreneurial solutions to global challenges and measuring and managing the social impacts of corporations, NGOs, and foundations. Each year he takes all of his MBA students to Africa as part of his course "Commercializing Technology in Developing Countries." In 2011, his book *Joining a Nonprofit Board: What You Need to Know* was published. In 2013, his book (with Eric G. Bing, M.D.) *Pharmacy on a Bicycle: Innovative Solutions for Global Health and Poverty* was released. And in 2014, the second edition of his book *Making Sustainability Work: Best Practices in Managing and Measuring Corporate Social, Environmental, and Economic Impacts* will be released.

His twenty authored or co-authored books and well over 200 professional papers have won numerous top academic, professional, and business awards.

Kristi Yuthas is the Swigert Endowed Professor of Management and Information Systems in the School of Business Administration at Portland State University in Portland, Oregon. Before joining PSU, Dr. Yuthas worked in accounting, financial analysis, and information system development. She has held faculty  positions at a number of universities, including American University and City University of New York, and has conducted research and training seminars in Asia, South America, and other places around the world.

Since joining PSU, Dr. Yuthas' academic work has focused on organizational, ethical, and financial issues associated with information and performance measurement systems. In recent years, her research has expanded to study microfinance, microentrepreneurship, and scaling in the nonprofit sector. Dr. Yuthas has been recognized as a top-50 researcher worldwide in accounting systems, and as a leading researcher in a number of other areas. She has more than 100 publications and presentations in the fields of business and development.

In her professional work, Dr. Yuthas has two major streams of interest. She consults with large multinational companies on corporate social responsibility and sustainability, helping organizations implement their strategies through effective performance measurement and reporting systems. She also consults with social sector organizations and investors on issues relating to measuring, scaling, and amplifying social and environmental impact.

She is currently working on a book on corporate social responsibility in India. The recently passed Indian Companies Act requires large companies to allocate 2 percent of their profits toward social and environmental impact. Through this work, she hopes to help Indian corporations maximize their social impact and to spread these pioneering ideas to other countries around the world.

Dr. Yuthas lives in Portland, Oregon, with her three children, where they enjoy hiking, traveling, and exploring food carts.

By Marc J. Epstein and Adriana Rejc Buhovac

Making Sustainability Work

Best Practices in Managing and Measuring Corporate Social, Environmental, and Economic Impacts, Second Edition

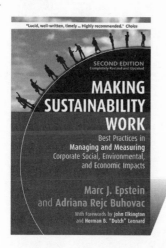

Updated throughout with new examples and new research, this is a complete guide to implementing and measuring the effectiveness of sustainability initiatives. It draws on Epstein's and Buhovac's solid academic foundation and extensive consulting work and includes best practices from dozens of companies in Europe, Asia, North America, South America, Australia, and Africa. This is the ultimate how-to guide for corporate leaders, strategists, academics, sustainability consultants, and anyone else with an interest in actually putting sustainability ideas into practice and making sure they accomplish their goals.

Praise for the first edition

"A welcome addition to the literature...Highly recommended."
   —Choice

Named one of *Sustainable Industries* magazine's Best Books of 2008

"An outstanding contribution to the field."
   —Strategic Finance

Hardcover, 288 pages, ISBN 978-1-60994-993-8
PDF ebook, ISBN 978-1-60994-994-5

BK Berrett–Koehler Publishers, Inc.
      www.bkconnection.com   **800.929.2929**

By Eric G. Bing and Marc J. Epstein

Pharmacy on a Bicycle

Innovative Solutions for Global Health and Poverty

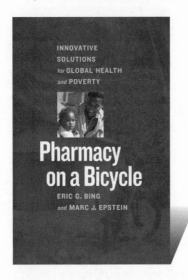

Millions of people are dying from diseases that we can easily and inexpensively treat simply because we can't get them what they need. They are dying not because we can't solve a medical problem but because we can't solve a logistics problem.

Eric Bing, an MD with an MBA, and Marc Epstein have an answer: a unique grassroots model that uses innovation, entrepreneurship, and building on existing infrastructures to deliver health care locally. They provide over 100 examples from organizations that are already using this approach to save lives in more than 35 countries throughout Africa, Asia, and Latin America.

"Demonstrates how, even in the most dire circumstances, entrepreneurs can develop cost-effective, sustainable, innovative solutions that have the potential for replication and scale."
—Professor J. Gregory Dees, cofounder, Center for the Advancement of Social Entrepreneurship, Duke University

Hardcover, 240 pages, ISBN 978-1-60994-789-7
PDF ebook ISBN 978-1-60994-790-3

Berrett–Koehler Publishers, Inc.
www.bkconnection.com   **800.929.2929**

✹ Berrett–Koehler
BK̄ Publishers

Berrett-Koehler is an independent publisher dedicated to an ambitious mission: *Creating a World That Works for All*.

We believe that to truly create a better world, action is needed at all levels—individual, organizational, and societal. At the individual level, our publications help people align their lives with their values and with their aspirations for a better world. At the organizational level, our publications promote progressive leadership and management practices, socially responsible approaches to business, and humane and effective organizations. At the societal level, our publications advance social and economic justice, shared prosperity, sustainability, and new solutions to national and global issues.

A major theme of our publications is "Opening Up New Space." Berrett-Koehler titles challenge conventional thinking, introduce new ideas, and foster positive change. Their common quest is changing the underlying beliefs, mindsets, institutions, and structures that keep generating the same cycles of problems, no matter who our leaders are or what improvement programs we adopt.

We strive to practice what we preach—to operate our publishing company in line with the ideas in our books. At the core of our approach is stewardship, which we define as a deep sense of responsibility to administer the company for the benefit of all of our "stakeholder" groups: authors, customers, employees, investors, service providers, and the communities and environment around us.

We are grateful to the thousands of readers, authors, and other friends of the company who consider themselves to be part of the "BK Community." We hope that you, too, will join us in our mission.

A BK Business Book

This book is part of our BK Business series. BK Business titles pioneer new and progressive leadership and management practices in all types of public, private, and nonprofit organizations. They promote socially responsible approaches to business, innovative organizational change methods, and more humane and effective organizations.

Berrett–Koehler
Publishers

A community dedicated to creating
a world that works for all

Dear Reader,

Thank you for picking up this book and joining our worldwide community of Berrett-Koehler readers. We share ideas that bring positive change into people's lives, organizations, and society.

To welcome you, we'd like to offer you a free e-book. You can pick from among twelve of our bestselling books by entering the promotional code **BKP92E** here: http://www.bkconnection.com/welcome.

When you claim your free e-book, we'll also send you a copy of our e-newsletter, the *BK Communiqué*. Although you're free to unsubscribe, there are many benefits to sticking around. In every issue of our newsletter you'll find

- A free e-book
- Tips from famous authors
- Discounts on spotlight titles
- Hilarious insider publishing news
- A chance to win a prize for answering a riddle

Best of all, our readers tell us, "Your newsletter is the only one I actually read." So claim your gift today, and please stay in touch!

Sincerely,

Charlotte Ashlock
Steward of the BK Website

Questions? Comments? Contact me at bkcommunity@bkpub.com.

Certified

Corporation
bcorporation.net